Global
Tourist Behavior

Global Tourist Behavior

Muzaffer Uysal, PhD
Editor

Routledge
Taylor & Francis Group

NEW YORK AND LONDON

First Published by
The Haworth Press, Inc., 10 Alice Street, Binghamton, NY 13904-1580 USA

Transferred to Digital Printing 2009 by Routledge
270 Madison Ave, New York NY 10016
2 Park Square, Milton Park, Abingdon, Oxon, OX14 4RN

Global Tourist Behavior has also been published as *Journal of International Consumer Marketing*, Volume 6, Numbers 3/4 1994.

The development, preparation, and publication of this work has been undertaken with great care. However, the publisher, employees, editors, and agents of The Haworth Press and all imprints of The Haworth Press, Inc., including The Haworth Medical Press and Pharmaceutical Products Press, are not responsible for any errors contained herein or for consequences that may ensue from use of materials or information contained in this work. Opinions expressed by the author(s) are not necessarily those of The Haworth Press, Inc.

Library of Congress Cataloging-in-Publication Data

Global tourist behavior/Muzaffer Uysal, editor.
      p. cm.
      "Also published as Journal of international consumer marketing, volume 6, numbers 3/4, 1994"--T.p. verso.
      Includes bibliographical references and index.
      ISBN 1-56024-471-2 (acid-free)
      ISBN 0-78900-096-2
      1. Tourist trade--Marketing. I. Uysal, Muzaffer.
G155.A1G495 1994
338.4'791--dc20
                                          94-21283
                                            CIP

Publisher's Note

The publisher has gone to great lengths to ensure the quality of this reprint but points out that some imperfections in the original may be apparent.

INDEXING & ABSTRACTING

Contributions to this publication are selectively indexed or abstracted in print, electronic, online, or CD-ROM version(s) of the reference tools and information services listed below. This list is current as of the copyright date of this publication. See the end of this section for additional notes.

- *ABI/INFORM Global (broad-coverage indexing & abstracting service that includes numerous English-language titles outside the USA available from University Microfilms International (UMI), 300 North Zeeb Road, P.O. Box 1346, Ann Arbor, MI 48106-1346)*, UMI Data Courier, Attn: Library Services, Box 34660, Louisville, KY 40232

- *ABSCAN, Inc.*, P.O. Box 2384, Monroe, LA 71207-2384

- *AGRICOLA Database*, National Agricultural Library, 10301 Baltimore Boulevard, Room 002, Beltsville, MD 20705

- *Communication Abstracts,* Temple University, 303 Annenberg Hall, Philadelphia, PA 19122

- *Contents Pages in Management*, University of Manchester Business School, Booth Street West, Manchester M15 6PB, England

- *Food Science and Technology Abstracts (FSTA)* Scanned, abstracted and indexed by the International Food Information Service (IFIS) for inclusion in Food Science and Technology Abstracts (FSTA), International Food Information Service, Lane End House, Shinfield, Reading RG2 9BB, England

(continued)

- *Foods Adlibra*, Foods Adlibra Publications, 9000 Plymouth Avenue North, Minneapolis, MN 55427

- *Journal of Health Care Marketing (abstracts section),* Georgia Tech-School of Management, Ivan Allen College-225 North Avenue NW, Atlanta, GA 30332

- *Management & Marketing Abstracts*, Pira International, Randalls Road, Leatherhead, Surrey KT22 7RU, England

- *Marketing Executive Report*, American Marketing Association, 250 South Wacker Drive, Chicago, IL 60606

- *Social Planning/Policy & Development Abstracts (SOPODA)*, Sociological Abstracts, Inc., P.O. Box 22206, San Diego, CA 92192-0206

- *Sociological Abstracts (SA)*, Sociological Abstracts, Inc., P.O. Box 22206, San Diego, CA 92192-0206

- *Textile Technology Digest*, Institute of Textile Technology, P.O. Box 391, Charlottesville, VA 22902-0391

- *The Business Education Index*, Eastern Illinois University, Department of Business Education and Administration Information Systems, Charleston, IL 61920

(continued)

SPECIAL BIBLIOGRAPHIC NOTES

related to special journal issues (separates)
and indexing/abstracting

☐ indexing/abstracting services in this list will also cover material in the "separate" that is co-published simultaneously with Haworth's special thematic journal issue or DocuSerial. Indexing/abstracting usually covers material at the article/chapter level.

☐ monographic co-editions are intended for either non-subscribers or libraries which intend to purchase a second copy for their circulating collections.

☐ monographic co-editions are reported to all jobbers/wholesalers/approval plans. The source journal is listed as the "series" to assist the prevention of duplicate purchasing in the same manner utilized for books-in-series.

☐ to facilitate user/access services all indexing/abstracting services are encouraged to utilize the co-indexing entry note indicated at the bottom of the first page of each article/chapter/contribution.

☐ this is intended to assist a library user of any reference tool (whether print, electronic, online, or CD-ROM) to locate the monographic version if the library has purchased this version but not a subscription to the source journal.

☐ individual articles/chapters in any Haworth publication are also available through the Haworth Document Delivery Services (HDDS).

ABOUT THE EDITOR

Muzaffer Uysal, PhD, is Professor of Tourism in the Department of Hospitality and Tourism Management at Virginia Polytechnic Institute and State University, Blacksburg. He has extensive experience in the travel and tourism field and has authored or co-authored more than eighty articles and several book chapters related to different aspects of tourism marketing, demand/supply interaction, and international tourism. Dr. Uysal is an associate editor of *Leisure Sciences* for tourism related areas and methods and serves on the Editorial Boards of three additional international journals. He is a member of the Travel and Tourism Research Association, the National Recreation and Park Association, and the International Association of Scientific Experts in Tourism. Recently, he was invited to serve on the Education Advisory Council of the National Tour Foundation.

Global
Tourist Behavior

CONTENTS

Introduction   1
Muzaffer Uysal

Marketing of Tourism Places: What Are We Doing?   5
G. J. Ashworth
H. Voogd

Visitor Expectations of Tourism Benefits in Zambia   21
Winston Husbands

Tourism Marketing Management in Small Island Nations:
A Tale of Micro-Destinations   39
Stanley D. Reid
Laurel J. Reid

Foreign and Domestic Escorted Tour Expectations
of American Travelers   61
Charles R. Duke
Margaret A. Persia

A Comparison of Package and Non-Package Travelers
from the United Kingdom   79
Sheauhsing Hsieh
Joseph T. O'Leary
Alastair M. Morrison

An Expert System for Promotion Budget Allocation
to International Markets   101
Paulo Rita
Luiz Moutinho

Cross-Cultural Tourism Marketing Research:
An Assessment and Recommendations
for Future Studies   123
      Frédéric Dimanche

Travel Motivation Variations of Overseas German Visitors   135
      Ute Jamrozy
      Muzaffer Uysal

Tour Operators' Role in the Tourism Distribution System:
An Indonesian Case Study   161
      William C. Gartner
      Thamrin Bachri

"De Higher de Monkey Climb, de More 'e Sho 'e Tail":
Tourists' Knowledge of Barbadian Culture   181
      Graham M. S. Dann

Long-Term Impact of a Mega-Event on International
Tourism to the Host Country: A Conceptual Model
and the Case of the 1988 Seoul Olympics   205
      Yong-Soon Kang
      Richard Perdue

Health Tourism: A New Positioning Strategy for Tourist
Destinations   227
      Jonathan N. Goodrich

Projecting Western Consumer Attitudes Toward Travel
to Six Eastern European Countries   239
      Ken W. McCleary
      David L. Whitney

Index   257

Introduction

Muzaffer Uysal

Today, tourism with its complex social, economic and physical impact dimensions has become an international phenomenon and is evolving into an accepted field of scholarly endeavor. The globalization of tourism has resulted in more culturally diverse travelers with different preferences, motivations, expectations, and needs. The movement towards democratization in different parts of the world has also created new destinations and made them more accessible than ever before. Consequently, tourism destinations have become highly competitive in accommodating changes and differences in travel behavior, and providing the kind of services and leisure activities desired.

The nature of this diversity in global tourist behavior and the reciprocal interaction between the traveler and destinations will naturally pose new challenges and create new opportunities for destination promoters, marketing professionals and social scientists examining tourist behavior.

The purpose of this collection on "Global Tourist Behavior" is to present examples of tourist behavior and tourism marketing research that incorporates the global nature of tourism as an integral component. As editor of this volume I wish to acknowledge Dr. Erdener Kaynak for his support and direction in developing this special issue.

As Editor, I owe a great debt to all the referees and authors for their help and comments. I sincerely thank the authors for submitting their papers. This issue would not have been possible without the help and assistance of the people listed below who gave both time and effort to act as referees. Their contribution is greatly acknowledged.

[Haworth co-indexing entry note]: "Introduction." Uysal, Muzaffer. Co-published simultaneously in *Journal of International Consumer Marketing* (The Haworth Press, Inc.) Vol. 6, No. 3/4, 1994, pp. 1-3; and: *Global Tourist Behavior* (ed: Muzaffer Uysal) The Haworth Press, Inc., 1994, pp. 1-3. Multiple copies of this article/chapter may be purchased from The Haworth Document Delivery Center [1-800-3-HAWORTH; 9:00 a.m. - 5:00 p.m. (EST)].

Kathleen Andereck, University of North Carolina at Greensboro
Kenneth F. Backman, Clemson University
Sheila J. Backman, Clemson University
Mark A. Bonn, Florida State University
G. Wesley Burnett, Clemson University
Michael A. Blazey, California State University-Long Beach
Gary Chick, University of Illinois at Urbana-Champaign
Kaye Chon, University of Nevada
John L. Crompton, Texas A&M University
John Crotts, University of Florida
Frédéric Dimanche, University of New Orleans
Charles Duke, Clemson University
Daniel Fesenmaier, University of Illinois at Urbana-Champaign
Joseph D. Fridgen, Michigan State University
Leslie Furr, California State University-Chico
William C. Gartner, University of Wisconsin-Stout
Richard Gitelson, The Pennsylvania State University
Jonathan N. Goodrich, Florida International University
Larry Gustky, North Carolina State University
William Hammitt, Clemson University
Mark Havitz, University of Waterloo
Stephen Holland, University of Florida
Jafar Jafari, University of Wisconsin-Stout
Stephen McCool, University of Montana
Ken McCleary, Virginia Polytechnic Institute and State University
Cary C. McDonald, Clemson University
Deborah Kerstetter, The Pennsylvania University
Mahmood A. Khan, Virginia Polytechnic Institute and State University
Bonnie Knutson, Michigan State University
Brian Mihalik, Georgia State University
Ady Milman, University of Central Florida
Sue K. Murrmann, Virginia Polytechnic Institute and State University
Francis P. Noe, National Parks Service
Joseph T. O'Leary, Purdue University
Richard Perdue, University of Colorado at Boulder
Laurel Reid, Brock University
Stowe Shoemaker, Cornell University
David Snepenger, Montana State University

Daniel J. Stynes, Michigan State University
Stephen L. J. Smith, University of Waterloo
Daniel R. Williams, Virginia Polytechnic Institute and State University
Bruce E. Wicks, University of Illinois at Urbana-Champaign
Stephen F. Witt, University of Wales-Swansea

Marketing of Tourism Places:
What Are We Doing?

G. J. Ashworth
H. Voogd

SUMMARY. The marketing of tourism places involves coming to terms with the character and intrinsic qualities of place-products. This article poses the questions: What is the tourism place-product? Who produces it? Who consumes it? What is the nature of the market? How is it marketed? The answers are applied to the case of the city of Groningen, The Netherlands. Conclusions are drawn on the necessity for developing a distinctive form of marketing for tourism places.

INTRODUCTION

The commodification of tourism as an aspect of leisure (see Kirby's arguments, 1985) and the application of what has been termed 'the industrial approach' (Sinclair and Stabler, 1992) to holiday-making has not occurred without critical comment (see Leiper, 1990; Hughes, 1991, among others). This article accepts that tourism destinations are being treated de facto as traded commodities by most of those involved in them whether as commercial operators, public sector managers or academic commentators. If this is so then the argument must be taken a stage further

G. J. Ashworth is Chair of the Department of Urban and Regional Planning, and H. Voogd is Dean of the Faculty of Spatial Sciences, both at the University of Groningen, Postbox 800, 9700AV Groningen, NL.

[Haworth co-indexing entry note]: "Marketing of Tourism Places: What Are We Doing?" Ashworth, G. J., and H. Voogd. Co-published simultaneously in *Journal of International Consumer Marketing* (The Haworth Press, Inc.) Vol. 6, No. 3/4, 1994, pp. 5-19; and: *Global Tourist Behavior* (ed: Muzaffer Uysal) The Haworth Press, Inc., 1994, pp. 5-19. Multiple copies of this article/chapter may be purchased from The Haworth Document Delivery Center [1-800-3-HAWORTH; 9:00 a.m. - 5:00 p.m. (EST)].

by examining the consequences of treating places as products and specifically treating holiday destinations as tourism place-products within a marketing system.

Some simple general questions must initially be posed so that the nature
and distinctive characteristics of tourism place marketing can be established. The same questions, and the conceptual discussion that they raise,
will then be posed in a specific case chosen so that some general observations for marketing tourism places can be drawn.

IS A TOURISM DESTINATION A PLACE-PRODUCT?

That places can be treated as if they were products is indisputable. Not
only is this widely performed, it has been done for many years (see for
example Brown's 1985 account of the selling of Victorian resorts) for
many purposes and to many markets. The nature of tourism as a commercial activity has lent itself particularly to this treatment because the complex of varied activities that comprise the holiday experience is most
conveniently, for both producer and consumer, bundled together into a
destination, a place-product.

There are, however, a number of intrinsic characteristics of place-products that are distinctly different from most traded goods and services.
Quite simply it needs stressing that place-products are places and thus
have certain intrinsic qualities of places. The effect of these characteristics
of the product upon the marketing process are quite fundamental and must
be understood before such marketing can be pursued effectively. The most
important of these can be summarised in four simple conceptual points,
each of which will re-emerge in the later discussion of practice in various
guises.

1. The place-product has intrinsic problems of definition and delimitation. The simple command, 'describe the product,' can receive two types
of response. The first is a varied, if necessarily incomplete inventory of
facilities, services, or locations within the place which are actually or
potentially used by tourists and which taken together encompass the holi-
day-maker's consumption at that place. The second is a set of attributes or
qualities relating to the place as a whole as perceived by either producers
or consumers. It matters little whether or not such attributes are derived
from only a part of a place or indeed whether consumers of the non-tourism place-product would perceive quite different attributes: the place
name describes, in a very real sense, the product.

It has been argued, not surprisingly principally by geographers, that
places are physical locations on the earth's surface and therefore are al-

ways capable of being physically delimited (Ashworth and de Haan, 1986). However, tourism places as defined above can be delimited in two quite different ways with different results. There is no need for an objection in principle to this, although it can lead to some conceptual confusion. There are, however, some practical implications when differently delimited places are used in different stages or by different operators in the marketing process. This frequently occurs, for instance, when area based production agencies market products produced at different spatial scales.

Thus, to describe a tourism destination as a tourist product is to treat a place simultaneously as both a container or stage for an assemblage of products and as a product in itself. It is not the vagueness and multifariousness of the first definition nor the subjective nature of the second that presents distinctive problems. Many other physical products are assemblages of varied elements, and many service products are equally subjectively defined by purchasers or producers. It is the inescapable duality of tourism place-product definition that is unique. This is not a contradiction but, as Jansen-Verbeke (1988) has argued in her attempt to define her 'Tourist-Recreation Product,' an unavoidable dichotomy that must be accommodated in the marketing process.

2. This line of reasoning can be taken a stage further. If the tourism place-product is an assemblage of highly varied elements located at, or relating to, a place, then clearly it is not the totality of all possible or potential elements which is in itself the product, despite the labelling of facility inventories in many planning reports as the 'tourism product.' The product is a 'packaged' selection. If it is the package that is the product then the two basic questions of definition and identification concern the nature of this packaging process and who performs it. In one sense, the tour operators and other intermediaries are selling an assembled group of items but equally each individual holiday is unique to the extent that the use and experience derived from each element in the place is unique to a particular consumer. One of the many consequences of this, some of which are investigated in more detail below, is that the tourism place-product being sold is likely to be different than that which is being bought.

3. A fundamental and intrinsic quality of all places is that they exist at a particular spatial scale and within a series of nesting hierarchies. Both the purchaser and the producer of the tourism place-product may simultaneously be trading the Arab world, the Eastern Mediterranean, Egypt, Cairo, The Nile Corniche and Sheppeards Hotel. Each is a place-product in itself but linked in various ways with the rest within the spatial hierarchy. This simple point has a large number of fundamental consequences. For example, the scale selected for selling by the producer may not be the

scale that is being purchased by the customer. Turkey may be sold by the National Tourist Office to visitors who are purchasing a much wider Mediterranean experience.

The situation is in practice frequently much more complicated than this simple scale discrepancy between the place bought and the place sold in the same transaction. Both are likely to be trading or consuming simultaneously various combinations of place-products at different scales but giving different weightings to each. Thus, the visitor in an apartment in a Grande Motte 'pyramide' may be principally consuming a local spatially very restricted 'activity space' while supplementing this from time to time with trips to other resorts along the Languedoc coast or to historic towns in South-West France. The seller equally is marketing a set of spatial scales but these are bounded by fixed jurisdictional boundaries established for quite different purposes. Thus, the Grande Motte tourism locality is most coterminous with the commune responsible for promoting it, and the visitors' regional product is not the same as the regional territory of the 'Mission' responsible for planning the number, distribution and promotion of tourism facilities on the regional scale. (A description of the operations of these scale discrepancies in practice in the case of Languedoc resorts can be found in Stabler et al., 1988, and de Haan et al., 1990.)

The extent to which such scale discrepancies matter will depend upon many factors. The most important for practical marketing purposes is the extent to which the different scale products complement or compete with each other and the degree to which markets can be segmented so that the promotion of each scale product at best reinforces or at least does not interfere with the promotion of others.

4. Places are sold as products not only to potential tourists but to many other groups of consumers. Few other goods and services are multisold in this way. Precisely the same physical space, and, also, in most tourism situations, the same facilities in that space are sold simultaneously to different consumers as quite different products. Not only is the tourism place and many of the facilities in it, sold as different tourism products (to, for example, heritage, culture, sporting, entertainment or numerous other 'adjectival' tourists), it is being sold to residents, shoppers, commercial operators, investors and many more markets. This is not quite the same as the well known situation where individual units of the same product are marketed to segmented market sections as differentiated products. In place-product marketing it is the same physical place and frequently the same actual physical spatial locations that are being multi-sold. This raises a number of distinctive and in same instances curious marketing situations.

Few customers 'buying' a city actually expect to return home with it, or parts of it. The entrepreneur who actually purchased London Bridge and re-erected it in Arizona caused it to cease, in the important respect being considered here, to *be* London Bridge. Trading in places, in the sense here, does not involve the transfer of property rights or even in most cases the temporary hire of any rights over place-products (hotel beds and theatre seats may be so hired but they form only one constituent element of a place-product). The consequences of this characteristic is that the sale of the product does not diminish the stock of that product held by the producer, its consumption by any one customer does not limit its possible consumption by others and the sale of different place-products occupying the same space does not occur in a zero-sum gain situation. At least the above assertions are valid unless, or possibly until, conflict between consumers occurs. Space is finite and place-products therefore have a finite dimension and this can be exceeded. Practical considerations of capacity and conflict between consumers of the same or different place products arise. This may seem so familiar as to arouse no comment but the point is that this space dimension is not intrinsic to the marketing process and this will be directly reflected in it unlike most product characteristics; it is extrinsic and normally treated as an external cost that is the concern of land-use planning or regulatory place management.

WHO PRODUCES THE TOURISM PLACE-PRODUCT?

If the holiday is to be treated as a place-product, then an important task is to identify the producer. This is self-evident in the case of most marketed products but the special nature of place-products, as described above, allows a number of different answers to be given to this question.

In the most obvious sense the producer is the assembler of the various elements in the holiday package, some of which will be located in the destination place (such as accommodation) while others (such as transport) may not be. This is then sold as an interpreted place-product directly or indirectly to the consumer. That tour operators consider themselves to be the producers is indicated by the widespread use of the term 'the tourism industry' as a catch-all description of commercial firms engaged in assembling elements of the holiday and then marketing and selling these packages.

However, there are at least two other plausible candidates for the role of producer. Governments and their agencies responsible for many place bound aspects of tourism often regard themselves as producers of national or local tourism place-products. They concern themselves with coordinating, stimulating, subsidizing and occasionally even operating various accommodation and tourism attraction facilities, as well as engaging in much generalised place promotion.

No package, however 'all-inclusive,' actually contains all purchased elements of the holiday experience, and even if it did individual tourists will value and appreciate different mixes of such elements. Each holiday is an individual experience and thus an individual and not standarised product. This argument can be made for many products–especially personal services–but tourism is again by definition so varied that the tourism product more than most, is in reality assembled by the tourist from the very many elements available and who is therefore in a very real sense the producer as well as the consumer.

The tourism place-product is multi-produced.

WHO CONSUMES THE TOURISM PLACE-PRODUCT?

The tourist is one of the important groups of place-product consumers but there are a number of complications in attempting to operationalise this statement. Two of these are well known and apply to tourism in general. These are first, the difficulty of answering the question of who is a tourist, or more accurately, when does a tourist become one, as this sub-species of humanity is only definable through the motive for the consumption at the moment when it occurs, not the activity indulged in. Almost any human activity can conceivably become a tourism activity if the motive of the participant is appropriate; equally almost anything performed by tourists is also someone else's non-tourism activity. Secondly, tourism demand cannot be safely equated with participation and certainly not with participation at a particular holiday destination. Tourism demand contains a particularly large element of not only anticipation and recollection but also latent and option demands of various sorts.

A third difficulty, which is intrinsic to place-products, is the equivalent on the consumption side to multi-selling on the production side. Place-products are multi-bought; the same physical locations and frequently also the same facilities and attributes of these locations are consumed simultaneously by different groups of consumers seeking different 'buyer benefits.' The most obvious differences are between tourists and residents.

A further complication has been argued by Stabler (1988) on the basis of Plog's (1973) distinction between 'allocentric' and 'psychocentric' tourists. For the first group the place is the important binding and identifying element in the total tourism package, and for the second the sense of place is less important and they cannot really be considered to be conscious place consumers at all although both groups may be consuming the same product at the same place.

IS THERE A TOURISM PLACE-PRODUCT MARKET?

To argue that a marketing analysis requires the existence of a market is again self-evident but the practice of tourism place-product marketing, especially in the public sector, is frequently conducted as if it was market-less marketing.

A market is a situation where the exchange concept is free to operate in three ways, namely, the consumer is offered a free choice of many comparable products, producers have free access to many potential customers, and a free exchange of product for some measure of value occurs. The mechanism governing these choices and allowing such an exchange to occur is a pricing system. The question, 'What is the price of the tourism place-product?' and its corollary, 'Who pays this price?' is, therefore, not only valid but must necessarily be posed. Economists (such as reviewed in Sinclair et al., 1990) have explored various forms of surrogate, opportunity cost or hedonic pricing of holiday packages. However the difficulty with place marketing is that prices are often indirect, intangible, expressed in non-monetary units, part of a 'social market exchange' (Torkildson, 1983) and charged widely to consumers and non-consumers alike, either of whom may, or may not, be aware of the price level and even that they are being so charged at all. It is not that place-products cannot be priced, for if that was so then place marketing would be logically impossible; it is only that such prices are extremely difficult to determine and equally difficult to present for payment to particular groups. Prices in some form must, however, be determined for otherwise neither consumers nor producers can operate in the market in pursuit of their distinct strategies of choice.

This argument is more than the demonstration of a logical difficulty; it has a number of very practical implications. It accounts for much of the notorious sluggishness of both tourism demands and tourism facility supply to changes in perceived market prices as well as the high levels of customer dissatisfaction with the complexity of much tourism pricing information and even the high levels of post-consumption product complaints. One of the main reasons why consumers make unsatisfactory product choices and producers fail to react responsively to shifts in customer demand is simply that tourism markets do not work as smoothly as many other markets. This can in part be attributed to failures of information about, or sensitivity to, the pricing systems which make free comparison and free exchange difficult.

A further consequence, so serious that it threatens the continued existence of the tourism industry in many places is that the costs and benefits resulting from the sale of tourism place products are only partly reflected in the internal pricing system. Many such costs and benefits are external to the tourism producer-consumer system and paid by, or accrued by, others at the place of consumption. This problem is much wider than the scope of this article, currently often appearing in the guise of a tourism versus natural environment conflict, but it is clear that inadequate pricing contributes to the difficulty of determining the levels of costs and benefits and degree of externality involved in them.

HOW ARE PLACES SOLD AS TOURISM PLACE-PRODUCTS?

There are many handbooks available that set out to provide practical information answering this question. Writers such as Lickorish (1985), Middelton (1988), Holloway and Plant, (1988), and Witt and Moutinho (1989) have outlined the various techniques and media available for the dissemination of place-product information. However there are two important complicating factors in dealing with place-products. The first relates to the previously discussed difficulty of identifying the producer which can be reformulated as the difficulty of allocating responsibility for different aspects of the place product production system among the multiplicity of organisations involved in it. Specifically, the selling of the same tourism place-product may be undertaken by different organisations with different techniques, goals and responsibilities. National or local tourism offices, local tourism enterprises, extraneous tour and travel operators may all be engaged in selling the same tourism place product sometimes largely oblivious of the efforts of each other. Equally, and potentially more serious in its consequences, is a misleading weakness of the analogy between place-products and assembled manufactured commodities. Different stages in the production process are handled by organisations that are not only quite different in their objectives, working methods and responsibilities but may lack any effective coordination between them. The organisation selling the place may not have assembled the place-product and is unlikely to have managed the resources used in its production. The agency selling a tourism place may be selling a product it has not constructed, composed of resources it does not control. This is not merely a failure of managerial coordination but the more fundamental failure to relate the narrow economic production system to the much wider place resource system.

Finally, the marketing measures available for place marketing are not confined only to promotion and indeed much of the crudely defined and vaguely targeted boosterism widely, if inaccurately, spread by many public sector tourism place promotion agencies barely counts as marketing at all. This may be the case with many products but, as Ashworth and Voogd (1990) have argued at length, places in particular can be sold through a whole series of physical structural, design and organisational measures which are frequently more effective than promotion, and certainly than advertising, alone.

A CASE: GRONINGEN (NL)

Where and Why?

The general questions raised above can now be posed for a particular case and, if not fully answered, at least reformulated in the light of practical experience. Place marketing has been practised most often with urban products to the extent that the term 'city marketing' is often synonymous. Therefore an urban case is chosen although other scales impose an ever present context.

The choice of Groningen in the northern Netherlands is justified by it being in many respects unremarkable. It is a multifunctional medium sized city (population around 160,000) serving as a self-standing, regional capital for a service catchment of around 500,000. It has experienced a thousand years of urban development which has left an appropriate legacy of surviving morphological structures and relict buildings which allows the 'historic city product' option to be pursued but is in no sense a fossilised historic museum town in which conserved structures are accorded automatic priority over modern functions. It fulfils a traditional and expanding role in serving the recreational demands of the region on the city entertaining around two and a half million day visitors. In addition it accommodates about 970,000 visitor-nights, a figure which has increased by an average 10% a year over the last decade (compared with a national average of 6%). About 15% of total overnight visitors are foreign of which 40% are from Germany (Dienst Ruimtelijk Ordening/VVV, Groningen, 1992). Tourism thus makes a welcome additional support to the urban economy and presents the option of further development but is not an overdominant activity (VVV, 1992).

Groningen is therefore typical of thousands of such towns in Europe. Unlike the historic gems of Bath or Heidelburg, the major tourism meccas of Venice or Oxford or the multi-million metropolitan capitals, like London or Paris, there are many development options and the answers to the marketing questions are not predetermined by the existing economic structure or resource endowment. Towns such as Groningen are actually the home of most Europeans and therefore provide the most relevant cases.

What Is Sold to Tourists?

This question would be regarded by many active in the tourism promotion of Groningen as both unnecessarily precise and paradoxically not precise enough. What is sold to the tourists is in many respects the same marketed product as is being sold to residents and a self-conscious tourism product is rarely differentiated but equally the question prompts the rejoinder, 'Which Groningen, to which tourists?'

Groningen is marketed to visitors mainly as an historic city, a culture city and a shopping city in its own right and more broadly as a service base for regional rural and water based attractions. However tourism markets have proved impossible to segment according to these clear-cut product divisions. Such studies as have been undertaken into visitor behaviour suggest that the supply characteristics mentioned above are not from the visitor's viewpoint the Groningen tourism product; they are merely elements in a visitor assembled product that includes various combinations of all of these. Secondly, not only are the same place elements also sold to residents from the city and region, these customers comprise most of the market. Thus Groningen's tourism product is either so multifaceted or so diffuse as to make facile descriptions of *the* tourism product of little value.

A recent study of Groningen as a heritage city, to take one of the major components of the tourism product, argued that there were in fact many different 'historic cities' being presented simultaneously, often to overlapping markets (Ashworth, 1990). These include:

- The historic city of the architect, archivist and historian was easily delimitable through the designations and monuments ascribed by this expert consensus on the basis of intrinsic criteria.
- The legislative historic city, although often derived from the historians' city, is in many ways significantly different. It is a palimpsest of area designations of ensembles of buildings, spaces and cityscapes shaped since around 1960.
- The urban planners' and managers' historic city was essentially a creation since the 1970s and combines morphological and functional elements in selected historic districts. Such policies involve far more than just building renovation but include appropriately antique street paving,

street furniture and more recently area nomenclature (Gemeente Groningen, 1990).

* The tourists' historic city is a small fragment of the historians' city in which selected buildings and ensembles are assembled with the help of 'historic city trails,' which lead visitors around selected 'themed' sites carefully avoiding discordant areas and functions.

These, and more such cities, could be identified for Groningen, as for most such towns. None are more 'real,' authentic or intrinsically better than the others nor can they be sharply differentiated either in spatial terms or in markets.

Thus not only are different tourist city products being sold in the same or overlapping physical space, other 'cities' are simultaneously being sold to quite different markets. Such 'multi-selling' may in turn lead to some physical conflict for space (notably in Groningen over inner city tourism coach and car parking). Negative local reactions to the tourist use of scarce city centre space is reflected in the currently popular sticker slogan, 'Groningen: Love it or leave it!'

Which Spatial Scale Is Sold and Which Bought?

The city of Groningen as an officially delimited jurisdiction is not the city which is bought and sold. The tourist may buy an image of the city formed of characteristics relating to the city as a whole but makes actual use of only a very restricted area within it. The city that is sold, although spatially limited, is in practice wider than that purchased by most visitors; the information supplied to visitors is wider in spatial extent than the sites actually visited.

The organisational place and the tourism place are differently bounded. This obvious discrepancy can give rise to difficulties and occasional conflicts. For example the tourist office responsible for promoting the city (V.V.V. Groningen) has jurisdiction over the province as a whole and thus faces the continual situation of marketing two different and, only sometimes related, spatial products. For some tourists the product, 'the city in the region,' is relevant but for others the distinctly rural, sporting attractions of the surrounding region are so different from the urban historical attraction of the city as to arouse a conflict of images.

Similarly the organisation responsible for promoting the Netherlands as a whole to foreign visitors and for developing a set of coordinated national tourist products is the Nederlands Bureau voor Toerism (NBT), which has focussed on the theme 'Netherlands-Waterland' as its principal tourism product. While this accords well with the established image of The Neth-

erlands abroad (composed of canals, water sports and windmills, with the
embellishment of tulips and clogs) it does little to support the historic city
image of towns such as Groningen. Even when specifically urban historic
promotion is undertaken by the NBT, the accent understandably is upon
the typical characteristics and history of the well known towns in the
Western Netherlands, the 'Holland city,' which diverges in many architec-
tural and historical respects from a northern city such as Groningen, whose
heritage is in many ways closer to the Hansa ports of the North Sea and
Baltic.

How Is Groningen Sold and by Whom?

Like most such cities, Groningen is largely sold through unintentional
images, originating from a wide variety of sources outside the influence of
tourism policy makers, projected to tourists long before they arrive in the
city. Recent research on the images of Groningen held elsewhere in the
Netherlands concluded that the city was seen as varied, sociable, cultural
and historic but was also seen to be relatively unknown and inaccessible
(VVV, Groningen). The official promotion of the city is undertaken by a
number of different agencies who are often operating upon different markets. The information service of the city council (the 'gemeente') and that of
the provincial council (the 'provincie') whose administrative offices are
located in the city, are principally concerned with promotion to local inhabitants but increasingly also with distributing selected information to potential commercial investors. 'Groningen City Promotions' is a local consortium mostly concerned with the organisation of local commercial, sporting
and social events. Many other public and private commercial organisations
are engaged in promoting aspects of the city, not least the University that
not only operates its own promotion of the city as an agreeable student town
but is also itself a major generator of visitors through conferences and other
academic activities. All these organisations project images of the city which
may reinforce, conflict or be irrelevant to the tourism product being sold by
the Provincial VVV, which is responsible for both attracting potential visitors from home and abroad as well as providing information and reservation
services to visitors already present in the city.

The promotional dilemma of whether to stress perceived city strengths or
to attempt to counter weaknesses has been tackled by an aggressive campaign that combines both strategies. The tourism marketing plan (VVV,
1992) recognises three strong points (reasonable quality/price, varied range
of urban activities, and cultural/historical attractions) and three weak ones
(uninteresting surrounding landscapes, national peripherality, and poor
transport accessibility). Information on the cultural, historical, gastronomic

and surrounding rural water based attractions is stressed but to this is added the potentially risky option of using the most evident weakness of the region as the main advertising slogan. The perceived peripherality and distant isolation of the northern region is recognised in the 'Top of Holland' promotion, with its slogan, 'There's nothing above Groningen' used nationally and internationally.

CONCLUSIONS

The three conclusions to emerge from the set of general questions posed and the brief description of their application in a single medium-sized city can be summarized in three statements:

* places are a distinctive type of product, and
* tourism place-products are a distinctive type of place-product, therefore,
* tourism place marketing is necessarily a distinctive form of marketing.

If these conclusions seem self-evident then their consequences in the practice of tourism place marketing, especially by public sector agencies, seem too often to have been rarely appreciated.

Place marketing is a legitimate form of marketing in the sense that the terminology, techniques and philosophies of marketing can be applied to places but equally if this is to be attempted successfully, then a special type of marketing has to be devised. All too often, discussion of marketing in the literature of tourism studies is at best crude attempts to apply disembodied techniques (such as product life cycle, product line positioning, market segmentation and the rest) divorced from their original conceptual contexts and at worst no more than just an arbitrary substitution of marketing jargon for previously used terminology.

The development and practice of the concepts of 'social marketing,' 'attitudinal marketing' and 'non-profit sector marketing,' developed over the last twenty years in marketing science and popularised notably by the much quoted writings of Kotler (1975), all contribute towards the possibility of constructing a specific tourism place marketing. This sort of marketing, it has been argued, (see Ashworth and Voogd, 1988) is in many ways a wider rather than narrower application of more general marketing. The goals of place marketing for example are likely to extend beyond quantitative product sales or producer profits to wider place management objectives over a longer period and for more diverse groups. Similarly the range of effective marketing measures available especially to public sector marketing organisations is likely to be much wider, including spatial design and planning characteristics, than those available in more conventional commercial product marketing.

In addition, however, explicit account has yet to be taken of the peculiar attributes of places as products. They possess intrinsic characteristics of multifunctionality and existence within spatial hierarchies as well as containing an enormous variety of elements which renders them quite different from the types of products for which marketing was initially devised and still today dominantly practised. Tourism in particular is notorious for its extreme variety and difficulty of definition. Almost any place facility can conceivably be part of some tourism product while few, if any, are exclusively used for tourism.

Similarly tourists as customers, tourism markets and the market pricing mechanisms that operate within them, as well as the sets of interventional measures designed to influence such markets, are all, as has been argued above, distinctive.

Although some progress has been made on understanding and accommodating a number of these elements separately, until this has been achieved in an integrated form, tourism place marketing remains an idea and an aim rather than a practical reality.

REFERENCES

Ashworth, G.J. and Stabler M. (1988). Tourism development planning in Languedoc: Le Mission Impossible? In Goodall, B. and Ashworth G.J. (eds) *Marketing in the tourism industry: the promotion of destination regions.* Beckenham: Croom Helm.
Ashworth, G.J. and Voogd H. (1988). Marketing the city: concepts processes and dutch applications. *Town Planning Review* 59(1) 65-80.
Ashworth, G.J. and Voogd H. (1990). *Selling the City.* London/New York: Belhaven/Columbia.
Brown, B.J.H. (1985). Personal perception and community speculation: a British resort in the 19th century. *Annals of Tourism Research* 12: 355-69.
Dienst Ruimtelijk Ordening/VVV Groningen (1992). *Toerisme Groningen in Cijfers* Groningen.
Haan, T.Z. de, Ashworth G.J. and Stabler M. (1990). The tourist destination as product: the case of Languedoc. In Ashworth, G.J. and Goodall, B. (eds) *Marketing Tourism Places.* London: Routledge.
Holloway, J.C. and Plant, R.V. (1988). *Marketing for Tourism.* London: Pitman.
Hughes, G (1991). Conceiving of Tourism. *Area* 23(3), 263-7.
Jansen-Verbeke, M.C. (1988). Leisure, recreation and tourism in inner cities: explorative case studies. *Netherlands Geographical Studies* 58 Utrecht/Nijmegen.

Kirby, A. (1985) Leisure as commodity: the role of the state in leisure provision *Progress in Human Tourism* 9, 64-84.

Kotler, P. (1975). *Marketing for non-profit organisations.* Englewood Cliffs: Prentice Hall.

Leiper, N (1990) Partial industrialisation of tourism systems. *Annals of Tourism Research* 17, 600-5.

Middleton V.T.C. (1988). *Marketing in travel and tourism.* London: Heinemann.

Plog, S.C. (1973). Why destination areas rise and fall in popularity. *Cornell HRA Quarterly*, November 13-16.

Sinclair T., Clewer A. and Pack A. (1990). Hedonic pricing and the marketing of package holidays: the case of tourism resorts in Malag. In Ashworth, G.J. and Goodall B. (eds) *Marketing Tourism Places.* London: Routledge.

Sinclair, T. and Stabler M. (1992). *The tourism industry: an international analysis* Farnborough: CAB International.

Stabler M.J. (1988). The image of destination regions. In Goodall, B. and Ashworth G.J. (eds) *Marketing in the tourism industry*, Beckenham: Croom Helm.

VVV Groningen (1992). *Beleidsplan 1993-1997* Groningen.

Witt, S.F. and Moutinho L.A. (eds). *Tourism marketing and management handbook.* Hemel Hempstead: Prentice Hall International.

Visitor Expectations of Tourism Benefits in Zambia

Winston Husbands

SUMMARY. The author conducted a survey of foreign guests at Mfuwe Lodge in South Luangwa National Park, Zambia, to investigate the role of various benefits in visitor expectations of a rewarding visit to Zambia, and to assess visitor satisfaction with the tourism benefits. It emerged that the Zambian tourism product is highly undiversified. Wildlife, scenery and opportunities for experiencing African culture were the benefits most sought by visitors, and visitors defined the entire tourism product and their experience of it according to those benefits. Long stay visitors and those aged 30-49 displayed the most rigourous demands for a satisfying visit, in terms of opportunities for experiencing African culture, travel around the country, and the desire for interesting cuisine.

INTRODUCTION

National parks form an almost exclusive theme in Zambia's tourism product. However, the success of tourism usually depends on the availability of a wide range of benefits which, together, form an integrated tourism

Winston Husbands is affiliated with the School of Applied Geography, Ryerson Polytechnical Institute, 350 Victoria Street, Toronto, Ontario M5B 2K3, Canada.

This research was supported by a grant awarded by the University of Zambia in 1987.

[Haworth co-indexing entry note]: "Visitor Expectations of Tourism Benefits in Zambia." Husbands, Winston. Co-published simultaneously in *Journal of International Consumer Marketing* (The Haworth Press, Inc.) Vol. 6, No. 3/4, 1994, pp. 21-38; and: *Global Tourist Behavior* (ed: Muzaffer Uysal) The Haworth Press, Inc., 1994, pp. 21-38. Multiple copies of this article/chapter may be purchased from The Haworth Document Delivery Center [1-800-3-HAWORTH; 9:00 a.m. - 5:00 p.m. (EST)].

21

product. In this regard, the objectives of the present study are as follows:
(1) to assess the importance of various tourism benefits in Zambia, from
the visitors' viewpoint, (2) to derive the various dimensions of the Zambian tourism product, and (3) to assess visitor satisfaction by comparing
visitors' expectations with their actual experience of the various benefits.

The data originate from a survey of foreign visitors at Mfuwe Lodge in
the South Luangwa National Park of Zambia (Figure 1), conducted in
1987. Respondents rated a number of benefits in terms of their importance
for a rewarding visit to Zambia, and indicated the extent to which they felt
satisfied with their experience of each benefit. In addition the questionnaire solicited respondents' sociodemographic and travel profile.

Visitor evaluation of tourism benefits may form the basis for altering
the product and/or its marketing. This is crucial for Zambia, where the
imperative for improving tourism's economic profile is indeed strong.
Within the context of Zambia's poor economic performance over the last
decade (Burdette 1988), it is necessary to re-examine the practical feasibil-
ity of national park tourism.

TOURISM BENEFITS AND VISITOR SATISFACTION

Benefits are the attributes of a destination that are of interest to tourists.
'Ease of travel' from place to place, interesting scenery, and opportunities
for viewing wildlife may all be regarded as benefits in a particular destination. All benefits have the potential to enhance or degrade the tourism
product in a particular destination, but not to the same degree.

Several researchers have approached the study of tourism benefits from
the perspective of benefit segmentation (Graham and Wall 1978; Mazanec
1984; Mills et al. 1986; Snepenger 1987; Thomson and Pearce 1980;
Woodside and Jacobs 1985). Researchers suggest that awareness of the
number and structure of the various segments facilitates a more efficient
marketing strategy. However, June and Smith (1987) have suggested that
basic questions concerning consumer behaviour are obscured by the segmentation approach to market research. In this light, segmentation usually
takes account of what tourists do (or did) or what they consider important,
but the relationship between actual experiences and prior expectations has
remained largely unexplored.

The extent to which tourists are satisfied with the many benefits offered
by a destination is a function of their prior expectations and their actual
experience in the destination (Francken and van Raaij 1981; Pizam et al.
1978; van Raaij 1986). Moreover, the concept of visitor satisfaction
should properly refer to specific aspects of the vacation, since relatively

FIGURE 1

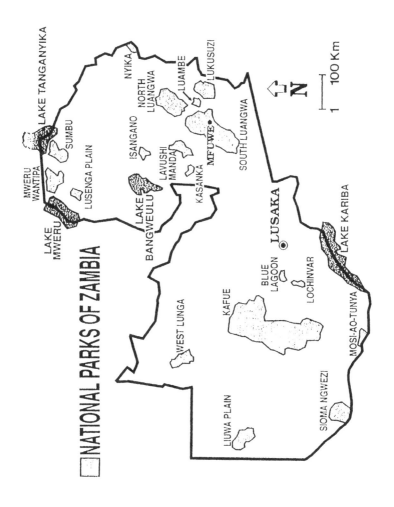

NATIONAL PARKS OF ZAMBIA

little information is disclosed by stated overall satisfaction (Buchanan 1983; Lounsbury and Hoopes 1985; Vaske et al. 1986).

A destination is usually characterised by several benefits. Among visitors, opinions are likely to differ concerning the importance of each benefit for a rewarding stay in, or experience of, the destination. It is likely, therefore, that benefits are evaluated in different combinations or packages, and the importance of any benefit reflects its relationship with the other benefits in the package (or packages) in which it occurs. What this means is that destinations should be multidimensional, in terms of the benefits and experiences produced by the destination and consumed by tourists.

NATIONAL PARKS AND TOURISM IN AFRICA

With the exception of Victoria Falls (which is not a national park in the usual sense), only four of Zambia's national parks are commonly accessible to visitors. These are Kafue (22,400 km^2), South Luangwa (9,050 km^2), Sumbu (2,020 km^2), and Lochinvar (410 km^2) (Figure 1). South Luangwa was established as a park in 1972, but has a much longer history as a game reserve. Large mammals are abundant in the park, there being large numbers of elephant, buffalo, hippopotamus, zebra, and a large variety of antelope. In addition, the park holds a large population of lions and a smaller number of leopards (Arid Lands Information Centre 1982; Clarke and Loe 1974). In 1978 (the last year for which published data are available), the number of visits to North and South Luangwa combined totalled 7,027, an increase of 135% since 1969 (Government of the Republic of Zambia 1970; 1979). This makes the Luangwa Valley (mainly South Luangwa National Park) the second most popular tourist attraction in Zambia, after Victoria Falls (Husbands 1989; Husbands and Thompson 1990).

The national parks of southern and eastern Africa (in which are included the Zambian parks) are home to "the last large-scale remnant of the tremendous variety of mammals of the Pleistocene" which included "the most remarkable array of mammal life this planet has known" (Myers 1972, 1255). Suttles and Suttles-Graham (1986) maintain that the "most impressive attributes [of Zambia] have to do with water" (p. 283), to which they also added wildlife and "bird-watching opportunities." Nolting (1987) suggests that while visitors to Kenya and Tanzania are rushed from park to park, in Zambia "the emphasis is on experiencing the bush and wildlife" through walking safaris, the best of which are available in Zambia (p. 161). Specific guidebook references to South Luangwa National Park indicate that the best walking safaris in Africa are available here (Nolting 1987, 160), and that "Luangwa has the most prolific animal populations in Africa" (*Traveller's Guide to Central and Southern Africa,* p. 208). But the guidebook picture is most sharply drawn by Crowther (1986). According to Crowther, "there's precious little worth seeing in Zambia apart from Victoria Falls and the national parks" (p. 708). It is reasonable to expect, therefore, that tourists in Zambia have an over-whelming interest in wildlife and that, with few exceptions, other benefits are incidental to this.

In the 1960s there was considerable optimism concerning the suppos-edly beneficial relationship between national parks, tourism and economic development (Thresher 1972). More recently, optimism has been replaced by skepticism. There has always been a suspicion that Europeans (under whose direction the African parks were established) gained more from wildlife tourism (as tourists) than the various indigenous African popula-tions (in economic rewards). Marshall (1988, 242) has argued along these lines, suggesting that wildlife tourism in Africa, in its present form, is an elitist enterprise that is only marginally "developmental." Myers (1972) and Branagan (1974) have documented cases in which the establishment of national parks in Africa resulted in a considerable cost in readjustment and loss of livelihood for populations displaced by the parks.

Pullan (1983) has noted that the economic performance of national parks in Africa (vis-à-vis tourism) has been decidedly disappointing. He proposed that "only a few parks are so located and have significant attrac-tions as to make international tourism in parks economically viable" (Pul-lan 1983, 4). In addition, only a few countries "have additional tourist attractions to combine with national park visits and there are often formi-dable distances between the different locations" (Pullan 1983, 5). Pullan concludes that national park management in Africa is characterized by "benign neglect" because parks absorb scarce financial resources without giving much in return.

Given Zambia's reliance on national parks in the country's tourism indus-try, serious questions exist about the depth of the current tourism resource base, and the necessity for Zambia to diversify its tourism product. The analysis to follow is therefore a partial test of Pullan's (1983) hypothesis regarding the severely undiversified nature of the Zambian tourism product.

METHODS

Foreign guests (non-residents of Zambia) at Mfuwe Lodge in South Luangwa National Park participated in a questionnaire survey from May to October 1987. Mfuwe Lodge is owned and operated by National Hotels Development Corporation (NHDC), a Zambian parastatal company. One copy of the questionnaire was distributed to each adult guest as part of the checking-in process, and guests were requested to turn in completed questionnaires at the time of their departure. Each spousal party received only one questionnaire, soliciting information from only one of the spouses. The final content and form of the questionnaire, as well as the mode of delivery, were based on the results of a pre-test carried out at Mfuwe one year earlier.

The following benefits were presented to respondents: opportunities for viewing wildlife (non-hunting), opportunities for experiencing local (African) culture, interesting scenery, opportunities for shopping (African art and craft), opportunities for rest and relaxation, ease of travel from place to place around Zambia, interesting cuisine, international hotel-type accommodation, nightlife, and diversity of attractions.

Respondents rated the anticipated importance of each benefit for a satisfying visit to Zambia, on a five-point scale (1 = very important; 2 = somewhat important; 3 = of average importance; 4 = somewhat unimportant; 5 = unimportant). In a second section of the questionnaire that also dealt with benefits (except that 'accommodation' was substituted for 'international hotel-type accommodation'), respondents indicated how satisfied they were with each of the benefits encountered on their stay in Zambia. Responses were recorded on a five-point scale (1 = very satisfied; 2 = somewhat satisfied; 3 = average satisfaction; 4 = somewhat dissatisfied; 5 = dissatisfied). These latter data are not, however, a measure of true satisfaction. Rather, they represent visitors' evaluation of their actual experience. A measure of true satisfaction with a specific benefit should normally take account of whether the visitor thought the benefit important in the first place.

The *relative importance* of various benefits is assessed by applying multidimensional scaling (MDS) to a proximities matrix of benefit importance. The MDS routine available in the SYSTAT statistical package was used for this task. It was expected that wildlife, culture and scenery should emerge as the most important benefits sought, while travel within Zambia, international hotel accommodation and nightlife should be the least important. The dimensionality of the importance data is an indicator of the *complexity* of the Zambian tourism product. Each dimension represents a different bundle or package of benefits (Goodrich 1977) that visitors seek in Zambia. For example, a one-dimensional solution would suggest that Zambian tourism is highly undifferentiated. A chi-square test was used to examine the relationship between judged benefit importance and visitor profile.

Respondents are considered to be *satisfied* with a benefit if they rated the benefit important for a rewarding visit (1 or 2 on the importance item) and if they also rated the actual experience as rewarding (1 or 2 on the experience item). Conversely, respondents are considered to be *dissatisfied* with a benefit if they rated the benefit important for a rewarding visit (1 or 2 on the importance item) but rated the actual experience as unrewarding (3, 4, 5 on the experience item). A chi-square test was used to examine the relationship between satisfied/dissatisfied and visitor profile.

The visitor profile consists of respondents' age group, country of origin, intended length of stay in Zambia, main reason for visiting Zambia, gender, estimate of whether or not Zambia is an expensive place to spend a holiday, and whether or not they had visited Zambia previously. No information on respondents' income was solicited because of the difficulty of comparing several different currencies.

Characteristics of the Sample

From a total of 300 questionnaires distributed, 135 usable questionnaires were returned. These 135 respondents represent one quarter of all non-residents staying at Mfuwe for all of 1987. Europeans accounted for the largest share of Mfuwe visitors (Table 1). However, the NHDC figures in Table 1 should be treated with caution since the nationality of every member of a party is sometimes not recorded.

Men outnumbered women in the sample (53% versus 46%). Respondents are relatively young: 38% were less than 30 years old and 65% were less than 40. Fifty eight percent of the respondents were in Zambia primarily on holiday, and the remainder were almost equally distributed between business, visiting friends and relatives, and 'other' purposes. The intended length of stay in Zambia ranged from 2 to 90 days, but the mean length of stay was 21 days (the mode and median were 8 and 14 days respectively). Respondents were almost equally divided on whether Zambia was an expensive or inexpensive place to holiday: 39% thought Zambia a costly destination, while 42% thought not, and 13% were unsure. The majority of respondents (81.2%) travelled to Zambia in the company of friends and/or relatives. Likewise, most persons (66.7%) spent the major part of their stay in paid accommodation. The sample was also dominated by persons visiting Zambia for the first time (77%).

A high proportion of respondents (43%) indicated that they would be visiting no other park. Of these, 34 were in Zambia on holiday. This means

TABLE 1. Distribution of Mfuwe Guests by World Region, 1987

Region	Mfuwe sample[1]		Total Mfuwe guests[2]	
	f	%	f	%
Africa	17	12.8	30	5.6
Asia	3	2.3	30	5.6
Caribbean	1	0.8	0	0.0
Europe	97	72.9	398	74.3
Middle East	1	0.8	0	0.0
North America	14	10.5	67	12.5
Oceania	0	0.0	11	2.1
Total	133	100.0	536	100.0

[1] Over the six month period of the survey; two respondents did not indicate country of residence.

[2] For the whole of 1987; developed from unpublished data supplied by National Hotels Development Corporation, Lusaka.

that almost half (47.5%) of those who travelled to Zambia for holiday would visit only one of the four parks commonly accessible to visitors.

Visitors should be in the final stage of the vacation sequence before they seriously consider the extent of their satisfaction (van Raaij 1986). In the Luangwa survey there were 58 persons who would visit no other park besides South Luangwa, and a further 22 persons indicated that they had visited some other national park before arriving at South Luangwa. Thus, 59.3% of the sample had already acquired as much first-hand knowledge of the parks as their itineraries would allow.

DATA ANALYSIS AND DISCUSSION

The Importance of Various Benefits

Opportunities for viewing wildlife and for experiencing African culture, interesting scenery, and local travel are generally important to visitors

(Table 2). Conversely, international hotel-type accommodation and night-life are relatively unimportant. Since visitors are virtually unanimous about the importance of wildlife, scenery, local culture and local travel, these benefits will not be discussed in relation to visitor profile. The visitor profile variables were recoded as shown in Table 3, while benefits were recoded as important (1 and 2 in Table 2), of average importance, and unimportant (4 and 5 in Table 2).

Only pairs of variables with statistically significant relationships are presented in Table 4. The search for rest and relaxation was considered important by return visitors, while those who thought this benefit unimportant or of average importance were almost exclusively first-time visitors. Interesting cuisine was judged unimportant mainly by persons on holiday, while those visiting Zambia for other reasons were anticipating interesting cuisine. International hotel-type accommodation was unimportant to younger visitors (20-29 age group) and important to older visitors (50 years old and over), but of average importance to the 30-49 years age group. Men, more so than women, were looking for nightlife; but the majority of women were not interested in this benefit. Respondents visiting Zambia for reasons other than holiday were not concerned with diversity of attractions. On the other hand, persons on holiday constituted the majority of those for whom this benefit was important.

However, these relationships notwithstanding, the benefits collapse along a single dimension that partially distinguishes the relatively important from the relatively unimportant benefits (Table 5). The matrix of inter-benefit dissimilarity was calculated on the original five-point importance scale. The low STRESS ($S_1 = 1$) shown in Table 5 indicates that a one-dimensional MDS solution is appropriate. Davison (1983, 91) and Kruskal and Wish (1978, 54) suggest that this solution should be accepted when $S_1 < .15$. Furthermore, the solution presented in Table 5, where I > 4R (I = the number of objects, R = the number of dimensions), means that S_1 is not sensitive to either I or R (Kruskal and Wish 1978, 52).

This single dimension is dominated by the contrast between wildlife, local culture, and scenery (wildlife tourism, nature, the non-urban, the traditional) on one hand, and nightlife (urban, modern) on the other. These attributes anchoring the extremes of the scale are those for which responses were almost unanimous. Respondents display various levels of diverging views for the benefits located between the extremes. However, these divergences are not substantive enough to necessitate additional dimensions.

Visitors have a reasonably consistent and clear-cut idea of what they seek in Zambia. The relative location of benefits on this single dimension (Table 5) coincides with the popular image of Africa: the supremacy of nature,

TABLE 2. Frequency of Respondents Indicating the Importance of Each Benefit for a Satisfying Visit to Zambia

Benefit	1. Very important f	%	2. Somewhat important f	%	3. Average importance f	%	4. Somewhat Unimportant f	%	5. Unimportant f	%	Total f	%
Viewing wildlife	124	93.2	8	6.0	1	0.8	0	0.0	0	0.0	133	100.0
Experiencing African culture	70	52.6	43	32.3	13	9.8	4	3.0	3	2.3	133	100.0
Scenery	72	56.3	45	35.2	8	6.3	3	2.3	0	0.0	128	100.0
Shopping	23	17.4	40	30.3	37	28.0	19	14.4	13	9.9	132	100.0
Rest and relaxation	38	28.8	45	34.1	33	25.0	7	5.3	9	6.8	132	100.0
Travel around Zambia	51	39.8	56	43.8	14	10.9	6	4.7	1	0.8	128	100.0
Interesting cuisine	20	15.5	42	32.6	42	32.6	18	14.0	7	5.4	129	100.0
Hotel-type accommodation	29	22.1	32	24.4	37	28.2	17	13.0	16	12.2	131	100.0
Nightlife	11	8.7	14	11.0	26	20.5	24	18.9	52	40.9	127	100.0
Diversity of attractions	18	14.0	46	35.7	40	31.0	8	6.2	17	13.2	129	100.0

TABLE 3. Visitor Profile Variables

Variable	Categories
Age group	20-29; 30-49; > 49
World region of residence	Africa; Europe; North America
Intended length of stay in Zambia (days)	2-14; > 14
Main reason for visiting Zambia	holiday; all other
Gender	male; female
Cost of holidaying in Zambia	expensive; not expensive; unsure
No. times visited Zambia	return visit; first visit

traditional cultures, and the non-Western. Visitors do not anticipate a highly complex product. Zambia appears to offer a stylised product appealing to a particularly specialised market. Visitors anticipate and expect that Zambia offers few benefits. The attributes sought are those most obviously associated with national park tourism: wildlife, nature, and the quaintness of local culture.

Visitor Satisfaction

It may be recalled that respondents are considered satisfied or dissatisfied with a benefit only if they initially judged the benefit very important/important. The intention in this section is to examine the relationship between satisfied/dissatisfied and the visitor profile. Here, 'satisfied' and 'dissatisfied' are not strictly 'either/or' categories. Furthermore, in most cases, the frequencies of 'satisfied' and 'dissatisfied' are not of sufficient magnitude to make the analysis of 'satisfied' versus 'dissatisfied' technically meaningful.

Table 6 shows that respondents were generally satisfied with opportunities for viewing wildlife and scenery-the same two benefits they identified as important for a successful visit (Table 2). Few respondents could be classified as satisfied with nightlife because only eleven persons considered this benefit important for a rewarding visit.

Statistically significant relationships between satisfaction and visitor profile variables are shown in Table 7. Wildlife, scenery and nightlife were excluded from this analysis because respondents were almost unanimous

TABLE 4. Relationship Between Visitor Profile and Benefit Importance

Profile variable	Benefits	n	Chi-square	df
Age group	accommodation	119	11.78[a]	4
Main reason for visiting Zambia	cuisine	115	8.65[a]	2
Main reason for visiting Zambia	diversity	115	6.75[a]	2
Gender	nightlife	126	7.76[a]	2
No. times visited Zambia	rest/relaxation	130	9.75[b]	2

[a] : $p < .05$

[b] : $p < .01$

TABLE 5. Relative Importance of Zambian Tourism Benefits: MDS Solution

Benefit	Scale value
Viewing wildlife	−1.46
Experiencing African culture	−1.06
Scenery	−0.94
Shopping	0.41
Rest and relaxation	−0.10
Travel around Zambia	−0.50
Interesting cuisine	0.21
Hotel-type accommodation	0.77
Nightlife	2.11
Diversity of attractions	0.56

Stress (S_1) = 0.11

TABLE 6. Visitor Satisfaction with Tourism Benefits: Satisfied

Benefits	Satisfied respondents f	%	Others f	%	Total
Viewing wildlife	125	95.4	6	4.6	131
Experiencing African culture	67	53.2	59	46.8	126
Scenery	102	82.3	22	17.7	124
Shopping	36	28.6	90	71.4	126
Rest and relaxation	71	55.5	57	44.5	128
Travel around Zambia	61	49.6	62	50.4	123
Interesting cuisine	36	29.0	88	71.0	124
Accommodation	49	38.3	79	61.7	128
Nightlife	10	9.0	101	91.0	111
Diversity of attractions	48	41.0	69	59.0	117

about the importance of wildlife and scenery, and about the lack of importance of nightlife. Visitors who were satisfied with opportunities for shopping were dominated by the youngest (20-29 years) and the oldest (50 years and over) age groups. Return visitors are more likely to be satisfied with opportunities for rest and relaxation. When compared to European and North American visitors, visitors from other African countries also appear satisfied with rest and relaxation. Short-stay visitors are more likely to be satisfied with opportunities for local travel than long-stay visitors.

Overall, there are no benefits with which visitors are generally dissatisfied (Table 8). However, the numbers of respondents dissatisfied with their experience of African culture and opportunities for travel around Zambia are large enough to warrant concern.

Statistically significant relationships between visitor profile variables and 'dissatisfied' and other visitors are reported in Table 9. This analysis was undertaken only for benefits with large numbers of dissatisfied respondents: local culture, shopping, local travel and cuisine. Respondents aged 30-49 were generally dissatisfied with opportunities for experiencing local culture. Similarly, the likelihood of disappointment with cuisine was greatest among the 30-49 age group. Dissatisfaction with opportunities for local travel was

TABLE 7. Relationship Between Visitor Profile and Visitor Satisfaction: Satisfied and 'Other' Visitors

Profile variable	Benefits	n	Chi-square	df
Age group	Shopping	114	6.14^a	2
World Region of residence	rest/relaxation	121	6.33^a	2
Length of stay in Zambia	local travel	121	11.36^{c*}	1
No. times visited Zambia	rest/relaxation	126	10.74^{b*}	1

^{a} : $p < .05$

^{b} : $p < .01$

^{c} : $p < .001$

* With Yates' Correction

TABLE 8. Visitor Satisfaction with Tourism Benefits: Dissatisfied

Benefits	Dissatisfied respondents		Others		Total
	f	%	f	%	
Viewing wildlife	5	3.8	126	96.2	131
Experiencing African culture	40	31.8	86	68.3	126
Scenery	12	9.7	112	90.3	124
Shopping	26	20.7	100	79.4	126
Rest and relaxation	12	9.4	116	90.6	128
Travel around Zambia	41	33.3	82	66.7	123
Interesting cuisine	24	19.4	100	80.6	124
Accommodation	11	8.6	117	91.4	128
Nightlife	14	12.6	97	87.4	111
Diversity of attractions	14	12.0	103	88.0	117

TABLE 9. Relationship Between Visitor Profile and Visitor Satisfaction: Dissatisfied and 'Other' Visitors

Profile variable	Benefits	n	Chi-square	df
Age group	culture	114	8.77[a]	2
Age group	cuisine	112	7.84[a]	2
Length of stay in Zambia	local travel	113	15.96[b*]	1
Cost of holiday in Zambia	culture	120	6.85[a]	2

[a] : $p < .05$

[b] : $p < .001$

* With Yates' Correction

most frequent among long-stay visitors. Persons who thought that Zambia was an expensive place to holiday are also likely to experience dissatisfaction with opportunities for experiencing African culture.

CONCLUSION

Overall, long-stay visitors and those in the 30-49 age group appear to exert the most rigorous demands for a satisfying visit to Zambia, especially in respect to experiencing local culture, opportunities for local travel, and the desire for interesting cuisine. Similarly, visitors who thought Zambia expensive also recorded noticeable dissatisfaction. On the other hand, younger visitors (20-29 years old) were more likely to be satisfied with their experience. Similarly, visitors whose stay in Zambia was of short duration (2-14 days) were usually satisfied with their experience. Not surprisingly, return visitors also tend to be satisfied, but these comprise less than a quarter of all respondents.

Visitors were generally satisfied with the benefits which they expected to be most important for a rewarding experience–wildlife, scenery and, to a lesser extent, local culture. However, visitors from other African countries (mainly neighbouring ones where wildlife also abounds) are impressed by opportunities for rest and relaxation in Zambia, as are return visitors. These findings are consistent with the earlier suggestion concerning the generally low level of diversification of the Zambian tourism product. Zambia therefore offers a very limited number of benefits. Certainly, a more diverse and well-rounded set of attractions, in addition to improved transportation infrastructure, should allow Zambia to attract visitors with different levels of interest in wildlife and local culture. Such a policy would, however, necessitate very comprehensive tourism planning to ensure that these different visitor interests are not destructive of the primary tourism resources associated with national parks.

Almagor (1985) has remarked that a visit to Africa represents an "escape to nature." Indeed, "escape to nature" seems an accurate description of the benefits sought and satisfaction obtained by visitors to Zambia. The dominant benefits are wildlife, scenery, and an experience of African culture, although visitors are divided about the satisfaction gained from the latter. As far as visitors are concerned, the Zambian tourism product is relatively uncomplicated, and visitors are single-minded in their expectations. The national parks of Zambia therefore appear to fulfill a very specialized tourism function.

REFERENCES

Almagor, U. (1985). A Tourist's Vision Quest in an African Game Reserve. *Annals of Tourism Research,* 12, 31-47.

Arid Lands Information Center. (1982). *Draft Environmental Profile of Zambia.* Washington, DC: U.S. National Park Service and U.S. Man and the Biosphere Secretariat.

Branagan, D. (1974). A Conflict Between Tourist Interests and Pastoralism in the Ngorongoro Highlands of Tanzania. In Centre for African Studies *Tourism in Africa and the Management of Related Resources.* Conference held at the University of Edinburgh, Scotland.

Buchanan, T. (1983). Toward an Understanding of Variability of Satisfactions within Activities. *Journal of Leisure Research,* 15, 39-51.

Burdette, M. (1988). *Zambia: Between Two Worlds.* Boulder: Westview Press.

Clarke, J. and Loe, I. (1974). *A Guide to the National Parks of Zambia.* Lusaka: Anglo-American Corporation.

Crowther, G. (1986). *Africa on a Shoestring.* Victoria, Aust.: Lonely Planet Publications.

Davison, M. (1983). *Multidimensional Scaling.* New York: John Wiley.

Francken, D. and van Raaij, W. (1981). Satisfaction with Leisure Time Activities. *Journal of Leisure Research,* 13, 337-352.

Goodrich, J. (1977). Benefit Bundle Analysis: An Empirical Study of International Travelers. *Journal of Travel Research,* XVI (2), 6-9.

Government of the Republic of Zambia. (1970). *Annual Report for 1969*. Lusaka: Department of Wildlife, Fisheries and National Parks, Ministry of Lands and Natural Resources.

Government of the Republic of Zambia. (1979). *Annual Report for 1978*. Lusaka: Department of Wildlife, Fisheries and National Parks, Ministry of Lands and Natural Resources.

Graham, J. and Wall, G. (1978). American Visitors to Canada: A Study in Market Segmentation. *Journal of Travel Research*, XVI (3), 21-24.

Husbands, W. (1989). Social Status and Perception of Tourism in Zambia. *Annals of Tourism Research*, 16 (2), 237-253.

Husbands, W. and Thompson, S. (1990). The Host Society and the Consequences of Tourism in Livingstone, Zambia. *International Journal of Urban and Regional Research*, 14 (3), 490-513.

June, L. and Smith, S. (1987). Service Attributes and Situational Effects on Customer Preferences for Restaurant Dining. *Journal of Travel Research*, XXVI (2), 20-27.

Kruskal, J. and Wish, M. (1978). *Multidimensional Scaling*. Beverly Hills, CA: Sage.

Lounsbury, J. and Hoopes, L. (1985). An Investigation of the Factors Associated with Vacation Satisfaction. *Journal of Leisure Research*, 17, 1-13.

Marshall, A. (1988). Tourists, Parks and Poverty: Wildlife Tourism and African Development. In J. Stone (Ed.) *The Exploitation of Animals in Africa*. Aberdeen: Aberdeen University African Studies Group.

Mazanec, J. (1984). How to Detect Travel Market Segments: A Clustering Approach. *Journal of Travel Research*, XXIII (1), 17-21.

Mills, A., Couturier, H. and Snepenger, D. (1986). Segmenting Texas Snow Skiers. *Journal of Travel Research*, XXV (2), 19-23.

Myers, N. (1972). National Parks in Savannah Africa. *Science*, 178 (December), 1255-1263.

Nolting, M. (1987). *African Safari: The Complete Guide to Ten Top Game Viewing Countries*. Pompano Beach, FL: Global Travel.

Pizam, A., Neumann, Y. and Reichel, A. (1978). Dimensions of Tourist Satisfaction with a Destination Area. *Annals of Tourism Research*, V, 314-322.

Pullan, R. (1983). Do National Parks Have a Future in Africa? *Leisure Studies*, 2, 1-18.

Snepenger, D. (1987). Segmenting the Vacation Market by Novelty-Seeking Role. *Journal of Travel Research*, XXVI (2), 8-14.

Suttles, S. and Suttles-Graham, B. (1986). *Fielding's Africa South of the Sahara*. New York: William Morrow.

Thomson, C. and Pearce, D. (1980). Market Segmentation of New Zealand Package Tours. *Journal of Travel Research*, XIX (1), 3-6.

Thresher, P. (1972). African National Parks and Tourism—An Interlinked Future. *Biological Conservation*, 4, 279-284.

Travellers' Guide to Central and Southern Africa. (1988). London: IC Publications.

van Raaij, W. (1986). Consumer Research on Tourism. *Annals of Tourism Research,* 13, 1-9.

Vaske, A., Fedler, A. and Graefe, A. (1986). Multiple Determinants of Satisfaction from a Specific Waterfowl Hunting Trip. *Leisure Sciences,* 8, 149-166.

Woodside, A. and Jacobs, L. (1985). Step Two in Benefit Segmentation: Learning the Benefits Realized by Major Travel Markets. *Journal of Travel Research,* XIV (1), 7-13.

Tourism Marketing Management in Small Island Nations: A Tale of Micro-Destinations

Stanley D. Reid
Laurel J. Reid

SUMMARY. Small islands have geographically imposed limits on their ability to capture an appropriate share of the growing global tourism market. These constraints can however be overcome by careful analysis of tourist behaviour and designing tourism strategies which make efficient use of the insights such an examination reveals. Tourism policy planners in small destinations should focus on maximising yield from tourist visitations and selectively pursue growth in tourism numbers.

INTRODUCTION

Small island nations have three attributes that give them a distinctive status among global tourism markets. These are size, geographical isolation and political autonomy. Size restricts the scale of tourism plant that can be established and rules out any dependence on the domestic internal

Stanley D. Reid is Professor of Management, University of the West Indies, Barbados, and Executive Director of the Centre for Management Development (Eastern Caribbean), University of the West Indies, P.O. Box 64, St. Michael, Barbados. Laurel J. Reid is Assistant Professor, Department of Recreation and Leisure Studies, Brock University, St. Catherine, Ontario, Canada L2S 3A1.

[Haworth co-indexing entry note]: "Tourism Marketing Management in Small Island Nations: A Tale of Micro-Destinations." Reid, Stanley D., and Laurel J. Reid. Co-published simultaneously in *Journal of International Consumer Marketing* (The Haworth Press, Inc.) Vol. 6, No. 3/4, 1994, pp. 39-60; and: *Global Tourist Behaviour* (ed: Muzaffer Uysal) The Haworth Press, Inc., 1994, pp. 39-60. Multiple copies of this article/chapter may be purchased from The Haworth Document Delivery Center [1-800-3-HAWORTH; 9:00 a.m. - 5:00 p.m. (EST)].

travel market as a source of tourists. Geographic isolation determines that tourism traffic be tied exclusively to sea and air transport modes. Political autonomy confers a sovereign status which makes it possible to negotiate aviation and maritime agreements for attracting international transport carriers. These three factors collectively distinguish small island states from the majority of tourist destinations that are the typical subject of tourism research.

Island destinations deserve special attention since relative size and geography are well recognised as critical planning considerations in developing tourism strategies (Gunn, 1988). However, normative approaches to planning and managing tourism focus on destinations whose tourism planning concerns are conceptually and operationally different from those of small island nations. These approaches, which argue for national, regional and local planning frameworks, are recommended for destinations that are typically in close physical proximity to or are part of a larger geographic market for domestic tourism that is directly and easily accessed by a variety of transit modes (e.g., bus, rail, ferry and automobile). As a result, the tourism marketing issues and concerns of small island destinations remain relatively untouched.

This paper, using island destinations in the Caribbean region as illustrative examples, provides insights into the marketing and management of micro-destination tourism. It explores the strategic issues that should be considered in designing tourism policies for microstates. Specific attention is paid to approaches that can be used for developing tourism promotion expenditures and visitor spending.

BACKGROUND

The task of developing a viable tourism industry for island states must begin with addressing the limitations and opportunities that size, geographical isolation and political autonomy create. These are presented in Table I and subsequently discussed.

SIZE

It is generally accepted that the size of a host economy limits the extent to which it can benefit from tourism as an industry (Khan, Seng and Cheong, 1990; Poon, 1990; Mathieson and Wall, 1982). This is particularly true for island microstates which are constrained by the absolute limita-

TABLE I. Major Factors Affecting Micro-Island Destination Tourism and Their Effects

Factors	Limitations	Opportunities
Size	**Disadvantages**	**Advantages**
	· Limits ability to attract sizeable capital investment and thus affects the pace and scale of tourism plant development · Potential for delivery of acceptable service levels constrained by presence of a minimum basic infrastructure · Highly fragile social and ecological systems that are sensitive to even small increases in tourist numbers · Market for domestic tourism nonexistent · Tourism promotion using mass market distribution channels and media unsuitable for small tourist numbers	· Selectivity of markets determined by ability to service · Selectivity of capital investment type and suppliers based on compatibility with market to be serviced · Holistic development of tourism product · Greater potential for retailing local services · Development of personalised guest-host relationships · Potential for accommodation of guest-house, family type hospitality sector · Greater use of informal and personalised promotion to market · Selectivity in origin market and segment afforded specific
Geographic Isolation	**Disadvantages** · Relative inaccessibility · Dependency on sea and/or air transportation modes	· Appeal to "allocentric" travellers (explorers) · Positioning of uniqueness
Political Autonomy	**Disadvantages** · Limits ability to negotiate with international transport carriers · Tourist vulnerability to national safety and security problems · Independent regulatory and bureaucratic requirements for traveller	· Can negotiate bilateral international transport arrangements to suit specific needs · Can negotiate special arrangements with other sovereign states · Cultural appeal as a distinctive nation · Special tax and regulatory climate can be used to encourage tourism travel

tion put on the volume of tourist visitations required to both justify and sustain particular levels of capital investment in a tourism plant (O'Reilly, 1988). The viability of tourism projects becomes even more sensitive to variations in tourism demand levels when small visitor numbers are under consideration (Weaver, 1990; Sessa, 1983). As a result the tourism product tends to be developed in small increments and is usually not in a position to have either the service levels or minimum basic infrastructure to attract further investment (Burnett and Uysal, 1991; Getz, 1983). An additional and increasingly critical consideration is the sensitivity of island ecosystems to small changes in tourism numbers (Holder, 1988; Krippendorf, 1982). These changes and their effects must be assessed in the context of carrying capacity for an entire island environment isolated by water from its neighbours.

Microstates have to rely exclusively on external markets for tourism since their small size effectively rules out any potential for domestic tourism. However accessing these markets involves considerable expenditure if conventional mass media methods of destinations promotion are used (Ogilvy and Mather, 1988). In many instances the absence of a critical mass in tourism plant makes it difficult for a destination to attract the network of facilitating intermediaries (travel agents and tour operators) who service international travel (Ryan, 1991). This situation is further compounded by the fact that many of the tourism channel intermediaries, typically sourcing island tourism traffic, exercise considerable bargaining power in their relationship with small destination markets (Poon, 1987).

Advantages of Small Size

While size does limit tourism growth it also confers some advantages to island states. Small geographic size assists in the promotion of a sense of community and personalised ties (Wheeller, 1991). This makes it easier to preserve local culture and identity, an important element in giving an island destination distinctiveness. It also affords an opportunity for being highly selective in choice tourism development approaches and tourism markets for promotion. In addition it is feasible to offer the highly personalized service which is a key feature of "small members" tourism.

POLITICAL AUTONOMY

Political autonomy confers on a microstate the jurisdictional authority over flows of goods, services, capital and people across its borders. It involves the setting up of legal conventions, bureaucratic rules and documentation for controlling and monitoring the movement of tourists. It also confers a responsibility for the security and safety of another country's citizens. Sovereignty makes an island particularly vulnerable to political acts of other sovereign states. For example embargoes that restrict travel and trade between a destination and a tourist origin nation can be imposed as in the case of Cuba or Haiti and the USA, or, travel advisories, identifying a destination as one to be avoided, may be issued as in the recent case of Barbados and the USA and the UK.

Advantages of Political Autonomy

Sovereign status allows the microstate to negotiate transport and other special agreements requiring bilateral and international approval. It also means the power to modify, remove or simplify a wide range of regulatory barriers which impact adversely on tourism flows. These barriers include regulations affecting traffic in goods and services, tax treatment of out of country expenses for activities such as conventions, quarantine procedures, travel entry documents and barriers to investment from foreign sources. Because of small size the regulatory concerns that typically require the coordination of national, regional and local levels of tourism planning can be centrally addressed. In general, political autonomy allows for integrated development of islands as destinations and the establishment of regulatory regimes specifically geared towards tourism development.

GEOGRAPHIC ISOLATION

Islands, as land masses surrounded by water, depend on sea and air transportation for physical linkage to other geographic areas. Convenient access from and to tourist origin markets depends exclusively on the reliability and frequency of international transport carriers. These transport modes are by definition mass transit carriers and typically move large numbers. It is these characteristics which are the most problematic issues in developing islands as tourist destinations since traffic volume is the single most important requirement for receiving a scheduled air and sea transport service.

Advantages of Geographic Isolation

Relative geographic isolation leads to the creation of habitats or ecosystems which give an island destination physical attributes that are unique and have special appeal. However, the "allocentric" crowd, initially drawn to islands that are "off the beaten track," often pave the way for the arrival of greater tourism numbers and increases in established communication and transport links that reduce an island's isolation. This means that tourism expansion has the potential to destroy the very qualities of an island destination which makes it initially attractive (Wheeller, 1991). However the fact of small size makes it easier for an entire eco-system to be more effectively managed. Island destinations thus have more scope for preservation of eco-systems and environmental control.

Small island states appear then to be in a paradoxical position because the joint effects of size, sovereignty and geography limit their potential to achieve an appropriate share of the world's fastest growing industry. Moreover, developing this potential means competing with other destinations who are in a more advantageous position to bargain with the network of intermediaries (tour operators, travel agents and transport carriers) that service international tourists. A premium is thus placed on finding strategies which can reduce constraints related to size (Burnett and Uysal, 1991; Morgan, 1991).

THE CARIBBEAN SETTING

The Caribbean region encompasses 32 countries, 28 of which are islands or island groupings (e.g., St.Vincent and the Grenadines). Of the total number of countries, half (16) have sovereign status (i.e., are self-governed) of which thirteen are islands. Tourism is a major industry for the region even though it accounts for only 2.4 percent of all international travel and 3.8 percent of world tourism receipts in 1986 (Waters, 1988). For example the tourism industry in most Caribbean countries is one of the principal sources of foreign exchange earnings and jobs (Caribbean Tourism Statistical Report, 1990).

Demand for Caribbean destinations is typically generated in European and North American markets which collectively account for the majority of international traveller trips in the region (see Table II). The USA, a primary source market, accounts for approximately 60% of all tourist arrivals with the United Kingdom and Canada being dominant secondary source markets for islands that are part of the British Commonwealth but are for the most part sovereign. France and Holland are important primary or secondary source markets depending on whether the island destination under consideration is linked to these countries as a political unit. The relative importance of these source markets for a representative group of island destinations is shown in Table II.

Examination of a sample of Caribbean nations provides some insights into the market development limitations previously mentioned. The geographic area encompassed by the relative population of these nations varies widely with the largest islands (Bahamas, Cuba, Dominican Republic/Haiti, Jamaica, Puerto Rico and Trinidad) accounting for approximately 93% of the total land mass and population of all twenty-eight Caribbean islands or island groupings. Most of these islands are less than 750 square kilometres in area. They have populations of 1/4 million or less, which in some instances are considerably less than the number of stay over tourist arrivals (see Table III). These data underline both the limited potential of an island destination, if any, for generating an internal tourism market and the constraints that are likely to exist on tourism carrying capacity.

Major differences exist between the tourism industry of each island. These are particularly evident when one examines the stages of tourism infrastructure, type of product offered (cruise vs. stopover), volume of tourist arrivals and the expenditures by national destination marketing organizations such as tourist boards (see Table III). Few islands exceed national tourism promotion expenditures of US$2 million of which more than 1/3 is typically for administrative expenses (Caribbean Tourism Statistical Report 1990). This naturally means that promotional campaigns to both consumers and the travel trade have to be efficiently designed and implemented. It also indicates the problems faced by microstates when competing with other destinations who, by comparison, are able to launch relatively large and well financed promotional campaigns.

Over half of the region's accommodation capacity is accounted for by hotels with over 100 rooms. These are either internationally affiliated or owned and have room rates and operating costs that are among the world's highest. Their profitability typically is among the lowest by international standards (Pannell, Kerr, Forster, 1987). The poor performance of these enterprises can be attributed to the joint impact of low productivity, an excessive burden of duties, quantitative restrictions on imports and a general burden of fiscal and regulatory policies that affect the industry's competitiveness.

The dominance of large accommodation units varies from island to island. In destinations such as Barbados, British Virgin Islands, Dominica, Grenada, St.Vincent and Grenadines, smaller establishments account for 75% or more of accommodation capacity. Many of these establishments are owner-managed and undercapitalized. They do not have links with computerized reservation systems (Poon, 1990) and depend on personal networks in the trade and customer referrals for generating business. Small hotels also lack the financial resources to conduct large scale promotion in origin markets and consequently depend on spillover awareness created

TABLE II. Distribution of Tourism Arrivals from USA, UK and Canada Origin Markets Excluding Caribbean for Selected Microstates (1990)

SELECTED MICROSTATES	USA, UK and Canada Origin Markets: % of tourist arrivals	USA, UK and Canada Key Origin Markets: % of all non-Caribbean tourist arrivals
Anguilla	69	75
Antigua and Barbuda *	54	
Barbados *	69	80
Bonaire	56 (est)	58
British Virgin Islands	73	74
Cayman Islands	88	95
Curacao	14	20
Dominica *	30	75
Grenada *	44	55
Montserrat	57	89
St. Christopher and Nevis *	51	84
St. Lucia *	64	88
St. Vincent and the Grenadines *	47	76
Total for region	72	85

* Sovereign Status

Source Caribbean Tourism Statistical Report 1990, Caribbean Tourism Organisation, Barbados, 1991

through destination promotion by large international tourism supplier and government tourism agencies. The extent of their dependence on these sources and the benefits secured is however unknown.

The above features point to major concerns that tourism policy makers in these island destinations have. They emphasize the need for tourism strategies that explicitly address the use of scarce resources. In addition, a fundamental question is posed, and that is, are the interests of micro-destinations best served by a focus on increasing tourism arrivals or on maximizing gains from existing levels of tourist visitations? It is from this perspective that size, geographical isolation and political autonomy weigh as critical considerations in developing tourism strategies for the microstate.

USA %	UNITED KINGDOM %	CANADA %
60	8	1
39	8	7
33	23	13
47	5 (est)	4
64	4	5
81	3	4
10	1	3
14	12	4
27	11	6
38	10	9
38	7	16
29	24	11
25	14	8
55	6	11

ECONOMIC EFFICIENCY, SIZE AND TOURISM STRATEGIES

Efficiency in resource use and maximization of social welfare gains are generally accepted as desirable goals for a tourism industry (Gunn, 1988; Pearce, 1981; Bryden and Faber, 1971). Within this framework it is necessary to understand the scope and potential of tourism for contributing to the development of other economic sectors, a feature that is considered as a major asset (Mathieson and Wall, 1982; Pearce, 1982). This potential can only be unlocked if markets are created for goods and services which can be serviced in or at the destination. The creation of entrepreneurial opportunities through tourist expenditures and consumption behaviour should therefore be a significant consideration in developing tourism policies.

TABLE III. General and Tourism Statistics for Selected Cor Microstates (1990)

Selected Micro-States	Area (sq. kms)	Population (000's)	National Tourist Board Expenditure (000's) US$
Anguilla *	91	8	511
Antigua and Barbuda	440	80	N/A
Barbados *	431	257	11,167
Bonaire	311	10	N/A
British Virgin Islands	150	13	876
Cayman Islands	260	27	11,143
Curacao	544	198	14,526
Dominica *	750	82	446
Grenada *	345	107	1,896
Montserrat	102	12	172
St. Christopher and Nevis *	269	45	674
St. Lucia *	616	151	1,813
St. Vincent and the Grenadines *	388	116	644
Total	4,799	1,106	N/A
Total for regions islands	239,374	32,660	N/A

* Sovereign Status

Source: Caribbean Tourism Statistical Report 1990, Caribbean Tourism Organisation, Barbadox, 1991

Source: J.A. Hall and R. Braithwaite "Caribbean Cruise Tourism—a business of transnational partnerships" *Tourism Management*, 1990 p.342

Stayover tourist arrivals (000's)	Cruise Passengers (000's)	Tourist accommodation (rooms)	Proportion of rooms in larqe hotels (100 rooms or over) %
31	59	741	0
206	224	2,752	0
432	363	6,650	20-39
41	5	1,038	60-69
161	97	1,121	10-19
253	362	3,064	20-39
208	159	1,631	60-69
45	7	570	0
82	183	1,105	10-19
17	11	233	0
76	34	1,402	0
138	102	2,370	60-69
54	79	1,058	0
1,761	1,685	23,735	N/A
11,842	7,450	124,191	50% (est)

Accommodation, food, leisure-based activities and gift purchases represent the main categories of tourist expenditure (Curtin and Sobers, 1987). It is both the magnitude and distribution of these expenditures that are critical issues in evaluating the viability of tourism policy initiatives designed to promote inter-sectoral linkages (Khan, Seng and Cheong, 1990). Such evaluations based on an understanding of tourism consumption patterns and decisions may show opportunities for developing viable inter-dependence between sectors. The tourism literature offers little guidance in this regard although there is suggestive evidence that the vacation expenditure decisions are influenced by family life cycle (Lawson, 1991) and country of origin (Keown, 1989). The extent to which similar behavioural influences on visitor spending is present among tourists to micro-destinations and its significance needs examining.

The above issues emphasize the economic relevance of small destinations understanding tourist behaviour. They suggest that both the absolute and relative magnitude of differences between tourist and domestic market expenditures should be considered when designing strategies for promoting tourism linkages with other sectors. This underscores the desirability of identifying and targeting tourist markets with consumption and expenditure patterns that fit output of services and goods of a destination where possible. In this manner tourism strategies can be pursued that are sensitive to a need for achieving both greater benefits from tourist spending and spending by tourists (Heng and Low, 1990). This is not an easy task, particularly where size and stage of economic development results in a very limited productive capacity. (Burnett and Uysal, 1991; Bogino, 1987).

TOURIST EXPANSION STRATEGIES

Destinations can use market concentration or market diversification as basic strategies for expansion. The first strategy focuses primarily on existing markets, with a view to increasing visitor length of stay, and/or encouraging multiple visits for shorter duration. It presumes a high destination satisfaction which can be translated into repeat visits. This approach depends on a *core market* which is incrementally extended by word-of-mouth, use of additional media and travel supplier networks. This core market can be segmented on the basis of activity, country of origin or any other relevant criterion.

The second approach, market diversification, relies on developing destination attributes and benefits that are sufficiently distinct in character to attract a variety of tourist markets. It typically involves the development of different travel products, intermediaries, networks and promotion channels for each market being targeted. The distinction between the two strategies is one of emphasis, since a destination's core attributes represent building blocks for both approaches.

The choice of expansion strategy has significant resource implications for a destination. Entry into new markets, the diversification approach, involves investments in both time, money and creativity in order to develop awareness and interest in the destination among prospective travel intermediaries and tourists. It often requires the establishment of new transportation linkages in addition to significant promotional expenditure. In contrast, a market concentration strategy leverages prior investments in familiar markets and is far more time efficient and less costly for the small island destination. It is from this perspective that the relevance of repeat visitors to the tourism strategies of small destinations should be assessed.

In spite of its desirability, repeat patronage (customer retention) receives little or no attention as an element in the tourism strategies of micro-nations. This distinctive buying behaviour signals the ability of a destination to generate loyalty in the form of repeat visits. Repeat visitor markets appear to be substantial, given the high levels of repeat visitation to Jamaica (33%) (Phipps, 1981) and Bahamas (42%) (Bahamas Tourism Statistics, 1987). Even higher repeat visitation levels are reported for island destinations outside the Caribbean (Gyte and Phelps, 1989; Gitelson and Crompton, 1984). This suggests that the importance of repeat visitors to island destinations, as a tourist market segment, cannot be overstated and deserves special attention.

A key concern then in the marketing strategy is knowledge of repeat visit characteristics such as visitation frequency, visit duration and period and market size. This knowledge helps in identifying a destination's competitive position and its potential for focusing on a market concentration strategy. Such a strategy would be aimed at achieving specific levels and rates of visitor conversion as evidenced by proportion of repeat visitations, their recency and frequency. The real issue then is establishing the net economic benefits (net of promotional costs) to be gained from a focus on repeat visitor markets in contrast to pursuing alternative markets.

Marketing strategies which strive to minimize foreign exchange leakages can also contribute to increasing the economic benefits of tourism. The number and type of channel intermediaries used to serve visitor travel influence the amount of net foreign exchange earned by the destination. These intermediaries (tour operators and travel agents) are typically based in tourist origin markets and may be integrated firms owning accommodation and ancillary services in destination markets with expected consequences for foreign exchange retention. For example, suppliers of all inclusive charter tours capture as much as 69 percent of tourist revenue if they own or control accommodation, ground handling and tour representation at the destination. However this percentage drops to 45 percent if these suppliers use independent accommodation and tour operator representation (Bull, 1990).

The relevance of channel intermediaries to islands can also be addressed from the perspective of size. Large package tour operators often secure heavily discounted prices from local accommodation suppliers because they are in a position to provide the traffic required to maintain viable occupancy levels, particularly during off season periods. They are typically involved with larger accommodation establishments in comparison to specialised operators (such as those offering nature tourism) who serve relatively fewer numbers, in some instances, less than 200 clients (Ingram and Durst, 1987).

Special markets, because of their smaller volume characteristics, should appeal to micro-destinations since they offer opportunities for more manageable relationships and greater selectivity in tourist visitor segments to be aimed at. However effective targeting and use of special markets requires a fairly extensive knowledge of how the travel industry is organized and holiday travel products distributed. Marketers must be particularly alert to differences in supplier and customer behaviour across national origin markets since travel industry structures typically show wide international variations.

ORIGIN MARKETS AND TOURISM BEHAVIOUR

Geographic origin is commonly used for categorizing tourism markets. This variable serves to focus a tourism marketing strategy since transportation routes, carriers, travel intermediaries and promotion channels are typically tied to national boundaries. Geographic origin represents the basis for collecting and interpreting tourism data in most regions. Consequently this criterion is universally employed to distinguish tourist segments.

Not surprisingly many of the differences in Caribbean tourist behaviour are identified in the context of national origin (Curtin and Sobers, 1987). For example, USA, Canadian, UK and European tourists to the Caribbean differ along several dimensions, including: average daily expenditure, length of stay, season visitation patterns, type of accommodation patronized, kind of meal package used and number of countries visited per trip (*North American Demand Study of Tourism, 1983; European Tourism Demand Study Update, 1983; Caribbean Tourism Statistical Report, 1987;*

Bogino, 1979; U.S. Travel Service, 1978). These studies imply significant differences in tourism behaviour according to national origin and seem to offer information that is of strategic use to tourism policy making in island destinations.

It should be noted that studies, such as those previously referred to, are based on data that is grossly aggregated. One should therefore exercise caution in interpreting the data these studies offer and assessing their validity. Aggregated data often obscures highly skewed distributions when presented in summary statistics such as "averages," conceals significant differences in tourism behaviour within and between markets, and when it aggregates country of origin markets into broader geographic areas effectively disguises any differences in traveller behaviour that may be significant to country-based marketing strategies used by a destination.

The European market is considered a single market and aggregated as such in Caribbean tourism data. However substantive differences exist in seasonal and destination visitation patterns among French, UK, German, Italian and Swiss travellers to the region (*Jamaica Annual Travel Statistics*, 1987; *Bahamas Tourism Statistics*, 1987; *European Tourism Demand Study*, 1983) These differences reflect biases in destination choice arising from historical, cultural and political links between origin and destination market which are formally represented in the presence of air and maritime transport services and travel intermediary networks. They merit significant consideration even though one recognizes that the type of trip may be a significant intervening variable affecting tourist expenditure behaviour.

It is difficult to say whether country of origin is really a factor that merits more substantive attention beyond its current practical use in defining the spatial location of potential tourist markets and tourism service suppliers. The research literature provides no evidence, apart from the well recognised impact of cultural affinity, to justify a continuation of consumption habits when individuals become tourists. Indeed, the fact of being a tourist may well lead to novel consumption activity. Notwithstanding these methodological reservations, destination marketers should be aware of any valid and significant country of origin differences in accommodation desired, consumption behaviour and visitation period since these provide opportunities for designing specially tailored tourism products and services.

Smaller geographic regions within countries such as states, provinces and cities warrant special attention by micro-destinations in their own right. They tend to be more accessible from an operational standpoint, have travelling populations that are easier to identify when compared to a country, typically contain population clusters of sufficient size and homogeneity to be viable tourist markets and offer opportunities for profiling travellers that are an appropriate fit to a micro-destination's characteristics.

Tourist visitations from national regions and sub-regions are of particular significance to the Caribbean area. For example, New York State accounted for nearly one-third of all US tourists visiting Barbados and one-sixth of all US visitors to the Caribbean region during 1990 (*Caribbean Tourism Statistical Report*, 1990). Similarly, more than seventy percent of all Canadian tourist arrivals to the region in the same year came from the province of Ontario, (Caribbean Tourism Statistical Report, 1990). Similar biases appear in the concentration of visitor arrivals from national sub-regions. For example, four cities in the provinces of Ontario and Quebec (Toronto and Ottawa, Montreal and Quebec City) account for nearly one-half of all Canadian travellers to Caribbean destinations (*North American Demand Study for Caribbean Tourism*, 1983).

The geographic concentration previously noted is likely to be a pervasive feature of most tourist origin markets. It questions the conventional focus by island destinations on tourism promotional efforts targeted at national markets. The scope for economies in promotional efforts and savings in promotional expenditures appear to be substantial if more specific geographic approaches are used. In addition it offers opportunities for precise targeting of particular geographic areas. A more focused strategy to tourism promotion such as that advocated here must recognise that there are also significant inter- and intra-group differences in tourist behaviour which have to be taken into account.

Although regional concentration in tourist origin markets occurs, this can be mediated by other variables such as seasonality (Jacobs, Glenesk and Woodside, 1986). For example the Canadian cities that account for nearly half of all Canadian visits to the Caribbean area represent only 36 percent of winter visits from that market. More specifically, Quebec City accounts for 17.4 percent and 9.4 percent of all Canadian visitors during summer and winter months, respectively. In contrast, Ottawa residents represent 1.3 percent and 4.6 percent of all Canadian visitors during the same periods. (*North American Demand Study for Caribbean Tourism*, (1986)). These seasonal variations suggest that when region of origin is considered in a destination's marketing strategy, there are other specific tourist behaviours that must still be taken into account. It is evident then that a focus on sub-regions in origin markets provides destination marketers with strategic flexibility and a variety of options in developing their tourism industry.

CRUISE PASSENGERS AS A MARKET

Island destinations in the Caribbean receive levels of cruise excursionist patronage that, in some instances, greatly exceeds tourist arrivals (*Caribbean Tourism Statistical Report*, 1990). However, policy making in the region is still driven by a major imperative of generating arrivals to meet accommodation capacity and are only now starting to give cruise excursionist travel any special attention. (Hall and Braithwaite, 1990). Ironically, little is known about cruise passengers who represent an important travel category. This group of travellers uses a transportation mode that covers a geographic area rather than specific destinations. Their travel involves short duration exposure to multiple island destinations. Such exposure serves to provide information that can help in selecting future destinations for alternative travel. It is this created awareness that offers a potential for systematic conversion of cruise passengers to stay over tourists if their identity is captured by the destination. This opportunity is not currently exploited and represents an area of strategic concern.

Travel expenditure statistics obscure the economic importance of cruise passengers as a market. For example, a 1986 Caribbean visitor spending study shows that this group spend less on a per day and per capita basis than stay over visitors (Curtin and Sobers, 1987). However, there is little difference between the daily expenditures of both groups when spending on accommodation and meals is factored out. In contrast data on aggregate expenditures by spending category shows that cruise visitors to the Caribbean spend almost the same amount per capita on duty-free items, gifts and liquors as longer-stay tourists. They also account for 60 percent of overall receipts in these expenditure categories and one-third of total expenditure on taxis and tours by all visitors (Seward and Spinrad, 1982). These findings suggest that, contrary to popular belief, the cruise ship market represents a significant economic contribution to the tourism industry and should be given a specific focus by Caribbean tourism decision makers.

WHAT SHOULD BE DONE?

Three central issues emerge in this discussion of tourism marketing management in sovereign micro-destinations. These are as follows:

1. Strategies for tourism expansion must focus on leveraging investments already made in infrastructure, creating destination awareness in origin markets and visitor patronage.

2. The search for opportunities for securing growth and greater yield from tourism should be guided by information on current cruise and stayover traveller behaviour.
3. Market segmentation and target marketing strategies offer the possibility of managing tourism within the constraints of size, geography and sovereign status.

Micro-destinations therefore need to bear the following considerations in mind when designing their tourism strategies.

TOURISM RESEARCH

More sophisticated, but useful, tourism research is vitally and urgently needed. This research is required to provide a more complete picture of current visitors and to identify market segments that can provide expenditure and consumption patterns consistent with that desired by a micro-destination. It would use, as its basis, information collected on both tourist and cruise ship visitors and if possible, archival data collected from accommodation facilities. Multivariate analyses of tourism data will have to be conducted so that more detailed visitor portraits are available. Within this context, the effectiveness of tourism promotion expenditures can be evaluated and the efficiency of present media programming in stimulating tourist visitations examined.

DIRECT MARKETING AND INFORMATION TECHNOLOGY

Specialized and niche markets can be reached through direct marketing. Comprehensive data bases using visitor entry forms and other methods need to be developed. These should be assembled, sorted and screened for use in direct marketing approaches. Using this approach, subscription or compiled lists of groups that match target market profiles can be rented. Promotional pieces are then directly mailed to names on these lists. This approach is the only method that allows for direct testing and measurement of promotional effectiveness. Such strategies present opportunities for cost-efficient use of promotional dollars and have been successfully used by tourism destination markets and tourism package suppliers (*Marketing News*, 1987, Snepenger, 1986). In addition, direct marketing can be tailored to fit any scale of promotion, from mass mailings by destination marketers to limited mailings by small hotels. In this respect a synergy can be created between tourism promotion at the industry level and that done by individual enterprises.

FOCUS ON MARKET SEGMENTS
AND SPECIALIZED PRODUCTS

Budgeting constraints make the amount that any Caribbean tourist organization can spend extremely small in comparison to well-financed competitors. Promotional efforts must therefore be directed toward offering specialized products to special interest and or niche markets. These markets have networks of travel and promotion channels which are particularly well placed to deal with small numbers. They permit more selective and focused media use and offer opportunities for strategic alliances with key actors who can effectively distribute and promote a destination.

POOLING RESOURCES

Strategic alliances are an obvious way for small destinations to overcome resource constraints. Pooling of resources can help to achieve critical mass and secure economies of scale and scope (Poon, 1987). Cooperative grouping, with the help of information technology, offers national tourist promotion agencies, accommodation suppliers and other ancillary enterprises the potential to

- share and manage information
- introduce inward-bound toll-free lines
- achieve bulk purchasing economies similar to that afforded large competitors
- use specialized management expertise technical skills and full-time service staff such as maintenance engineers and accountants
- have access to facilities and services for both own use and customers
- create a pool of trained personnel for managing information and providing the required product development
- engage in joint marketing efforts and product development.

CONCLUSION

Strategies for encouraging, limiting or managing tourism growth for micro-destinations must have the common objective of *securing tourism markets that match their resources and use their competitive and comparative advantages*. Pursuit of this objective must take into account that:

a. Caribbean destinations, collectively and individually, represent minor markets in world tourism,
b. tourism is an important, if not the key economic sector for many Caribbean islands and
c. each island destination has a unique identity and competitive potential that can be easily overlooked.

Irrespective of whether a small island destination has a "mature" or "developing" tourism industry, the mere fact of sovereignty is significant. Sovereignty indicates that microstates have absolute jurisdictional responsibility for the strategic direction of their destination's tourism industry. In this context, two strategic options are available. Destinations with tourism industries that are approaching their limits to physically carry and sustain tourism visitations must place their policy and managerial focus on maximizing local tourism spending, and maintaining or improving the physical integrity or quality of the tourism product. Destinations with developing tourism industries should focus on attracting and building markets that are consistent with their revealed advantages and distinctiveness.

Intelligent management is therefore a prerequisite for micro-destinations to benefit from the benefits of tourism. Knowledge of visitors' demographics, consumption habits and spending, and the tourism product they desire is the key to designing effective tourism marketing programmes. A systematic policy of market segmentation and product innovation aimed at satisfying market niches and retention of past patrons offers significant potential for microstate destinations to achieve the economic benefits they desire from tourism.

REFERENCES

Bahamas Tourism Statistics. (1987). Ministry of Tourism. Nassau, Bahamas.

Bogino, P. (1987). The Economic Impact of Tourism in Guadeloupe. In *Caribbean Tourism Policies and Impacts*, (ed) J. Holder. Barbados: Caribbean Tourism Research and Development Centre, 226-294.

Bryden, J. and M. Faber. (1971). Multiplying the Tourist Multiplier. *Social and Economic Studies*, 20, part 1, pp. 61-82.

Bull, A. (1990). Australian Tourism: Effects of foreign investment. *Tourism Management* (December), pp. 325-331.

Burnett, G.W. and M. Uysal. (1991). Dominica-Geographic isolation and tourism prospects. *Tourism Management*, (June) 12, (2) pp.141-145.

Caribbean Tourism Statistical Report 1990. (1991). Barbados, Caribbean Tourism Organisation.

Curtin V. and A. Sobers (1987). *Visitor Spending in the Caribbean in 1986*. Barbados: Caribbean Tourism Research and Development Centre.

European Tourism Demand Study Update (1983), Barbados: Caribbean Tourism Research Centre, Vol. II.

Frank, K.E.R. (1968). Market Segmentation: Research and Implications. *Applications of the Sciences in Marketing Management*, (eds.) F. Bass, C. King and E. Pessemier. New York: John Wiley & Sons, Inc.

Getz, D. (1983). Capacity to Absorb Tourism: Concepts and Implications for Strategic Planning. *Annals of Tourism Research*, 10, 2, 239-263.

Gitelson, R.J. and J.L. Crompton. (1984). Insights into the repeat vacation phenomena, *Annals of Tourism Research* 11, pp. 199-218.

Gunn, C.A. (1988). *Tourism Planning*, New York, Taylor and Francis.

Gyte, D.M. and Phelps A. (1989). Patterns of destination repeat business: British tourists in Majorca, Spain. *Journal of Travel Research*, 28, (1), pp. 24-28.

Hall, J.A. and R. Braithwaite. (1990). Caribbean Cruise tourism. A business of transnational partnerships. *Tourism Management*, (December), pp. 339-347.

Holder, J. (1988). Pattern and Impact of Tourism on the Environment of the Caribbean." *Tourism Management*, June, pp. 119-127.

Ingram C.D. and Durst P.B. (1987). Nature-Oriented tour operators: Travel to developing countries. *Journal of Travel Research*, 28, (2), pp. 11-15.

Jacobs, L.W., G. Glenesk and A. Woodside. (1986). Segmenting International Travel Markets by Seasons: Implications for Tourism Marketing Strategy *Tourism Services Marketing: Advances in Theory and Practice*, (eds.) W. Joseph, L. Moutinho and I. Vernon. Special Conference Series, V. II, Cleveland, Ohio: Academy of Marketing Science and Cleveland State University, 97-106.

Jamaica Annual Travel Statistics. (1987). Kingston, Jamaica: Ministry of Mining, Energy and Tourism.

Keown C. (1989). A model of tourists' propensity to buy: The case of Japanese visitors to Hawaii, *Journal of Travel Research*, 27, (3), pp. 31-34.

Khan H., C.F. Seng and W.K. Cheong. (1990). Tourism multiplier effects on Singapore, *Annals of Tourism Research*, 17, (3), pp. 408-418.

Krippendorf, J. (1982). Towards New Tourism Policy–The Importance of Environmental and Socio-Cultural Factors. *Tourism Management*, 3 (September), pp.135-148.

Lawson R. (1991). Patterns of tourist expenditure and types of vacation across the family life cycle. *Journal of Travel Research*, 29, (4), pp. 12-18.

Marketing News. (1987). Direct Marketing in the Travel Industry, 20, (14) July, 1987.

Mathieson, A. and G. Wall. (1982). *Tourism, Economic, Physical and Social Impacts.* New York: Longman.

Morgan, M. (1991). Dressing up to survive-marketing Majorca anew, *Tourism Management.* (March), pp 15-20.

Nolan, S.D. (1976). Tourists use and evaluation of travel information sources: Summary and conclusions. *Journal of Travel Research*, 14, pp. 6-8.

North American Demand Study for Caribbean Tourism. (1983). Barbados: Caribbean Tourism Research Centre, V. 3.

Ogilvy and Mather. (1988). *Trends in Travel and Tourism Advertising Expenditures in the United States Measured Media, 1983-1987*. New York: Ogilvy and Mather Ltd.

O'Reilly, A.M. (1988). Tourism in the Eighties from the Commonwealth Caribbean Perspective: Change, Challenge and Renewal. *Tourism: An Exploration*, 2nd ed. (Ed.) J. Van Harssel. New York: National Publishers of the Black Hills, pp. 213-224.

Pannel, Kerr, Forster. (1987). *Trends in the Hotel Industry: International Edition, 1987*. Houston, Texas: Pannel, Kerr and Forster.

Pearce, D. (1981). *Tourism Development*. New York: Longman Group Limited.

Poon, A. (1990). Flexible specialisation and small size: The Case of Caribbean Tourism. *World Development* 18, (1), pp. 109-123.

_____. (1988). Innovation and the Future of Caribbean Tourism. *Tourism Management*, (September), 213-220.

_____. (1987). *Information Technology and Innovation in International Tourism: Implications for the Caribbean Tourist Industry*. Sussex, England: University of Sussex, Science Policy Research Unit.

Ryan, C. (1991). Tourism and Marketing–a symbiotic relationship? *Tourism Management*, 12(2), (June), pp. 101-111.

Seward, S.B. and B.K. Spinrad. (1982). *Tourism in the Caribbean–The Economic Impact*, Ottawa, Canada: International Development Research Centre.

Sessa, A. (1983). *Elements of Tourism Economics*. Catal, Rome.

Snepenger, D.J. (1986). Segmenting the Alaskan Market by Tourist Style. *Tourism Services Marketing: Advances in Theory and Practice*, (eds.) W. Joseph, L. Moutinho and I. Vernon. Special Conference Series, V. II. Cleveland, Ohio: Academy of Marketing Science and Cleveland State University, pp. 107-118.

U.S. Travel Service. (1978). *Profiles of Travel to the United States from Selected Major Tourism Generating Countries*. Washington, DC: U.S. Department of Commerce.

Waters, Somerset R. (1988). *Travel Industry World Yearbook: The Big Picture 1988*. New York: Child and Waters, Inc.

Weaver D. (1990). Grand Cayman Island and the Resort Cycle Concept. *Journal of Travel Research* 29 (2), pp. 9-15.

Wheeller B. (1991). Tourism's troubled times. *Tourism Management* (June), pp. 91-96.

Foreign and Domestic Escorted Tour Expectations of American Travelers

Charles R. Duke
Margaret A. Persia

SUMMARY. A national survey of American escorted tour participants showed differences in expectations between domestic tours and foreign tours. Foreign travelers had higher expectations for tour comfort and value along with need for adequate stops, adventure, and educational aspects. Both groups expected the tour to be the best way to see as much as possible with a congenial atmosphere. Additionally, both groups expected comfort, scenery, and experienced tour guides. Tour planning can ensure that expectations are met.

INTRODUCTION

Tourism is a major world industry, but the dominant issues addressed in research have been related to promotion instead of other components of

Charles R. Duke is Assistant Professor, Department of Marketing, 245 Sirrine Hall, Clemson University, Clemson, SC 29634-1325. Margaret A. Persia is a doctoral candidate, Department of Parks, Recreation, and Tourism Management, Clemson University, Clemson, SC 29634.

Data collection assistance for this project was provided by the management and member firms of the American Society of Travel Agents and the National Tour Association.

[Haworth co-indexing entry note]: "Foreign and Domestic Escorted Tour Expectations of American Travelers." Duke, Charles R., and Margaret A. Persia. Co-published simultaneously in *Journal of International Consumer Marketing* (The Haworth Press, Inc.) Vol. 6, No. 3/4, 1994, pp. 61-77; and: *Global Tourist Behavior* (ed: Muzaffer Uysal) The Haworth Press, Inc., 1994, pp. 61-77. Multiple copies of this article/chapter may be purchased from The Haworth Document Delivery Center [1-800-3-HAWORTH; 9:00 a.m. - 5:00 p.m. (EST)].

marketing (Ryan 1991). While promotion is important, other issues need to be considered in creating a quality product. Tour product development has often been interpreted in terms of physical, tangible components alone without reference to the type of travelers that are attracted or to what these tourists want and expect from the tour experience (Middleton 1988). Although awareness of features and benefits of a tour is needed, a more critical issue for managers is that the expectations held by the tourist should be consistent with the reality of the tour itself (Ryan 1991). Tour designers must understand consumer wants, needs, and perceptions to determine benefits sought to create tour experiences that meet these needs (Calantone and Mazanec 1991). To measure the consistency required between consumer needs and the services delivered, important cognitive issues must be measured including expectations, satisfaction, attitude, image, perceived risk, and cognitive dissonance. A micro-approach to management which looks at these cognitive issues in a disaggregate, segmentation analysis is necessary to fully understand market needs (Calantone and Mazanec 1991).

EXPECTATIONS AND SATISFACTION

Consumer satisfaction is a fundamental element of services marketing (cf. Zeithaml, Berry, and Parasuraman 1988) and serves as a surrogate measure for quality of recreation service (cf. LaPage 1983). However, satisfaction is difficult to measure and to track (Hunt 1976). But by modifying some portion of the product mix in response to consumer feedback, increased consumer satisfaction will lead to a higher probability of business success. Satisfaction may occur when evaluation of the product is at least as high as expectations (cf. Engel, Blackwell, and Miniard 1990). To meet these expectations, travel companies must understand what consumers expect prior to the tour experience.

One approach to satisfaction determination is the expectancy-disconfirmation model (cf. Erevelles and Lockshin 1991). This notion suggests that consumers have certain beliefs about the attributes that a product has or should have (cf. Tolman 1932; Oliver 1977, 1980). Post-purchase consumer evaluations compare the perceived product experience with prior expectations to determine if expectations have been met. Unmet expectations may cause dissatisfaction and may decrease the consumer's inclination to repurchase (Engel, Blackwell, and Miniard 1990; LaTour and Peat 1979; Tse and Wilton 1988). Additionally, expectations provide an anchor point for further processing of satisfaction determination which may operate independently of disconfirmation effects (Oliver and DeSarbo 1988).

EXPECTATIONS AND TOUR PLANNING

Expectations of travelers should serve as a basis for tour planning and design (Mancini 1990). Escorted tour participants likely have relatively *high expectations* because the tour purchase, accompanied by its high cost relative to unescorted trips, is a decision of great consequence. Expectations have been considered in tour planning research (Cunningham and Thompson 1986; Lopez 1980, 1981; Pearce 1984; Quiroga 1990; Sheldon 1986; Thompson and Pearce 1980). In applying expectation issues to tour planning, some prior researchers have developed models based on consumer demographics (cf. Sheldon and Mak 1987). However, no prior work has investigated the expectation differences among consumers of foreign versus domestic travel. By understanding these differences, travel professionals can best plan for product offerings which suit the different expectations of these market segments. In addition, little work has been done to examine reactions of travelers across a large number of tour companies and tour destinations. Prior literature exploring tour expectations have concentrated on a specific application. To enhance the ability of managers to act on generalized information, multiple tours from a wide variety of suppliers should be studied.

Among discussions of cross-boundary tourism marketing, Ziff-Levine (1990) suggested that global marketing (similarities in product offerings across boundaries) should be used as a basis for tour development where commonalities in consumer response exist. This approach attempts to make the best use of limited resources. However, basic cultural differences suggest that each tourist nationality or ethnic origin may require a different marketing approach, and possibly more resources, to be successful. Whereas operators may offer certain services for domestic tourists, foreigners may require other services. Conversely, travelers from a single country may differ in their expectations for domestic travel versus foreign travel.

Group travel have been recognized as a major force in the tourism industry (cf. Sheldon 1986). Touring (such as escorted motorcoach tours) represents the largest segment of escorted group travel, approximately 30 percent (Longwoods 1990). These escorted tours represent a special travel segment where more service is expected. This segment is expected to grow modestly through the mid-1990s creating a highly competitive market in which both agencies and operators need to provide excellence in service (Ostrowski 1990). To provide that service, firms must be aware of and be able to address the specific expectations of the consumers.

Study Objectives

This study explored similarities and differences in a profile of tourist expectations for travel inside their country (domestic) versus travel outside their country (foreign). The investigation concentrated on a single nationality, citizens of the United States, with a national sample of escorted tour participants from a large number of agencies and operators. The specific objectives of the study were (1) to profile the level of expectations for all travelers on an upcoming tour experience and (2) to determine the similarities and differences in expectations between purchasers of domestic escorted tours and purchasers of foreign escorted tours.

METHOD

Design

Expectations were compared for American tourists preparing to go on either domestic or foreign tours. This sample design is meant to profile the similarities and differences between the two groups for consumer-generated expectation issues.

Sampling Procedure

Travel agencies and tour operators from throughout the United States were asked to assist in data collection. Agencies were selected from a list of those approved by the Airline Reporting Corporation, the widest sample frame available. Tour operators were selected from a list of members of the National Tour Association (NTA). Firms were asked to distribute a maximum of five surveys to escorted tour clients booked on upcoming tours. To maintain confidentiality, responses were not associated with the distributing firm. Of the 555 questionnaires distributed by the travel firms, responses were obtained from 133 tour participants.[1] This represents an appropriate sample size for Longwoods' (1990) estimate of America's touring market (2,975,200) at a confidence interval of 99 percent and a tolerance of 10 percent given the widest standard deviation resulting from the questionnaire's scale responses (cf. Tull and Hawkins 1991; Lehmann 1989). Agency clients provided 52 percent of the responses and operator clients provided 48 percent. More importantly, domestic travelers composed 47 percent of the sample with the remaining 53 percent traveling to foreign destinations.

Respondent characteristics, shown in Table 1, are similar to those for domestic escorted tours (Longwoods 1990). Additionally, these demographics are similar to a previous Spanish escorted tour study (Quiroga 1990). The majority of respondents were female, and most participants were between the ages of 61 and 75. Education level was relatively high. Respondents reported that they were experienced group travelers with a large majority having participated in previous escorted tours. European tours outnumbered all other foreign destinations which included a highly diverse set of destinations. Approximately one-third of the respondents indicated that they had visited their tour destination before. Tours occurred in every month of the year except January. Respondents resided in 29 different states.

Instrument

Printed questionnaires requested respondents to provide information on their tour plans and expectations. Prior tour research does not provide a consistent framework of similar measures, features, or benefits (cf. Um and Crompton 1991; Ross and Iso-Ahola 1991; Yau and Chan 1990; Chon 1990). However, a situational research approach may be appropriate given the variability of travel experiences available. Expectation statements used in this study were derived from an exploratory study of American escorted tour participants (Persia and Duke 1991). Specific statements generated from this exploratory study reflected consumer concerns in their own terminology which increases content and external validity from the consumers' perspective (cf. Peter and Ray 1984). Issues of concern to travelers included such classic expectations as itinerary, personal satisfaction, social interaction, services provided, and scenery. Additional external validity for the expectation statements was obtained by soliciting suggestions from industry research professionals. The research departments from the National Tour Foundation and the American Society of Travel Agents reviewed the statements and suggested refinement, consolidation, or elimination based on their experiences with field data collection. The final statements (Table 2) were pretested and considered appropriate by consumers who were not a part of final data collection. Respondents in the data collection phase of this study used the statements to complete Likert scales (+2 = strongly agree, − 2 = strongly disagree) rating tour expecta-

TABLE 1. Respondent Characteristics

Variables		Number	Percent
Gender:	Male	49	36.8
	Female	84	63.2
Age:	20-40	8	6.0
	41-60	21	15.8
	61-65	27	20.3
	66-70	40	30.1
	71-75	23	17.3
	76-85	14	10.5
Education:	Less than High School	12	9.0
	High School Diploma	37	27.8
	Technical/Vocational	9	6.8
	Associate Degree/Some College	31	23.3
	Bachelor's Degree	27	20.3
	Graduate Degree	17	12.8
Tour Experience:	Never on Tour Before	5	3.7
	1-3 Tours	32	24.1
	4 or More Tours	96	72.2
Destination:			
Domestic:	United States	62	46.6
Foreign:	Canada/Mexico	18	13.5
	Europe	27	20.3
	Other "Overseas"	<u>26</u>	<u>19.6</u>
Total Foreign:		71	53.4
Month of Tour:	January	0	0.0
	February	3	2.3
	March	4	3.0
	April	1	.8
	May	5	3.7
	June	32	24.0
	July	19	14.3
	August	7	5.3
	September	33	24.8
	October	16	12.0
	November	4	3.0
	December	9	6.8

TABLE 2. Expectations of Escorted Tour Participants

Expectation Statements
• I expect the scenery will be a source of enjoyment on this tour.
• I expect to be treated as a special person.
• I expect the tour escort in particular to make this tour enjoyable.
• I expect to be comfortable on this tour.
• I expect to make friends with other passengers on this tour.
• I expect the atmosphere among the group to be friendly.
• I don't expect to be alone often.
• I expect to learn new things about myself on this tour.
• I expect to get my money's worth on this tour.
• I expect to relax on this tour.
• I expect this tour will be the best way I personally could visit this destination.
• I expect I won't have to make major decisions on this tour.
• I expect to do what I couldn't do alone on this tour.
• I expect we will see as much as possible.
• I expect this tour to be adventurous.
• I expect never to be bored on this tour.
• I expect that stops at interesting places will be long enough to see what is important.
• I expect to be shown the most important attractions during this tour.
• I expect this tour to be educational.
• I expect to be safe from harm or injury on this tour.

tions along with other scales indicating the importance of each expectation (+2 = very important, +1 = important, 0 = neutral, − 1 = unimportant).

RESULTS

Expectations of All Tourists

Tourists indicated high expectations in several areas regardless of tour destination (Table 3). Nineteen of the 20 statements received a mean score within the "strongly agree" to "agree" range, indicating that these were appropriate expectations for tour participants. The highest rated expectations indicated that participants expected to be shown important attractions and expected that scenery would be enjoyable. Issues concerning the structure of the tour, such as stopping long enough to see what is important and seeing as much as possible, along with comfort and safety were rated highly. Also highly rated was the expectation that the tour was the best way to visit the destination. Participants next expected good value for their tour expenses and a friendly atmosphere along with competent escorts and the ability to do things they could not do alone. Other items received moderate ratings. The lowest rated statement "I expect to learn new things about myself" did not appear to be important to this group.

Foreign versus Domestic Expectations

Although foreign travelers indicated higher expectations in virtually all areas (Table 4), few of the differences were statistically significant at conventional levels (alpha = .05 or less). On foreign tours, travelers have significantly higher expectations of comfort. Additionally, these travelers expect to "get their money's worth." However, some of the expectations were marginally higher (alpha = .06 to .10) with this sample and might be considered as potential issues in future studies. Foreign tourists had marginally higher expectations for stops to be long enough to see those things which are important. Also, foreign tours created marginally higher expectations of being more adventurous and more educational. Support for considering these marginal expectation differences come from the importance attached to them (Table 5). Foreign travelers placed significantly higher importance to the expectation of tours being adventurous and educational. No other significant or marginal differences in expectation importance ratings were evident.

TABLE 3. Overall Tour Expectation Levels

Statement: "I expect . . ."	Mean[1]	(s.d.)
	(n = 133)	
I. to be shown the most important attractions.	1.64	(.58)
2. the scenery will be a source of enjoyment.	1.63	(.61)
3. stops long enough to see what's important.	1.55	(.62)
4. to be comfortable on this tour.	1.52	(.56)
5. we will see as much as possible.	1.51	(.69)
6. to be safe from harm or injury.	1.49	(.67)
7. this tour will be the best way I personally could visit this destination.	1.47	(.83)
8. to get my money's worth on this tour.	1.46	(.63)
9. atmosphere among group to be friendly.	1.40	(.59)
10. to do what I couldn't do alone on this tour.	1.37	(.88)
11. escort to make this tour enjoyable.	1.36	(.73)
12. I won't have to make major decisions.	1.25	(.85)
13. to relax on this tour.	1.08	(.91)
14. this tour to be adventurous.	1.06	(.85)
15. to make friends with other passengers.	1.03	(.72)
16. (not) to be alone often.	.97	(.88)
17. this tour to be educational.	.97	(.84)
18. to never be bored on this tour.	.92	(1.00)
19. to be treated as a special person.	.90	(1.00)
20. I will learn new things about myself.	.30	(.90)

[1] Listed in order of highest expectation

(+2 = Strongly Agree; − 2 = Strongly Disagree)

GLOBAL TOURIST BEHAVIOR

TABLE 4. Expectation Levels: Domestic versus Foreign Tours

Statement: "I expect . . ."	Expectation Means[1] Domestic (n = 62)	Foreign (n = 71)	t-Value	prob.
1. to see important attractions.	1.60	1.72	1.24	.22
2. scenery to be enjoyable.	1.55	1.70	1.48	.14
3. tour to be best way to visit.	1.50	1.48	.15	.88
4. to see as much as possible.	1.48	1.51	.19	.85
5. to be safe.	1.47	1.61	1.25	.21
6. to be comfortable.	1.43	1.63	2.10	.04[2]
7. friendly group atmosphere.	1.42	1.42	.03	.97
8. stops will be long enough.	1.42	1.61	1.71	.09[3]
9. to get my money's worth.	1.40	1.62	2.14	.03[2]
10. to do what I couldn't do alone.	1.32	1.45	.87	.39
11. escort to make tour enjoyable.	1.24	1.41	1.29	.20
12. not to make major decisions.	1.23	1.21	.10	.92
13. to relax.	1.10	1.07	.16	.87
14. to make friends.	1.06	1.06	.07	.95
15. not to be alone often.	1.02	.92	.66	.51
16. tour to be adventurous.	.94	1.17	1.63	.10[3]
17. never to be bored.	.87	1.07	1.20	.23
18. to be treated special.	.84	.94	.61	.54
19. tour to be educational.	.83	1.10	1.77	.08[3]
20. to learn about myself.	.29	.31	.13	.90

[1] Listed in order of highest expectation to Domestic travelers
 (+2 = Strongly Agree; −2 = Strongly Disagree)

[2] Significant (alpha = .05)

[3] Marginal significance (alpha = .06 to .10)

TABLE 5. Expectation Importance: Domestic versus Foreign Tours

Statement: "I expect . . ."	Importance Means[1] Domestic (n = 62)	Foreign (n = 71)	t–Value	prob.
1. to see important attractions.	1.92	1.72	1.34	.18
2. tour to be best way to visit.	1.75	1.54	1.09	.28
3. to get my money's worth.	1.71	1.73	.14	.89
4. to see as much as possible.	1.68	1.55	1.02	.31
5. stops will be long enough.	1.68	1.73	.50	.62
6. to be safe.	1.68	1.65	.17	.87
7. to be comfortable.	1.68	1.68	.01	.99
8. scenery to be enjoyable.	1.63	1.69	.54	.59
9. escort to make tour enjoyable.	1.58	1.58	.03	.98
10. friendly group atmosphere.	1.53	1.55	.15	.88
11. to do what I couldn't do alone.	1.44	1.45	.11	.92
12. not to make major decision.	1.16	1.27	.74	.46
13. to relax.	1.13	.96	.96	.34
14. to be treated special.	.89	.87	.07	.94
15. never to be bored.	.84	.96	.70	.49
16. to make friends.	.84	.82	.10	.92
17. tour to be adventurous.	.66	1.08	2.28	.02[2]
18. not to be alone often.	.63	.39	1.16	.25
19. tour to be educational.	.42	.89	2.48	.01[2]
20. to learn about myself.	.11	.20	.40	.69

[1]Listed in order of importance to Domestic travelers
 (+2 = Very Important, +1 = Important, 0 = Neutral, −1 = Unimportant)

[2]Significant (alpha = .05)

DISCUSSION

To begin the process of satisfying their consumers, travel firms must first understand the expectations of tourists. The results of this study provide some insight into the profile of escorted tour customer expectations. The expectation statements used to develop the traveler profiles should be useful to managers and researchers in continuing to develop more competitive tours. These statements, using consumer terminology and reviewed by industry researchers, reflected both the level of expectations and the importance of the issues to the consumer.

Common and Divergent Expectations

Expectation ratings were used to rank issues from most critical to least critical for the traveler. Top ranked expectations should be considered critical and must be met by the tour operator. Once these top expectations are met, then customers look to the lower issues to discriminate among tours and companies. In this case, the highest ratings were given to issues which expressed the basic attributes of the tour structure (important attractions, enjoyable scenery, appropriate stops, see as much as possible, providing the best way to visit, safety, comfort). The expense and time spent on an escorted tour may cause the traveler to require the tour provider to deliver a high level of service on these identifiable structural issues of a tour. These attributes, which were also common across both domestic and foreign tours, might be considered as "tangible" parts of the tour experience. Consumers use these issues as determining factors in deciding which tour to book. Firms should assume that these basic issues must be met simply to exist in the industry. The structural elements held in common by both domestic and foreign tours reflect American cultural beliefs and attitudes for escorted tours which are stable regardless of destination. This may illustrate an American attitude of escorted tours as being good values for efficient sight-seeing as the best way to visit a destination.

After higher level expectations are met, firms must compete on whatever level of issues are not yet met. Moderate level issues indicated social requirements such as friendly group atmosphere and an enjoyable escort. These issues are only partially under the control of the firm, but some training for escorts can improve the potential for satisfying these needs. The lower rated needs relate to personal benefits and enjoyment. Meeting these expectations (after meeting all higher rated needs) should make a tour more satisfying and help a firm to become more competitive in the industry. Personal issues such as relaxation, no decision making, and special treatment allow the traveler to reduce cognitive effort and create a less stressful experience. Firms can often meet these needs easily by meticulous preparation, by providing concise and complete information on important issues, and by providing small service details which make the tourist feel special.

This ranking of expectations underscores the reliance of prospective tour participants on the expert knowledge of the tour operator and escorts to structure the tour so that the basic expectations are met. Tradeoffs between conflicting tour features, which must be developed for all tours, should emphasize the need for meeting basic expectations first. The expectation of participants for definite procedures and structure support previous findings concerning purchase characteristics of prospective tour participants (Persia and Duke 1991).

Significant differences between foreign and domestic travelers relate to the uncertainty of personal issues and to a need for something other than an ordinary vacation. Personal safety and comfort are more important when travelers are not familiar with the customs and culture of the country that they will be visiting. Because the trip is unlikely to be duplicated in the future, travelers want to be assured of the value of their trip (financial risk, time used, and effort expended) and expect to be able to spend sufficient time to be able to enjoy their foreign destinations. On the other hand, these uncertainties are a part of the attraction of foreign locations which increase the sense of adventure and create an atmosphere of learning for the traveler. Therefore, uncertainty and higher risk are not only detriments to some portions of a foreign tour experience, but they are also a part of the attraction of the tour.

Limitations

Although selection of travel agents and tour operators was controlled to enhance the probability of a national sample, there is a potential that their actions in distributing the questionnaires may have biased the study. Instructions were detailed and callbacks to agents and operators indicated that their procedures were consistent with the spirit of obtaining a representative sample. Non-experienced tour travelers were not represented in this sample. However, the relative stability of expectations across experience levels might indicate that even inexperienced travelers would have similar responses. Additional research can verify this idea. Additionally, nonresponse bias may be important. If there were significant differences between those who chose to return questionnaires and those who did not, the expectations noted might be different from those presented. However, because of the method used in selecting potential tour participants for the study, it was not possible to probe for nonresponse bias. Client mailing lists were considered to be proprietary information and were not released by either tour operators or travel agencies.

Expectation differences developed here between domestic and foreign tours could possibly be explained in terms of perceived risk. With higher expense (financial risk) and longer vacations (personal time investment), consumers may generate higher expectations. In this study, no control was made for either cost or length of stay. Future studies could delineate these issues and contribute to the intriguing question of whether foreign travel itself or other risks (expense, length of stay, etc.) is the primary contributor to higher expectations.

This study focused on the profile differences between domestic and foreign escorted tour travelers for a specific set of expectations. Additional research might show the underlying dimensions of these expectations. Expectation, motivation, and attitude dimensions literature in tourism is diverse (cf. Um and Crompton 1991) and requires considerations beyond the scope of this profile analysis. Future studies could focus on these underlying issues.

Unescorted tour package offerings may generate a different set of expectations and importance ratings. Additionally, short tours (lasting for a single day or less), might generate less involvement and expectation by the participants. These issues must be considered in additional studies. Finally, although expectations and importance are critical to success, continued work is needed to relate post-trip satisfactions to understand how participants view their experience after the tour is completed.

CONCLUSION

From experience, travel professionals are aware that all tour participants want to see important attractions and scenery while feeling comfortable about their trip. The empirical results of this study expand these impressions to show the importance rankings and ratings of escorted tour participants. Tour destination and associated attractions were the most critical elements of all tours. While no service provider can guarantee perfect service delivery, meticulous preplanning and explicit attention to consumer needs can lead to the creation of a satisfying tour experience.

American domestic travelers have many of the same expectations as Americans traveling to foreign destinations. By acknowledging and addressing differences between these domestic and foreign travel expectations, tour providers can begin the process of satisfying the traveler. Foreign tour expectations are generally higher. Structure, safety, and comfort in providing access to appropriate locations and information are critical for foreign tour success. Planners must attempt to deal with the conflicting issues of providing comfort and security with the need for adventure. Increasing use of special interest tours may help to meet these conflicting needs.

NOTE

1. The Airline Reporting Corporation list contained approximately 30,000 firms. The NTA membership list contained 570 firms. From these sample frames, a random selection of 909 firms (272 operators and 635 agencies) were invited to participate. Of those, 111 firms (41 operators = 15% response; 70 agencies = 11% response) requested questionnaires to distribute. Participating firms were provided 5 questionnaires each (total 555), distributed a total of 248, and returned any that were not given to clients. Useable responses were received from 23.9% of questionnaires provided to participating firms and 53.6% of questionnaires distributed to consumers.

REFERENCES

Calantone, R. J. and Mazanec, J.A. (1991). Marketing Management and Tourism. *Annals of Tourism Research,* 18 (1), 101-119.
Chon, K.S. (1990). Traveler Destination Image Modification Process and its Marketing Implications. *Developments in Marketing Science: Proceedings of the Thirteenth Annual Conference of the Academy of Marketing Science,* Vol. 13, R.L. King (ed.). New Orleans: Academy of Marketing Science, 480-482.
Cunningham, L.F. and Thompson, K.N. (1986). The Intercity Bus Tour Market: A Comparison Between Inquirers and Purchasers. *Journal of Travel Research,* 25 (2), 8-12.
Engel, J.F., Blackwell, R.D. and Miniard, P.W. (1990). *Consumer Behavior.* New York: Holt, Rinehart and Winston.
Erevelles, S. and Lockshin, L.S. (1991). The Development of the Concept of Consumer Satisfaction in Marketing Thought. In *Marketing: Toward the Twenty-First Century,* R.L. King (Ed.). Richmond, VA: Southern Marketing Association, 406-414.
Hunt, H.K. (1976). *Conceptualization and Measurement of Customer Satisfaction and Dissatisfaction.* Cambridge: Marketing Science Institute.
LaPage, W.F. (1983). Recreation Resource Management for Visitor Satisfaction. *Journal of Park and Recreation Administration,* 1 (2), 37-44.
LaTour, S.A. and Peat, N.C. (1979). Conceptual and Methodological Issues in Consumer Satisfaction Research. In *Advances in Consumer Research,* Vol. 6, W.L. Wilkie (Ed.). Ann Arbor, MI: Association for Consumer Research, 431-437.
Lehmann, D.R. (1989). *Market Research and Analysis,* 3rd Edition. Boston: Irwin.

Longwoods Travel (1990). *National Tour Foundation Group Travel Report.* Longwoods International, USA.

Lopez, E.M. (1980). The Effect of Leadership Style on Satisfaction Levels of Tour Quality. *Journal of Travel Research,* 18 (4), 20-23.

_____. (1981). The Effect of Tour Leaders' Training on Travelers' Satisfaction With Tour Quality. *Journal of Travel Research,* 19 (4), 23-26.

Mancini, M. (1990). *Conducting Tours: A Practical Guide.* Cincinnati, OH: Southwestern.

Middleton, V.T.C. (1988). *Marketing of Travel and Tourism.* Oxford: Heinemann, 57-64.

Oliver, R.L. (1977). A Theoretical Reinterpretation of Expectation and Disconfirmation Effects on Post-Exposure Product Evaluations: Experience in the Field. In *Consumer Satisfaction, Dissatisfaction, and Complaining Behavior,* R.L. Day (Ed.). Bloomington: Indiana University, 2-9.

_____. (1980). A Cognitive Model of Antecedents and Consequences of Satisfaction Decisions. *Journal of Marketing Research,* 17 (November), 460-469.

_____, and Desarbo, W.S. (1988). Response Determinants in Satisfaction Judgments. *Journal of Consumer Research,* 14 (March), 495-507.

Pearce, P.L. (1984). Tourist-Guide Interaction. *Annals of Tourism Research,* 11 (1), 129-146.

Persia, M.A. and Duke, C.R. (1991). Determining Expectations of Tour Participants. In *Interface: 1991.* Council on Hotel, Restaurant, and Institutional Education, 1991 Annual Conference Proceedings, D. Hayes, ed. Houston, TX: CHRIE.

Peter, J.P. and M.L. Ray (1984). *Measurement Readings for Marketing Research.* Chicago: American Marketing Association.

Quiroga, I. (1990). Characteristics of Package Tours in Europe. *Annals of Tourism Research,* 17 (1), 185-207.

Ross, E.L.D. and Iso-Ahola, S.E. (1991). Sightseeing Tourists' Motivation and Satisfaction. *Annals of Tourism Research,* 18 (2), 226-237.

Ryan, C. (1991). Tourism and marketing: a symbiotic relationship? *Tourism Management,* 12 (June), 101-111.

Sheldon, P.J. (1986). The Tour Operator Industry: An Analysis. *Annals of Tourism Research,* 13 (3), 349-365.

_____. and Mak, J. (1987). The Demand for Package Tours: A Mode Choice Model. *Journal of Travel Research,* 25 (3), 13-17.

Thompson, C.M. and Pearce, D.G. (1980). Market Segmentation of New Zealand Package Tours. *Journal of Travel Research,* 19 (2), 3-6.

Tolman, E.C. (1932). *Purposive Behavior in Animals and Men.* New York: Appleton-Century.

Tse, D.K. and Wilton, P.C. (1988). Models of Consumer Satisfaction Formation: An Extension. *Journal of Marketing Research,* 25 (May), 204-212.

Tull, D.S. and Hawkins, D.I. (1991). *Marketing Research: Measurement and Method,* 5th Edition. New York: Macmillan.

Um, S. and Crompton, J.L. (1991). "Development of Pleasure Travel Attitude Dimensions." *Annals of Tourism Research.* 18 (4), 500-504.

Yau, O.H.M. and Chan, C.F. (1990). Hong Kong as a Travel Destination in Southeast Asia: A Multidimensional Approach. *Tourism Management,* 11 (June), 123-132.

Zeithaml, V.A., Berry, L.L. and Parasuraman, A. (1988). Communication and Control Processes in the Delivery of Service Quality. *Journal of Marketing,* 52 (2, April), 35-48.

Ziff-Levine, W. (1990). The Cultural Logic Gap: A Japanese Tourism Research Experience. *Tourism Management,* 11 (June), 105-110.

A Comparison of Package and Non-Package Travelers from the United Kingdom

Sheauhsing Hsieh
Joseph T. O'Leary
Alastair M. Morrison

SUMMARY. The development of package tourism has been a significant feature in the post-war expansion of tourism. The package tour provides many benefits to both travelers and tourism service groups and has become one of the greatest influences in the travel and tourism industry. This paper provides a comparative profile of package and non-package travelers from the United Kingdom. The profiles were developed using sociodemographics, travel characteristics, and information sources. In contrast to earlier studies on packaged vacations, travel philosophy, benefit sought, and product preference were included to understand the choice and decision-making patterns of package and non-package travelers.

Sheauhsing Hsieh is a graduate student specializing in the areas of International Travel and Tourism, Forestry & Natural Resources Department, Purdue University, West Lafayette, IN 47907. Joseph T. O'Leary is Professor, specializing in Recreation Participation and Behavior, Forestry & Natural Resources Department, Purdue University, West Lafayette, IN. Alastair M. Morrison is Associate Professor, specializing in Tourism Marketing, Restaurant, Hotel, Institutional, and Tourism Management Department, Purdue University, West Lafayette, IN.

The data utilized in this paper were made available by Tourism Canada. The data for the United Kingdom Pleasure Travel Market Study, 1989 was originally collected by Market Facts of Canada. Neither the collector of the original data nor Tourism Canada bear any responsibility for the analysis or interpretations presented here.

[Haworth co-indexing entry note]: "A Comparison of Package and Non-Package Travelers from the United Kingdom." Hsieh, Sheauhsing, Joseph T. O'Leary, and Alastair M. Morrison. Co-published simultaneously in *Journal of International Consumer Marketing* (The Haworth Press, Inc.) Vol. 6, No. 3/4, 1994, pp. 79-100; and: *Global Tourist Behavior* (ed: Muzaffer Uysal) The Haworth Press, Inc., 1994, pp. 79-100. Multiple copies of this article/chapter may be purchased from The Haworth Document Delivery Center [1-800-3-HAWORTH; 9:00 a.m. - 5:00 p.m. (EST)].

INTRODUCTION

The development of package tourism has been a very significant feature in the post-war expansion of tourism (Pearce, 1988). The packaging of travel service is unique and different from the packaging of consumer products in a general store. A package tour is identified as a trip planned and paid for in a single price far in advance, which covers both commercial transportation and accommodation (often meals and sightseeing are also included) (Morrison, 1989). Packages are popular with customers because they make travel easier and more convenient. At the same time, package tours help the industry to increase business in off-peak periods and attract specific or new target markets (Morrison, 1989). The package tour, therefore, provides many benefits to both travelers and tourism service groups and has become one of the greatest influences in the travel and tourism industry.

Market Segmentation

Any travel and tourism organization has to understand the composition of the market in order to provide products and services that meet client needs. Business can be more effective if marketing efforts are directed toward a limited number of well-defined market segments (Dickson & Ginter, 1987; Stynes, 1985). Since package tours have become an important market for the tourism industry, a travel market might be divided into two submarkets–package tours and non-package tours.

Market segmentation has been considered as one of the concepts to understand the market efficiently. Market segmentation is the process of partitioning markets into segments of potential customers with similar characteristics (Frank, Massy, & Wind 1978; Morrison, 1989; Stynes, 1985). This strategy will adjust a product or service and its price, promotion, and distribution to meet the needs and wants of discrete target segments. Segmentation usually results in a more efficient allocation of marketing resources and a more precise setting of market objectives. Therefore, market segmentation can offer significant advantages as a competitive strategy and as a guide to market planning and analysis.

In general, a market can be segmented in many ways with a variety of variables. These variables are usually classified into four broad categories: geography, demographics, psychographics, and product-related (Kotler, 1980; Morrison, 1989; Stynes, 1985).

Demographics and socioeconomics appear to be the most prevalent form of market segmentation. Socioeconomic characteristics of the household as well as the individual have been used to identify population segments. These include such characteristics as age and sex of household members, income, education, occupation, and ethnicity (Anderson & Langmeyer, 1982; Graham & Wall, 1978). Psychographic classification of consumers is based upon personality, attitudes/philosophy, opinions, motivation, and benefit sought. Davis, Allen, and Cosenza (1988) segmented Florida residents with respect to their AIO (Attitudes, Interests, and Opinions) toward tourism. In addition, there are alternative ways of defining and describing psychographic or lifestyle segments such as VALS (Values and Lifestyles) and PRIZM (Potential Ratings in Zipcode Markets). A study conducted by Gilmore Research Group (1989) for GTE Travel Enterprises found that American travelers can be categorized into seven attitude groups: adventure-seekers, older stay-at-homes, fun-seekers, family travel planners, solitude-seekers, intense travelers, and no-nonsense travelers. The demographics, travel behavior, and vacation activities were different across these seven categories.

Some researchers consider benefit segmentation to be the best segmentation base (Goodrich, 1978; Morrison, 1989; Woodside & Jacobs 1985). It groups customers according to similarities in the benefits they seek in specific products or services. Goodrich (1978) clustered eleven travel motivation factors of international travelers into four benefit bundles: entertainment, purchase opportunities, climate for comfort, and cost. Linking to these different travel motivation types, marketers could develop advertising campaigns through words and pictures. Crompton (1979) suggested that it is possible to identify specific directive motives guiding the tourists toward the selection of a particular type of vacation or destination relative to all the alternatives of which the tourist is aware. To accomplish this, he identified seven socio-psychological motives: escape from a perceived mundane environment, exploration and evaluation of self, relaxation, prestige, regression (less constrained behavior), enhancement of kinship relationships, and facilitation of social interaction. In international travel and tourism studies, Woodside and Jacobs (1985) applied different market positioning strategies to Japan, Mainland U.S.A., and Canadian market segments based on the different travel benefits realized. According to the results, the advantages of segmenting the markets by benefits would offer a significant and competitive strategy and guide market planning and promotional strategies.

Product-related segmentation in recreation and tourism has been based upon three categories of variables: participation in recreation or travel activities, frequency or volume of use, and equipment ownership (Morrison, 1989; Stynes, 1985). In the travel and tourism studies, Bryant and Morrison (1980) segmented the recreation activities and opportunities of

Michigan into four distinct groups–young sports activities, outdoorsman/ hunters, winter/water types, and resort types. In the international travel and tourism research by U.S. Travel and Tourism Administration and Tourism Canada (Market Facts of Canada Limited: United Kingdom, 1990), the British travel market was divided into sports and entertainment, outdoors and native, comfort and culture, beach, developed resort, and culture and nature segments. It was suggested that recreation and tourism businesses could target respective segments and design appropriate activity and facilities according to customers/travelers needs. In addition, the phenomena of recreation and tourism activity is linked to equipment. For example, Michigan campers were aggregated into four major segments (tent, camping trailers, travel trailers, and motor home) based on the type of equipment utilized on each trip (Mahoney & Stynes, 1986). Further, a purpose of trip segmentation can be selected as a primary segmentation base. Morrison (1989) suggested that a travel market can be split into two groups–business travel as well as pleasure and personal travel. He further noted that the number of times a service is purchased (e.g., use-frequency or volume) can also be useful. Additionally, portions of the population tend to purchase specific services or products more frequently than others. Stynes and Mahoney (1980) segmented the downhill ski market in Michigan to heavy half and light half skiers by the number of days spent skiing.

Clearly, the examples show that product-related segmentation is a useful way of describing customer groups with needs and wants that correspond to certain types of hospitality and travel services. Since package tours are a particular type of product that corresponds to certain types of service and equipment a customer seeks, and since it is becoming more important in the travel industry, it will be used in this study as a basis for segmentation.

Factors Affecting the Choice of Package and Non-Package Tours

Package and non-package tour research has most often examined the number of people purchasing package tours (Askari, 1971; U.S. Travel Data Center, 1985). Sheldon and Mak (1987) presented a model that explained a traveler's choice of independent travel vis-à-vis travel on package tours to the Hawaiian Islands. The results indicated that travelers' decisions for vacation mode were related to certain sociodemographic attributes and travel characteristics. Although these studies provided useful information, they did not examine the differences between package and non-package travelers in terms of psychographic attributes. In the past, literature in the travel area has focused on demographics because it was easy to do and readily understood. Nevertheless, understanding people's demographics and past travel behavior may only be one facet that helps to interpret vacation choice. There is sufficient evidence in the literature to suggest an understanding of psychographic factors influencing travel can serve travelers more effectively and profitably than only focusing on sociodemographic factors especially if we try to understand different products like package or non-package tours. In fact, these factors may actually determine why people will travel and the specific products and vacation styles they will choose (Mayo & Jarvis, 1983; Plog, 1987). The study conducted by Woodside and Pitts (1976) found that life-style information may be more important in predicting foreign and domestic travel behavior than demographic variables. Similarly, Abbey (1979) concluded that tour travelers prefer tours designed with vacation life-style information to those designed with demographic information. He noted travel suppliers might seek to create a package that is more compatible with the motivations, attitudes, and opinions of the tour travelers. Later, Schul and Crompton (1983) used two separate multiple regression procedures to examine the relative effects of six psychographic factors and the sociodemographic variables on two measures of external search behavior-travel planning time and the number of external travel organizations consulted for British travelers. They found that travel-specific psychographics would be more effective than sociodemographics for predicting external search behavior. Thus, they suggested that using psychographics for tour suppliers and marketers becomes increasingly important in aiding the development of effective copy and promotional themes as well as in the selection of appropriate media for advertising.

Most of the studies in travel behavior were based on domestic and not international long-haul travelers. The factors affecting travel choice may be more complicated for international than domestic travel. Thus, not only sociodemographic but psychographic attributes (travel philosophy and travel benefit sought) will be used to understand the traveler in this study. In contrast with other research, travel preference will be considered by examining British travelers in terms of travel characteristics and travel product preferences. Therefore, understanding differences between package and non-package travelers in terms of travel psychographic factors such as philosophy, benefit sought, and product preference may help influence tourism development and planning as well as promotional and marketing strategies.

The Purpose of This Study

In 1989, the United Kingdom ranked fourth, following Canada, Mexico, and Japan, in terms of number of visitors to the United States and represented the second largest tourist-generating country to Canada (Waters, 1990). In addition, British travelers represented the largest proportion of tourists from European countries to North America. Since international travel is different from domestic travel, it is important to know whether there are differences between international and domestic package tours in terms of socioeconomic and demographic factors. In addition, the choice of package and non-package tours may interact with a large variety of other factors such as travel type, travel party, information sources, travel behavior, etc.

Since British travelers represent such an important component of the North American travel market, it is important to conduct further analysis to understand more about this group. The British travelers will be segmented into package and non-package submarkets based on a priori segmentation. The objectives of this study are to: (a) provide a comparative description of package and non-package tours from the United Kingdom travel market; (b) identify the variables which distinguish the choice of package and non-package tours, and (c) provide recommendations to travel and tourism organizations of host countries.

METHODS

Questionnaires

Data from the Pleasure Travel Markets Survey for the United Kingdom were collected from May 9 to June 6, 1989. A total of 1,209 personal, in-home interviews were conducted. All respondents were 18 years of age or older who took an overseas vacation in the past three years or intended to take such a trip in the next two years.

The sample was drawn from England, Scotland, and Wales, excluding only the most sparsely populated rural areas and council estates with the worst poverty and unemployment. Northern Ireland was not included in the survey. Households were screened by interviewers who followed a predetermined walk pattern from a total of 126 computer-selected starting points. In households with more than one qualified respondent, a random selection was made using the next birthday method. The incidence of qualified respondents was determined by recording the results of these screening procedures (Market Facts of Canada Limited: United Kingdom, 1989).

In the data-processing stage, weights were applied to correct for an apparent female bias. The survey collected information on: (a) socioeconomic and demographic variables–age, gender, income, education, occupation, life cycle, and region; (b) travel characteristics–party size, length of stay, trip description, travel season, and travel with whom; (c) travel philosophy, benefit, and product; (d) the most important information sources used to plan a trip; (e) the places visited on most recent and second most recent trips, etc.

Data Analysis

The dependent variable was whether the respondent's flight or accommodation was included as part of a package with anything else. In this study there were 846 respondents who did take trips in the past three years, with 251 respondents (29.8%) taking package tours and 595 respondents (70.2%) who took non-package trips in the past three years.

The independent variables selected to identify the differences among package and non-package travelers were:

a. According to the *Pleasure Travel Markets To North America:United Kingdom* (Market Facts of Canada Limited: United Kingdom, 1989), three major factors–philosophy, benefit sought, and product– were developed. Travel philosophy was based on a series of 25 agree-disagree statements relating to how people think about travel in an overall sense as well as how they prefer to travel. The statements took in a variety of issues ranging from making travel arrangements to preferences for different kinds of trips. Respondents were asked on a 4-point Likert-type scale (1: strongly agree; 2: agree somewhat; 3: disagree somewhat; 4: strongly disagree) how much they agreed or disagreed with each statement in order to obtain on overall profile of their travel philosophy or attitudes. In addition, benefit sought was identified based on the importance ratings of a series of 30 items relating to reasons people might want to go on vacation and experiences they might be looking for. The product preference was based on the importance ratings of 53 different activity features, and amenities that are important in the selection of a vacation destination. Both travel benefit and product preference were based on a 4-point Likert-type scale ranging from "very important" to "not at all important."

b. Socioeconomic and demographic factors: income per year, age, sex, and marital status.

c. Travel characteristics such as length of trip, party size, trip description, and travel with whom.

d. The information sources used most.

The Chi-Square test of homogeneity of proportions for categorical variables and T-Test for continuous variables were used to examine whether differences existed between package and non-package travelers.

RESULTS

Travel Destination

The United States was the most popular destination for both package (65.9%) and non-package travelers (57.5%) in the past three years. The second most popular destination for package travelers were the Far East/ Asia and other Pacific Islands (23.5%), followed by Mexico, the West Indies/Caribbean/Hawaii/Guam/American Samoa (18.6%). For non-package travelers, there was more interest in visiting Canada (25.6%) and Australia/New Zealand (18.1%) than package travelers (Table 1).

TABLE 1. Destinations for Package and Non-Package Tours

Subject	Package Tour	Non-Package Tour
	251	595
	---Percent([a])---	
U.S.A.	65.9	57.5
Canada	9.0	25.6
Mexico, West Indies/Caribbean & Hawaii/Guam/American Samoa	18.6	11.2
Central/S. America & Central/S. Africa	9.9	13.5
Far East/Asia & other Pacific Islands	23.5	21.7
Australia/New Zealand	11.0	18.1
Other	1.5	0.9

([a]) Based on 1224 trips comprised of most recent and second most recent trips. Percentages were based on multiple responses.

Sociodemographics

Package tours attracted more travelers (21.5%) whose ages were from 35 to 54 than non-package tours (17.6%). Travelers over 65 years of age accounted for 18.3% of non-package travelers, compared with 11.6% of package tours. In contrast to earlier studies, older travelers in this study showed more interest in non-package tours. However, the Chi-Square test for age groups between package and non-package travelers was not significant (Chi-Square = 10.4, P ≤ 0.11) (Table 2).

Gender can be one of the factors that distinguish package and non-package travelers. Female travelers preferred to travel on package tours (58.3%) and males showed more interest in non-package opportunities. There were no significant differences between package and non-package tours in terms of marital status. However, travelers who were married showed slightly more interest in package tours, and non-package tours attracted more single travelers. Household income differences were significant between package and non-package tours (Chi-Square = 23.6, P ≤ 0.00). Lower-income travelers (£8,000 or less) preferred to travel independently. Respondents who were in the middle income level earning between £20,001-30,000 pounds per year liked to travel on package tours (Table 2).

Travel Characteristics

Travel characteristics varied between package and non-package travelers. Respondents who traveled on non-package tours took longer trips, averaging 43.7 nights. Package travelers spent only 22.8 nights on their trips. The T-Test of the length of trip showed a significant difference between package and non-package travelers (Table 3). Those who traveled on package tours liked to travel in small parties, especially two and four persons. Respondents taking non-package tours liked to travel independently (31.2%) or with one other person (41.2%). The party size difference between package and non-package travelers was significant (Chi-Square = 87.8, P ≤ 0.00). Package travelers preferred to travel with relatives and friends or travel alone. Non-package travelers liked to travel alone or with business associates/colleagues. Most package travelers liked to take resort trips or visit friends and relatives. On the other hand, 88% of the non-package travelers visited friends and relatives during their trips. In addition, trips combining business and pleasure accounted for 17% of non-package tours (Table 3).

Finally, package travelers preferred to book their package tours from travel agents and tour operators or holiday companies. Very few reported booking directly with an airline. Most of the package tours included flights (96.4%) and accommodations (68.6%) (Table 3).

TABLE 2. Demographics of Package and Non-Package Tour

Subject	Package Tour	Non-Package Tour	Chi-Square
	251	595	
	--- Percent ---		
Age group			10.4
18-24	14.2	15.2	
25-34	18.6	19.9	
35-44	21.5	17.6	
45-54	15.3	15.6	
55-64	18.6	13.0	
65 or more	11.6	18.3	
Not stated	0.3	0.4	
Sex			6.0*
Male	41.7	50.9	
Female	58.3	49.1	
Marital status			8.4
Single	20.2	23.7	
Married	65.7	59.2	
Living together	1.3	3.6	
Divorced/separate/widow	12.3	13.5	
Other	0.5	0.0	
Household income			23.6**
£8,000 or less	8.0	15.6	
£8,001-11,000	8.8	7.8	
£11,001-15,000	5.9	9.5	
£15,001-20,000	12.6	13.2	
£20,001-30,000	17.9	9.3	
£30,001-40,000	6.4	5.2	
£40,001-50,000	3.2	2.0	
Over £50,000	1.5	1.4	
Refused	35.6	36.1	

* $p \leq 0.05$. **$p \leq 0.01$.

TABLE 3. Travel Characteristics for Package and Non-Package Tours

Subject	Package Tour	Non-Package Tour	Significance Test
	251	595	
	--- Mean ---		
Length of trip (# of nights) (std. = 25.4) (std. = 48.6)	23.3	39.9	t = − 6.5**
	--- Percent ---		
Party size			Chi-Square = 87.8**
One	6.2	31.2	
Two	51.1	41.2	
Three	9.1	9.7	
Four	19.3	9.5	
Five	3.4	3.4	
Six	1.4	1.4	
Seven	0.7	0.5	
Eight	0.7	0.0	
Nine or more	7.9	1.8	
Not stated	0.3	1.3	
Person with whom traveled on trip			N/A(a)
Traveled alone	29.5	88.5	
Wife/husband/girlfriend/boyfriend	0.0	0.0	
Child(ren)	10.2	2.8	
Father/mother	2.8	3.2	
Other relatives	43.3	11.0	
Friends	20.0	4.2	
Organized groups/club	6.4	0.2	
Business assoc./colleagues	10.2	17.0	
Trip description			N/A(a)
Visit friends & relatives	29.5	88.5	
Touring trip	0.0	0.0	
City trip	10.2	2.8	
Outdoor trip	2.8	3.2	
Resort trip	43.3	11.0	
Exhibition, spec. event, theme park	20.0	4.2	
Cruise	6.4	0.2	
Combined business & pleasure	10.2	17.0	

TABLE 3 (continued)

Subject	Package Tour	Non-Package Tour	Significance Test
	251	595	
	--- Percent ---		
Where package vacation booked?			
Travel agent	81.2	N/A[b]	
Tour operator/holiday	10.1	N/A	
Directly with airline	0.8	N/A	
Other	7.9	N/A	
Components included package tour			
Flight	96.4	N/A[b]	
Accommodation	68.6	N/A	
Rented car	26.2	N/A	
Guided tour	31.0	N/A	
Flight/accommodation	24.8	N/A	
Flight/accommodation/ guided tour	23.5	N/A	

[a]   Based on 1224 trips comprised of most recent and second most recent trips. Percentages were based on multiple responses.

[b]   Percentages were based on multiple responses. Only package travelers answer these questions.

* $p \leq 0.05.$ ** $p \leq 0.01.$

Information Sources

The travel agent was the most important information source for both package and non-package travelers. Brochures/pamphlets and friends/family also played important roles for package travelers when planning their overseas travel. Apart from travel agents, friends and family represented the second important information source for non-package travelers (Table 4).

Travel Philosophy

In comparing the individual travel philosophy item, although both package and non-package travelers agree that value for vacation money is important, they still have different travel philosophies. Package travelers usually have things arranged before traveling. They like to buy all-inclusive

TABLE 4. Most Important Sources of Information Used in Planning a Long Haul Trip for Package and Non-Package Tours

Subject	Package Tour	Non-Package Tour
	251	595
	--- Percent[a] ---	
Travel agent	36.6	38.7
Brochures/Pamphlets	22.8	5.1
Friends/Family	15.4	29.0
Airline	0.7	4.0
Tour operator/Company	5.1	1.4
Newspapers/Magazine/Articles	0.4	2.3
Books/Library	3.5	3.4
Automobile association	4.6	2.1
Government tourism office/board	0.0	0.4
Embassy/Consulate	2.3	1.7
Clubs/Associations	2.2	1.8
Advertisements	4.1	2.3
Personal/Previous experience	2.6	1.3
Someone else made reservation	1.6	1.2

[a] Percentages based on multiple responses.

vacations from travel agents and feel that it is worth paying more for extras and luxuries. They also prefer traveling to different places on each new vacation. Non-package travelers enjoy making their own vacation arrangements and traveling inexpensively. Language-speaking is an important issue for non-package travelers, probably because of the independent nature of their trip. They like to choose vacation places they have already been to (Table 5).

TABLE 5. Travel Philosophy for Package and Non-Package Tours

Subject	Package Tour	Non-Package Tour	T-Value
	251	595	
		--- mean(a) ---	
Like to have things arranged before I go	1.5	1.7	− 3.4**
Take short pleasure trips/opportunity	1.7	1.9	− 1.8
Maj. trip arrangements a bother/do not travel	3.5	3.5	0.2
Choose vacation places already been to	3.1	2.8	3.4 **
Money spent on travel is well spent	1.4	1.4	− 0.1
Prefer short trips over one long trip	2.7	2.7	0.0
Rather spend money on things beside travel	3.2	3.0	1.6
Enjoy making own vacation arrangements	2.3	2.0	4.0**
Like to stay put at vacation destination	3.1	3.1	0.6
Worth paying more for extras/luxuries	1.6	2.1	− 4.2**
Prefer guided tours on overseas vacations	2.5	2.8	− 3.9**
Don't have to travel to enjoy vacation	2.6	2.5	1.3
Don't have to spend a lot of money to enjoy	1.9	1.8	1.6
Like different place on each new vacation	1.9	2.0	− 2.6*
Choose vacation trips/friends have been to	2.3	2.4	−0.9
Important that people speak my language	2.9	2.7	2.3*
Usually travel reduced air fares	2.7	2.3	5.0**
Like to make vacation arrangements as I go	2.6	2.2	4.5**
Usually use travel agent to decide place	2.5	2.9	− 5.7**
Prefer leaving others to do organizing	2.7	3.0	− 3.1**
Usually buy vacation with accom./transp. inc.	1.9	2.9	− 12.2**
Prefer traveling place to place	1.8	1.9	− 0.8
Inexpensive travel to country is important	2.2	2.0	3.0**
Usually travel on all-inclusive vacation	2.2	3.1	− 12.7**
Value for vacation money is important	1.5	1.5	− 0.7

(a) 4: strongly disagree; 3: disagree somewhat; 2: agree somewhat; 1: strongly agree.
* $p \leq 0.05$. ** $p \leq 0.01$.

Travel Benefit Sought

For travel benefits sought, both package and non-package travelers like to see as much as possible and experience new and different lifestyles while traveling overseas. However, non-package travelers seek the benefit of family togetherness. They prefer to visit friends/relatives and places that their family originally came from (Table 6).

Travel Product Preference

In terms of travel product preferences, the destination environment such as good weather, cleanliness, warm welcome, and outstanding scenery are very important for both package and non-package travelers. Package travelers have more interest in high quality restaurants, first class hotels, resort areas, and guided tours to see everything. In contrast, non-package travelers prefer to see a museum and historical sites, and pay more attention to local issues such as the friendly local people and public transportation (Table 7).

CONCLUSIONS AND IMPLICATIONS

This research paper provides a comparative profile of package and non-package travelers from the United Kingdom. These profiles were developed using socioeconomic and demographic factors, travel characteristics, and information sources. In contrast to earlier studies on package vacations, travel philosophy, benefit, and product preference were included to understand the choice and decision-making patterns of package and non-package travelers. While significant differences between package and non-package travelers in terms of their socioeconomic/demographic characteristics might have been anticipated, the role of travel characteristics, travel philosophies, benefits sought, and product preferences appear to also be important in understanding the package product.

The results show that non-package travelers are twice as large a group as package travelers. Package travelers prefer to leave their arrangements to travel agents and co-travelers. Most of them take trips because they want to learn new things and increase knowledge. Usually, they have more interest in comfort, well-developed resorts, and entertainment. In contrast, non-package travelers make their own travel arrangements, take vacations for social reasons and to be with family and friends, and prefer destinations where they feel safe and secure. They normally like to take outdoors/ native as well as culture/nature trips.

TABLE 6. Travel Benefit Sought for Package and Non-Package Tours

Subject	Package Tour	Non-Package Tour	T-Value
	251	595	
	\-\-\- mean([a]) \-\-\-		
Reliving past good times	2.7	2.5	2.4*
Experiencing new & different lifestyles	1.5	1.5	− 0.7
Trying new foods	1.9	1.9	0.0
Traveling to places historically important	2.1	2.0	0.7
Being free to act the way I feel	1.7	1.7	1.2
Family is together	2.0	1.9	2.0*
Meet people with similar interests	2.1	2.1	− 0.1
Seeing & experiencing a foreign destination	1.4	1.4	− 1.8
Going places friends haven't been	3.0	3.0	0.7
Talking about trip after return home	2.4	2.4	0.3
Sports participation	3.1	3.1	− 0.0
Sports spectating	3.1	3.0	2.1*
Safe/secure travel	2.0	2.0	0.4
Having fun/being entertained	1.9	1.9	0.5
Seeing as much as possible	1.5	1.6	− 2.0
Rediscovering myself	2.9	2.7	1.9
Visit friends/relatives	2.7	1.9	10.9**
Visit places family came from	3.0	2.7	3.7**
Physical activity	2.4	2.3	1.5
Change from busy job	1.9	2.0	− 1.1
Being daring and adventuresome	2.6	2.6	0.5
Doing nothing at all	2.9	2.9	1.0
Learning new things/increase knowledge	1.8	1.8	0.4
Indulging in luxury	2.1	2.2	− 1.8
Roughing it	3.4	3.2	3.6**
Escaping from the ordinary	1.9	1.9	0.0
Feeling at home away from home	2.2	2.0	2.4*

[a]   4: Not at all important; 3: not very important; 2: somewhat important; 1: very important.

* $p \leq 0.05$. ** $p < 0.01$.

TABLE 7. Travel Product Preference for Package and Non-Package Tours

Subject	Package Tour	Non-Package Tour	T-Value
	251	595	
	--- mean[a] ---		
High quality restaurant	2.1	2.3	− 3.5**
Budget accommodation	2.4	2.3	1.4
Seaside	2.4	2.4	− 0.8
Golf and tennis	3.4	3.4	0.1
Big modern cities	3.0	3.0	0.9
Historic old cities	2.3	2.2	1.5
Nightlife and entertainment	2.5	2.6	− 1.2
Outstanding scenery	1.6	1.5	1.3
Good shopping	2.1	2.1	− 0.6
Reliable weather	1.4	1.5	− 1.4
Standards of hygiene/cleanliness	1.4	1.5	− 1.0
Mountainous areas	2.4	2.3	1.5
Local cuisine	1.8	1.8	− 0.1
Personal safety, even when traveling alone	1.4	1.5	− 1.0
Snow skiing	3.5	3.5	1.1
Interesting small towns/villages	1.9	1.9	1.3
Good beaches for swimming/sunning	2.0	2.0	− 0.6
Casinos and gambling	3.5	3.6	− 1.3
Campgrounds and trailer parks	3.4	3.4	0.2
Local festivals	2.3	2.2	1.8
Amusement/theme parks	2.6	2.7	− 1.3
Museums/art galleries	2.5	2.3	2.3*
Warm, sunny climate	1.4	1.5	− 1.4
Wilderness and undisturbed nature	2.1	2.0	1.6
Interesting/friendly local people	1.6	1.4	2.8**
Wide open spaces to get away from crowds	1.9	1.8	0.9
Local crafts/handiwork	2.3	2.2	0.7
Outdoor activities	3.0	2.9	0.5
Inexpensive restaurant	2.2	2.1	2.4*
Public transportation	1.8	1.8	0.1
Live theater/concerts	2.6	2.6	0.2
Resort areas	2.3	2.4	− 2.2*
Unique/different native cultural groups	2.4	2.3	1.9
Unique/different immigrant cultural groups	2.5	2.5	0.4

TABLE 7 (continued)

Subject	Package Tour	Non-Package Tour	T-Value
Subject	251	595	
		--- mean[a] ---	
National parks and forests	2.0	1.9	2.3*
Inexpensive travel in destination country	1.9	1.7	2.7**
Variety of short guided excursions/tour	2.1	2.3	− 2.8**
Exotic atmosphere	2.3	2.4	− 1.2
Warm welcome for tourists	1.6	1.6	− 0.3
Lakes and rivers	2.0	1.9	1.4
Culture different from my own	2.0	1.9	0.3
Good fishing	3.6	3.4	3.3**
Good hunting	3.7	3.6	1.9
First class hotels	2.7	3.0	− 2.8**
Spectator sporting events	3.2	3.0	3.0**
Historical/military/archeological sites	2.6	2.5	1.3
See wildlife/birds I don't usually see	2.1	2.0	1.3
Opportunity to increase knowledge	1.7	1.7	1.0
Manageable size/able to see everything	2.2	2.4	− 2.1*
Water sports	2.9	3.0	−1.1
Fast food restaurants	2.9	2.9	− 0.7
Environmental quality of air, water, and soil	2.0	2.0	0.6
Cruise of one or more nights	3.0	3.0	0.8

[a]: 4: not at all important; 3: not very important; 2: somewhat important; 1: very important.
* $p \leq 0.05$. ** $p \leq 0.01$.

The United States and Far East/Asia/Other Pacific Islands are the most popular destinations for U.K. package travelers. Although the United States of America is also the number one destination for non-package travelers, Canada ranks second, slightly ahead of the Far East/Asia/Other Pacific Islands.

Demographically, package travelers tend to be middle-aged, female, married, and prefer to travel with relatives and friends in small parties (2 or 4 persons) for resort trips or to visit friends or relatives. They like to get information from travel agents or family/relatives, or use brochures and pamphlets in planning trips. They prefer to book trips with travel agents or tour operators/holiday companies. On the other hand, non-package travel not only attracts younger (18-34 years) but also older (65 years or more) travelers. Non-package travelers tend to travel alone or with fewer people in the travel party, and like to take trips to visit friends/relatives or combination business/pleasure trips. They take longer trips and prefer to get information from travel agents and family/relatives.

Implications

This research study should provide useful marketing information for those interested in outbound travel from the United Kingdom. Destinations, suppliers, carriers, and travel trade intermediaries located within or serving the United States of America, Canada, the Far East/Asia/Other Pacific Islands may benefit most from these data.

Two important findings that emerge are the tendency for package travelers to seek out new places to visit versus non-package groups who tend to go back and visit the same place more than once. Non-package travelers are also inclined to follow this pattern by staying with friends and family. In some research (Sheldon & Mak, 1987), package travelers have shown a higher propensity to visit places once and then look for new areas to move on to. The inclination is to limit repeat visitation and build a "life list" of places visited. In these data it is not apparent from the philosophy or benefit items that package and non-package travelers are different in their search or choice of new or different opportunities. However, for those who might choose to visit a destination more than once, how should they be approached? Should the first time visitor be presented with promotion and information the same way we would with the repeat visitor? Recent research by O'Malley (1991) suggests that repeat visitors to Canada have a different image of the place than the first time visitor. Knowing that there are differences between package and non-package travelers and the fact that a substantial proportion are female suggests attention must be paid to these issues. The higher tendency for U.K. package travelers to be female also suggests that advertising in publications with high female-male ratios in readership may be effective.

The differences also underscore communication channel impacts. Non-package travelers are twice as large a group as their package counterparts and have a high representation in the "social safety" benefit category underscoring the issue of language, repeat visitation, and perhaps the pattern of visiting friends and relatives (VFR).

Perhaps one of the least understood areas in travel and tourism is dealing with this VFR travel. These people tend to travel longer than package travelers, certainly seeking things to see and do. They rely on friends and relatives to help with putting the information together. This dependency among the non-package traveler suggests that an emphasis be placed on mentioning and/or illustrating family ties in advertising copy and photography. Another more novel approach may be to appeal to the friends and relatives of U.K. citizens residing in the United States, Canada, Australia and elsewhere. Developing information for and with the family for use by visitors could improve the experience of these visitors and address the needs that many have on their repeat visits to find new things to do and see, particularly if it involves family. This same approach might also be examined relative to Asian and Mexican residents and visitors.

What is surprising about the results is the lack of difference between the product items. Since doing things on a tour or with friends and family will affect how activities are carried out, there is probably some need to look in greater detail at the way in which places are used or activities pursued before we would accept this finding as definitive. Follow-up research with focus groups of travelers might begin to provide the depth of information that will clarify this issue.

In the case of the U.K. market, there is a heavy reliance on travel agents along with the advice of friends and relatives. Any destination interested in this market should develop a close liaison with selected travel agents and tour wholesalers, and with the airlines who service the U.K. The selection of these agents and wholesalers should be most effective by carefully matching the destination's segment focus to the sociodemographic profiles and preferred pursuits of the clients of each agency or wholesaler.

REFERENCES

Abbey, J. R. (1979). Does life-style profiting work? *Journal of Travel Research, 18*(1), 8-14.

Anderson, G., & Langmeyer, L. (1982). The under-50 and over-50 travelers: A profile of similarities and differences. *Journal of Travel Research, 20*(4), 20-24.

Askari, H. (1971). Demand for package tours. *Journal of Transport Economics Policy*, 40-51.

Bryant, B. E., & Morrison, A. J. (1980). Travel market segmentation and the implementation of market strategies. *Journal of Travel Research, 18*(3), 2-8.

Crompton, J. L. (1979). Motivations for pleasure vacation. *Annual of Tourism Research, 6*(4), 408-424.

Davis, D., Allen, J., & Cosenza, R. M. (1988). Segmenting local residents by their attitudes, interests, and opinions toward tourism. *Journal of Travel Research,* 27(2), 2-8.

Dickson, P. R., & Ginter, J. L. (1987). Market segmentation, product differentiation, and marketing strategy. *Journal of Marketing, 51,* 1-10.

Frank, R. E., Massy, W. F., & Wind, Y. (1978). *Marketing segmentation.* New Jersey: Prentice Hall.

Gilmore Research Group. (1989, May). *Travel benegraphic segmentation.* Seattle, WA: Report prepared for Travel Enterprises.

Goodrich, J. N. (1978). The relationship between preferences for and perceptions of vacation destinations: application of a choice model. *Journal of Travel Research, 17*(2), 8-13.

Graham, J. E. J., & Wall, G. (1978). American visitors to Canada: A study in market segmentation. *Journal of Travel Research, 16*(3), 21-24.

Kotler, P. (1980). *Principles of marketing.* Englewood Cliffs, New Jersey: Prentice Hall.

Mahoney, E. M., & Stynes, D. J. (1986). *1984 Michigan commercial campground marketing study.* East Lansing, MI: Michigan State University, Department of Park and Recreation Resources.

Market Facts Of Canada Limited (1989). *Pleasure travel markets to North America: United Kingdom.* A report prepared for Tourism Canada. Montreal: Toronto.

Mayo, E. J. & Jarvis, L. P. (1981). *Psychology of leisure travel.* Boston, MA: CBI Publishing Company, Inc.

Morrison, M. A. (1989). *Hospitality and Travel Marketing.* Albany, NY: Delmar Publishers.

O'Malley, G. L. (1991). *The role of past experience in U.S. travelers' destination images of Canada.* Unpublished master's thesis. West Lafayette, IN: Purdue University. Department of Forestry and Natural Resources.

Pearce, D. (1988). *Tourism today: a geographical analysis.* England: Longman Scientific & Technical.

Plog, S. C. (1987). Understanding psychographics in tourism research, In J. R. B. Ritchie and C. R. Goeldner (Eds.), *Travel, tourism and hospitality research* (pp. 203-214). New York: Wiley.

Schul, P. and Crompton, J. L. (1983). Search behavior of international vacationers: travel-specific lifestyle and sociodemographic variables. *Journal of Travel Research, 22*(2), 25-30.

Sheldon, P. J., & Mak, J. (1987). The demand for package tours: A mode choice model. *Journal of Travel Research, 25*(3), 13-17.

Stynes, D. J. (1985). Marketing tourism. *Journal of Physical Education and Dance, 54*(4), 21-23.

Stynes, D. J., & Mahoney, E. M. (1980). *1980 Michigan downhill ski marketing study: segmenting active skiers* (Research Rep. No. 391). East Lansing, MI: Michigan State University, Department of Park and Recreation Resources.

U.S. Travel Data Center (1985). *Special studies in travel economics and marketing–U.S. market for package tours.* Washington, DC: U.S. Travel Data Center.

Waters, S. R. (1990). *Travel industry world yearbook, the big picture–1990.* New York: Child & Waters.

Woodside, A. G., & Jacobs, L. W. (1985). Step two in benefit segmentation: Learning the benefits realized by major travel markets. *Journal of Travel Research, 24*(1), 7-13.

Woodside, A. G., & Pitts, R. E. (1976). Effects of consumer life styles, demographics and travel activities on foreign and domestic travel behavior. *Journal of Travel Research, 14*(3), 13-15.

An Expert System
for Promotion Budget Allocation
to International Markets

Paulo Rita
Luiz Moutinho

SUMMARY. This article's main thrust is centered on the analysis and discussion of the findings generated from interviews undertaken with a sample of European National Tourist Offices (NTOs). These in-depth interviews were carried out as part of a research methodology that underlies the knowledge acquisition process to build TOUREX, an expert system aimed at assisting NTOs in the allocation of promotion budget sums to international travel markets. The fieldwork interviews produced a number of useful results whereby the particular model and demonstration system could be enhanced.

INTRODUCTION

The tourism industry has grown to international importance over the last three decades and is now the world's largest industry. As a mass market pursuit, tourism has a major impact on the wealth and development

Paulo Rita is a doctoral research associate, and Luiz Moutinho is Professor of Marketing, both at Cardiff Business School, University of Wales, Colum Drive, Cardiff CF1 3EU, United Kingdom.

Paulo Rita wishes to acknowledge support from the Portuguese Research Council for Science and Technology (JNICT).

[Haworth co-indexing entry note]: "An Expert System for Promotion Budget Allocation to International Markets." Rita, Paulo, and Luiz Moutinho. Co-published simultaneously in *Journal of International Consumer Marketing* (The Haworth Press, Inc.) Vol. 6, No. 3/4, 1994, pp. 101-121; and: *Global Tourist Behavior* (ed: Muzaffer Uysal) The Haworth Press, Inc., 1994, pp. 101-121. Multiple copies of this article/chapter may be purchased from The Haworth Document Delivery Center [1-800-3-HA-WORTH; 9:00 a.m. - 5:00 p.m. (EST)].

of many countries. It contributes to the Gross National Product (GNP), representing 5.5 percent of the world's GNP, and stimulates the economy of problematic areas through the increasing entrepreneurial activity and the deriving employment opportunities, accounting for over 100 million jobs world-wide.

Incoming tourism as an export and an earner of foreign exchange for the destination countries assumes vital importance. During the 1980s, world international tourism arrivals increased by 42 percent, and expenditure on international tourism doubled, rising one-third faster than world GNP. In the 1990s, tourism will continue to be a major growing economic factor in the world with real growth rates of 4.3-5.0 percent and a creation of 38 to 55 million new jobs (Hawkins and Ritchie 1991). International travel is heavily concentrated, with Europe alone accounting for two-thirds of total international arrivals and one-half of receipts. But Europe's rate of growth is slowing and is losing market share while the East Asia/ Pacific region is booming.

A National Tourist Office (NTO) is the officially recognized expert body on tourism matters in any country. This organization is in charge of expanding a country's incoming tourism. To achieve this goal it must promote the destination country in the international travel markets. Therefore, the key task to be accomplished by an NTO is the effective and efficient defence of a country's stake in the enormous international market with its massive implications for foreign currency, earnings and employment (Jefferson 1990).

Strategic decisions in an NTO include issues such as: which markets are most attractive; in which markets are a specific country's 'products' most competitive; how promotional budgets should be allocated for greater effectiveness; and what type of promotional message should it convey (Henshall and Roberts 1985). The crucial and most difficult decision to be taken by NTO management at annual intervals is that of the allocation of financial resources over the leading tourism generating countries (Heneghan 1976).

PROMOTION BUDGETING IN TOURISM

Conventional wisdom dictates that the promotion business does well in recessionary eras. However, current promotional budgets are not offering the same degree of power as in previous recessions. Promotion marketers in the tourism industry must look beyond the immediate concerns of short-term sustainability and consider the strategic imperatives of making meaningful progress in the long-run. The full value and potential of promotions cannot be realised if underlying concepts are forced to stop and start over a period of days, weeks or months. Building promotional equity depends on allowing big ideas to grow and improve over a period of years. Staying with tried-and-true promotional concepts offers the opportunity to be more dynamic since promotional repetition builds a degree of steady credibility (McElnea 1991). The tried-and-true promotional campaign framework relies on the assumption that because specific copy and media strategies used in the past by the NTO or any major direct competitors have performed well by producing positive results, these same strategies could be applied as the building blocks of future promotional efforts. Nevertheless, the evaluation stage of any promotional campaign suggests that critical changes may be required when one takes into account changing demographics, economic conditions, targeted market areas, non-controllable social-political events as well as other key variables included in the decision-making process. In response to the current economic recessionary period, marketing experts foresee increased and broadened incentive programmes designed to strengthen the market positions (Rosenthal 1991) and increased press release activity in response to smaller promotional budgets (White 1991).

National Tourist Offices need to plan effectively the allocation of financial resources to promotional efforts. Ad hoc marketing expenditure allocation decisions can lead to possible imbalances in the marketing expenditure mix and ineffectiveness of the total marketing effort. NTOs have successfully used segmentation strategies to maximize the impact of their promotional efforts. The most obvious reason is the need to make the most efficient use of fixed promotional budgets.

Birks and Southan (1990) suggested that the development of a formal marketing information system would promote and improve: (1) long-range planning and objective setting; (2) development of a holistic communications strategy; (3) greater control of operations; and (4) the ability to audit a range of functions within the organisation, measure cost-effectiveness, control expenditures and improve budgeting.

Basu and Batra (1988) developed ADSPLIT, a computer-based interactive marketing model, which optimally allocates a given corporate promotional budget among individual brands that compete for limited resources. The model has been constructed because budgeting models developed previously are single-product maximizing models that ignore the reality of corporate funds constraints. ADSPLIT requires either regression-based response function coefficients based on historical data or judgements on what sales should be for different values of price and advertising expenses for the brands. A flexible form that permits both concave and S-shaped relationships is used to model the advertising-sales response function. Sales are related to price through a constant elasticity, Cobb-Douglas function. The estimated or input functions are employed to compute the optimal budget allocation for the brands with an upper bound for the total promotional expenditures and upper and lower budget bounds for every brand, using non-linear optimisation heuristics. Optimal prices are also computed for the brands.

An important part of effective promotional planning is measuring results. Developing a promotional budget is difficult because proving the value of promotion is a complex task. The key dilemma involves determining what is expected of promotion and if it is possible to find out exactly what it achieves. NTO's marketing managers should not consider promotion as a form of marketing activity with only a short-term payoff and should acknowledge that its sales (tourist arrivals) effects cannot be measured accurately. It is unfortunate that advertising is most often evaluated through sales volume and over a short-term time frame. There is a dangerous trend towards viewing short-term sales measurement as the answer to measuring the impact of advertising (Broadbent 1988). The productivity of advertising can be tracked more effectively if managers identify specific goals to be achieved within a given period. The implementation of measurable goals would enable NTO's managers to know the return on promotional investments. An effective tourism promotion management process balances the short and the long term.

EXPERT SYSTEMS IN TOURISM

Expert systems are designed to cope with problems or decisions that conventional computer tools are not capable of handling because the solution relies on the knowledge and inferential reasoning capabilities of human experts. Expert computer systems have applications in the tourism industry, which already makes extensive use of conventional computers in routine tasks. There is substantial scope for the expanded application of computer-based techniques to facilitate management decision making in corporate strategic planning and marketing. Expert systems in the tourist industry could find applications in the areas of: (1) accommodation; (2) transportation; (3) tourism development; (4) wholesaling and retailing; (5) finance; and (6) government tourism offices (Crouch 1991).

Expert systems are extremely productive, but a pure expert systems approach is limited by the skill of the experts, the experts' ability to articulate their knowledge, limited range of available knowledge representation and inference methods, and inadequate knowledge bases. Fortunately, artificial intelligence is widening the scope of the next generation of knowledge systems to include: (1) greater reliance on problem solving from principles; (2) use of more powerful inference methods; (3) data processing interfacing; and (4) improved user interfaces. Among the new generation are the TRACE project, sponsored by the Alvey Directorate and aimed at the travel and transport industries (Vaughan 1988).

THE PRELIMINARY MODEL

The development of the preliminary model has been undertaken with the objective of assisting NTOs in the allocation of promotion budget sums to international travel markets in order to optimize their marketing objectives. The high-level concept construct of the TOUREX (TOURism EXpert system) model is shown in Figure 1.

An application rule-based demonstration has been developed for demonstration purposes using an expert system development tool (shell), Leonar-

FIGURE 1. High Level Concepts in the TOUREX Model

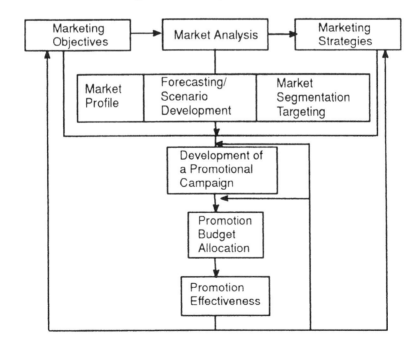

do. The demonstration system performs as a marketing consultant providing advice on the markets to select and on the allocation of promotional budget sums to those markets in order to attract tourists from generating international travel markets to a particular destination country.

During the course of a consultation the user first enters the NTO's marketing objectives. The main objective may be maximize visits or it may be maximize spending. Secondary objectives may be extend regional and seasonal spread of visits. Some of these objectives may be in conflict with each other; for example, the maximum stimulation of economic growth may be in conflict with the protection of the natural environment. Therefore, the user is asked to rank them in terms of their importance. The marketing objectives are translated into the identification of key market segments to be addressed; for example, the senior citizens and the special interest segments in the case of seasonal spread.

The second stage of the consultation process consists of the analysis of each of the generating markets, whereby markets are profiled and their level of attractiveness assessed. The user first selects the more relevant factors within each dimension (for a detailed explanation of each of these dimensions and associated factors, the reader is referred to Rita 1991b). Second, the user attaches priorities in the form of weights (subjective estimates) to each of the factors selected using pairwise comparisons. Third, the user rates each of the factors against each of the markets. The system then calculates the complete composite scores on each dimension. The user is also asked to compare the relative importance of each dimension for the computation of the overall market attractiveness index.

The forecasting/scenario subcomponent of the model allows for the analysis of future trends regarding their probability of occurrence and level of impact. For example, a market showing an aging population is likely to favour a boost on non-seasonal travel, long-haul travel, length of stay, international travel, and package/inclusive tours. The user is also asked to identify the major market segments within each market and to target these.

Marketing Strategies constitute also an important component in the model since they assist in guiding the allocation of resources to the foreign markets.

The model takes into account the development of a promotional campaign for each of the target markets. The campaigns—derived from marketing objectives and strategies, and market analysis—help managers to identify cut-off points for each market, i.e., minimum platforms below which it does not make sense to spend on promotion, as well as minimum reach and frequency criteria.

The measurement of promotion effectiveness is also another important component of the model. For example, conversion methods are used to measure promotion to consumer effectiveness. Other important measures taken into consideration are carry-over effects such as delay-response effect and customer-retention effect.

The system ranks the various markets into primary, and secondary categories according to their market attractiveness indexes, promotion effectiveness, future scenarios, market segmentation and targeting, marketing strategies, and promotional campaigns.

KNOWLEDGE ACQUISITION METHODOLOGY

The bottleneck in the development of expert systems is in extracting the knowledge from the expert(s), that is, in knowledge acquisition. There are two classes of methods for revealing what experts know. Direct methods (e.g., interviews, questionnaires), as opposed to indirect methods (e.g., repertory grid analysis), ask the expert to report on knowledge he/she can directly articulate (Olson and Rueter 1987).

Interviews are the most common method for eliciting knowledge from the expert. In conversation, the expert reveals the variables he/she thinks are critical (factors or objects), how they are related or organized (relationships), and the processes he/she goes through in making a judgement, solving a problem, or designing a solution (inferences). Questionnaires, on the other hand, are also very useful in discovering the objects of the experts, the important subdomains, as well as uncovering relationships. They are particularly appropriate for eliciting uncertainty about particular inferences an expert has reported, since normal verbal responses from people are not very reliable in revealing this kind of information.

In order to acquire the relevant knowledge to improve and expand the model and the knowledge base, a fieldwork methodology has been developed. This comprises both in-depth interviews to a sample of twelve European NTOs and mail questionnaires to all NTOs worldwide, i.e., a census approach (for a more detailed description of the research methodology underlying the knowledge acquisition process to build TOUREX, the reader is referred to Rita 1991a).

An in-depth personal interview technique, having the interviewer (knowledge engineer) asking the questions to the respondents (domain experts) in a face-to-face situation, was the method employed first. The sampling unit was selected using a nonprobability judgemental approach to make sure that world leading European destination countries would be included.

The interviews were carried out with 22 senior managers of the twelve selected European NTOs: marketing directors, heads of strategic planning, and directors of research. All the interviews were taped with the previous agreement of the respondents. Approximately 24 hours of relevant taped material was yielded by the interviews.

The main interview objective was to identify and analyse the most relevant variables, their relationships and inferences affecting promotion budget allocation decisions to foreign markets. The interviews were based around the following seven questions/issues:

1. Critical Steps in Promotion Budget Allocation;
2. Marketing Objectives;
3. Market Segmentation and Targeting;
4. Marketing and Promotion Strategies;
5. Promotion Effectiveness Measures Used;
6. Factors Influencing Promotion Budget Allocation;
7. Scenarios: If-Then Rules/Criteria.

Qualitative content analysis of data was used instead of formal statistical techniques due to the small sample unit size, non-random method of sample selection, and the semi-structured format of the interviews.

Since more than one expert is involved in knowledge acquisition, there is a need of achieving some type of consensus on the issues mentioned above in order to build/expand the knowledge base. A crude method to solve this problem would be to consider the knowledge elements which show a majority of agreement between the managers. However, the technique that will be used takes also into account the size of each NTO's budget and the importance of tourism within its country's GNP. Each of these criteria will be given a weight to attach to the knowledge elicited.

EMPIRICAL RESULTS

Critical Steps in Promotion Budget Allocation

The real essence of a strategic decision is that scarce resources will be allocated to one project and denied to another. Therefore, resource allocation is at the heart of the strategic market planning process.

The allocation of promotion budget sums to overseas markets follows two distinct approaches:

i. Central Office makes actual allocation
   of promotion budget sums to each market;

ii. Each Representative Office proposes a budget
   which is then judged by the Central Office.

Some NTO's head offices make the actual allocation of the overall promotion budget by market. Here, the head office is concerned about the allocation of budget sums between the markets, whereas the actual use of these sums is left to the market representatives/directors as they have the responsibility of delivering the targets set by the head office. The representative offices have to decide, for example, on how they must spend the budget in terms of consumer and/or trade promotion approaches (promotion mix and strategy decisions).

Other NTO's central offices bear judgement on proposed promotion budgets from representative managers. Here, the starting point of budget allocation by market is constituted by the proposals from representative managers bearing in mind the guidelines (including budget constraints) produced by the central marketing director.

The promotion budget allocation process consists of six critical steps:

1. Spread versus Concentration of Markets
2. National/Government Goals
3. Marketing Objectives
4. Market Research, Segmentation and Targeting
5. Weighting and Classification of Markets
6. Allocating Promotion Budget

The first step is to look at the NTO's overall policy in terms of spread versus concentration of markets. A broad spread of markets mitigates any sudden drop in traffic from individual markets as a result of external factors (e.g., USA and the Gulf War), and allows for the development of new markets and a good return on investment in the long-term. The second step is to consider national or government goals (e.g., employment creation) which determine implicitly or explicitly the third step of the process – the definition of the NTO's overall marketing objectives (e.g., optimizing tourism earnings, regional spread).

The fourth step is to conduct market research in order to collect and analyse information from each market: present and future trends (economic, demographic, social, environmental, political); segmentation of markets; product/market fit analysis (matching each market and segment wants with suitable products offered by the destination country). This analysis, complemented with representative managers' knowledge of the markets and intuitive judgement, enables NTOs to set volume and expenditure targets for each of the market and segment areas.

The fifth step is to weight each market according to the revenue target that it is to produce, attaching more weight to the markets and segments generating larger proportion of revenue. Markets are grouped into three major categories: primary, secondary, and tertiary markets. Primary markets are the backbone of incoming tourism, and they are given high priority for budget allocation by NTOs which usually have an office there, and use all the available instruments (providing information, press and public relations, working with the trade, participating in joint promotions, and marketing directly to the consumer). Secondary markets are given medium priority by NTOs which have normally only some marketing activities (supply information and services for the consumer and travel industries) and a small budget allocated to these markets. Tertiary markets are given low priority by NTOs which do not undertake any marketing activity in these markets. The factors outlined below are used as the criteria to allocate each market to one of these three groups, and then if it is an important market to allocate resources to it. A key management decision lies on how to allocate budget sums/funding between these three categories. In reality, about 70% of the budget goes to primary markets, 30% to secondary markets and 0% to tertiary markets. Therefore, the resources are allocated to primary and secondary markets.

Marketing Objectives

Establishing objectives is a key step within the strategic marketing planning process. After a suitable definition of the organization's business has been established and a comprehensive situation analysis carried out, the organization will be in the position to establish objectives.

The set of objectives should meet certain criteria. First, each objective should be stated in an unambiguous and measurable form with an appropriate time frame within which the target is to be achieved. Second, the various objectives should be internally consistent. Third, the objectives should be stated hierarchically with lower objectives being clearly derived from higher objectives. Fourth, the objectives should be attainable but sufficiently challenging to stimulate maximum effort (Kotler 1988).

As a nonprofit organization, an NTO is in a position where no profit measure or ready identifiable end output is available for use as an indicator of efficiency. There are marketing costs but no return attributable to the same organization which has incurred the costs. Therefore, any attempt of budget allocation by maximizing a profit variable is unfeasible (Mazanec 1986).

The NTO's marketing objectives are government inspired to an extent. As government agencies, the NTOs must address government guidelines and national goals (e.g., job creation). Therefore, government policy is implicit or explicit in the NTO's objectives.

As shown in Table 1, NTOs establish several key objectives in carrying out their responsibilities to promote tourism to the destination country. The major objective is to optimize tourism revenue and share of earnings for visitor spending from key international travel markets, weighted for regional and seasonal spread of visits.

Broad promotion objectives, such as "to remind," "to inform," and/or "to persuade" tourist audiences can be found embedded in the listing of specific marketing objectives included in the study questionnaire (for example, "to increase repeat visits," "to develop new tourist products," "to promote less visited regions of the country" or "to increase the average length of stay"). The aforementioned broad promotion objectives were found not to be widely cited by NTO's managers when designing a promotional campaign and setting its budget appropriations. Nevertheless, promotional campaign objectives and budget allocation are intrinsically linked with the specified goals of the NTO's marketing plan.

Market Segmentation and Targeting

Strategic planning involves market segmentation, which entails breaking down the market for a particular product or service into segments of customers which differ in terms of their response to marketing strategies (Wind and Douglas 1972).

Segmentation is a prerequisite for selective market operation and takes into account tourist attitudes, travel behaviour, and demographic or socioeconomic profiles. Thus, when targeting a marketing effort to selected segments one can reduce the competitive pressure that would prevail if all tourist services were indiscriminately offered to the same market (Vavrik and Mazanec 1990).

TABLE 1. Marketing Objectives

1. Optimize tourism earnings
2. Extend regional and seasonal spread of visits
3. Maintain a broad spread of markets
4. Maintain/increase market share in developed/new market
5. Maintain/increase volume traffic (arrivals, bednights)
6. Strengthen country's image as an attractive tourism destination

Segmentation of potential tourist markets has a number of benefits for governmental tourist agencies who have limited promotional resources. Promotional messages and travel incentives can be better tailored to receptive market segments and will lead to greater effectiveness of promotional spending (McQueen and Miller 1985).

The key market regions and segments identified are presented in Table 2. The most used segmentation technique is 'purpose of visit' (overall and by market): holiday independent, holiday inclusive, visiting friends and relatives (VFR), business travel, special interest, study, and miscellaneous. Markets are also commonly segmented on distance travelled (short-haul and long-haul), number of previous visits (first-time and repeat visitors), buying habits (independent and inclusive traveller), length of stay (short-break and long stay), demographic characteristics (e.g., age, family composition, education, income), season visited (high season and off-peak), and travel method (air, sea, land).

NTOs use a product/market fit table in order to target each market and segment. This table facilitates the matching of the right product against the right market and the right segment within that market. This method ensures that the marketer will be specific in directing the right message to the right target group.

Marketing targets are identified regarding receipts (expenditure per day and total expenditure), volume and annual growth of overall visitors, holiday visitors, and first time holiday visitors, as well as average length of stay, and employment creation. In identifying the targets, NTO's managers are very much influenced by a certain number of primary factors. For example, generating markets performing well on basic economic indicators (e.g., income, relative price), and with a high volume of outbound traffic are looked at as being potentially more fruitful markets to work in than those in economic recession and with a low volume of outbound

TABLE 2. Markets and Segments

Key Markets:	Western Europe
	North America
	East Asia/Pacific
Key Segments:	Holiday
	Business travel
	Special interest
	Senior citizens
	Youth

traffic. In addition, NTO's managers are also conscious of the overall state of the tourist market in the generating countries as far as preferences and tastes are concerned. Despite the difficulty in assessing the perceptions of managers and its range, these should be based on hard market research data, and are accounted in the model by using a system of ratings, i.e., confidence factors (0-100%), in relation to market research input.

Marketing and Promotional Strategies

Marketing strategy describes the direction the organization will pursue within its chosen environment and guides the allocation of resources (Day 1984). The purpose of promotional strategy is to allow tourism organizations to decide priorities and goals before allocating money and resources.

The marketing strategies formulated by NTOs are listed in Table 3. The promotional strategies formulated follow the push/pull principle. That is to say, the manager has the option of operating through distribution channels and through them pushing the product to the consumer (Push), or alternatively the appeal can be directed to the consumer, who will ask for the product (Pull). Depending on the characteristics of each market, and the budget available, certain markets are almost totally consumer-oriented, other markets are totally trade-oriented, and yet other markets are targeted with both trade and consumer promotion.

Trade promotion is undertaken in markets and segments where most of the tourists are travelling abroad in package/inclusive tours, whereas consumer promotion is conducted in markets and segments where most of the outgoing tourists are independent travellers. Trade promotion is undertaken in order to increase the tour operators and travel agents' awareness and knowledge about the destination country and to ensure that the des-

TABLE 3. Marketing Strategies

1. Emphasize the attractions of less visited regions
2. Promote areas in the country which could attract more tourists and where unemployment is high
3. Emphasize the attractions of the destination country in off-season periods
4. Improve product quality and innovation constantly in order to take advantage of the consumers' rapidly changing wishes
5. Distinguish destination country from the competition through a powerful positioning

tination country is featured in all major travel trade programs. Trade promotion is mainly conducted through trade exhibitions and joint advertising schemes, whereas consumer promotion is mainly undertaken through media advertising (TV, radio, magazines, newspapers) and consumer exhibitions in major generating countries.

Promotion Effectiveness Measures Used

The evaluation of marketing/promotional programs is a must in order to determine what is and is not working, to determine positive and negative consequences, to determine relative program performance, to guide subsequent resource allocations and to justify program expenditures (Wynegar 1989).

The most used promotion effectiveness measures by the NTOs are summarized in Table 4. NTO's promotion is a small effort within a vast overall promotion effort (carriers, hotel chains, competition, etc). Objective testing is difficult and involves estimation and professional judgement. But there is a second area for test, the marketing operations themselves, which often provides useful and clear indications of results. These vary according to the media. The simple tests used include analysis of

TABLE 4. Promotion Effectiveness Measures

Consumer:

Coupon replies to media advertising
No. enquiries to information offices
Percentage of enquirers who bought the product
Quality of brochures
Literature sales and advertising revenue
Visitor satisfaction

Industry:

Satisfaction of NTO's activities
National travel trade interest
Non-Government funding raised
Number national participants in travel fairs
    together with NTO

replies (particularly coupon replies to advertising). But there are dangers–not all coupon replies are turned into bookings.

A second test measures quality by checking if the enquirer bought the product. Analysis of literature sales and advertising revenue, enquiries by mail (including reply to advertisements) and by phone to enquiry or information offices are also important performance tests used. In addition, ratios such as No. enquiries/No. staff, minutes per enquiry, tourist spend/No. staff, and percentage of visitors who got information from NTO's representative offices before travelling to the destination country are used as performance indicators.

Public relations activities, such as visits by journalists, result in press coverage and this is counted as well as travel trade visits. Number of exhibitions and workshops by special sample surveys also show business generated.

Factors Influencing Promotion Budget Allocation

As seen in Table 5, there are a number of factors identified by the NTOs as being fundamental in formulating a managerially actionable framework for evaluating travel markets and allocating promotion budget sums to those markets. These are mainly economic, tourist-related and marketing factors.

Within a 5 point scale, from least important (1) to most important (5) each of the primary factors was weighted in terms of its importance. The weighting as well as the list of factors change dynamically from one market to another. However, although some of the factors might vary, the final decision would not vary because only a very few factors are heavily weighted, i.e., have a real impact on the final decision. Ultimately, weighings, which are partially historical, are attached on the basis of specific target markets and the value of these markets by meeting NTOs marketing objectives. Economic benefits derived from tourism are directly linked to the level of expenditure by tourists (revenue target).

The managers' level of confidence on the quality of the existing data is an important consideration that should be borne in mind for decision making. Managers have a high confidence on the accuracy of some data such as staff resources and knowledge, travel distance and costs, transportation links, marketing/promotional and operational costs, and travel intensity. They have medium confidence on the quality of data like expenditure per visit, average daily expenditure, length of stay, first time/repeat visitors, GDP and disposable income figures, and destination awareness/image. Finally, they have low confidence on the accuracy of data such as

TABLE 5. Primary Factors Influencing Budget Allocation

Economic Factors	
Disposable Income	Relative Price
Daily Expenditure	Expenditure per Visit
Market Size	Market Potential
Market Growth Rate	
Tourist-Related Factors	
Length of Stay	Buying Habits
Travel Intensity	Repeat/First-Time Visitors
Marketing Factors	
Market Share	Competitive Pressure
Marketing Costs	Operational Costs
Product Position	Marketing Gaps
Potential for Non-Government Funding	
Staff Resources and Knowledge	
Other Factors	
Travel Distance/Costs	Political Factors

marketing gaps, level of autonomous demand, and private sector interest in the market.

The issue of data quality to be incorporated in the knowledge base is a critical factor since the whole argument for the development of the proposed tourism expert system lies heavily on finding and using reliable and valid data. Four measures are proposed in order to increase the degree of accuracy related to data acquisition and utilization. First, a validation procedure is set up to check for a high degree of correspondence between the data inputted by the user and available key tourism statistics. Second, greater weight and emphasis has been placed on the data and key indicators supplied by some large NTOs included in the achieved sample since they were recognized as possessing a more reliable and valid management information system. Third, consistency loops and checks within the nested rule base can be applied to the rule matching process implemented by the inference engine of the expert system shell; warning screens to the user can also be used. Finally, "library" screens can be added to the system designed to indicate to the user the most suitable sources of information which should be utilized at each decision point.

Scenarios: If-Then Rules/Criteria

In extracting knowledge from NTO's managers, a problem analysis technique was used whereby the managers were presented with a series of realistic problems (scenarios) to solve aloud, probing for the rationale behind the reasoning steps.

Alternative future analysis, using scenarios, can serve as an organizing framework within which the elements of environmental risk can be systematically identified and evaluated (Zentner 1982). Scenario development forces managers to explicitly state their assumptions about risk and helps to focus attention on causal processes and decision points.

Examples of rules for TOUREX applied to different knowledge subdomains are given in Table 6. To achieve regional and seasonal spread objectives, the senior citizens and business travel segments are particularly targeted and their major markets specially weighted. Note that if the business travel segment includes a significant independent business travel subsegment then the NTO's strategy for this particular subsegment is to convince business travellers to bring their spouse and extend their length of stay and regional spread in the destination country.

The language skills of the potential tourists have an important effect on their buying habits and consequently on the promotion strategy to be employed. On the one hand, when English is the mother language or a second good language in the generating market then language skills are high, and consequently tourists tend to travel independently; a pull strategy is applied here. On the other hand, when English is not the mother language or a second good language in the generating market then language skills are low, and consequently tourists tend to travel inclusive; a push strategy is more appropriated here.

As seen above, markets are normally grouped into primary, secondary and tertiary categories, and are allocated budgets only when they fall within the first two categories. If a market moves from the secondary to the primary category it will get increased funding in its first 2 to 3 years to catch up. So, to increase funding to that market the tourist office must decrease funding to another market. When the confidence in the decision is low (certainty) or the market falls within the middle category (secondary markets) one should also look at secondary factors. Note that the confidence on the decision tends to be higher when it falls within the primary (90%) or tertiary (100%) categories than when it falls within the secondary one (60-70%).

TABLE 6. Examples of Rules for TOUREX

<u>To Select Market Segments</u>

IF Marketing_Objectives include 'regional spread'
AND Marketing_Objectives include 'seasonal spread'
THEN Market_Segments include (senior citizens, business travel)

<u>To Determine Promotion Strategy</u>

IF English_Language is 'mother language'
OR English_Language is 'second good language'
THEN Language_Skills are high

IF Language_Skills are high
AND Visitors are 'repeat visitors'
THEN Buying_Habits are independent

IF Buying_Habits are independent
THEN Promotion_Strategy is pull

<u>To Determine Market Priority</u>

IF Expenditure_per_Visit is low
AND Staff_Resources_and_Knowledge are good
AND Length_of_Stay is long
AND Marketing_Gaps are 'very significant'
THEN Market is 'secondary priority' (low certainty)

A market may fall within the secondary category, with low certainty, if expenditure per visit is low, staff resources and knowledge are good, length of stay is long, and marketing gaps are very significant. Rationale: the low expenditure per visit (which would tend to indicate a tertiary market) is balanced out by marketing gaps, staff resources and knowledge and length of stay. This particular market would fall within the tertiary category by looking at secondary factors showing, for example, a low propensity to travel, indirect transportation links (mainly if the market is a short-haul market), and a low number of passport holders, even if its GDP would show high growth, and demographics (e.g., age) were changing positively.

Sensitivity (What-If) analysis, having a set of external events analysed in terms of their direction (positive or negative) and degree of impact (strong, medium or weak) on individual markets, showed that, for example, a political factor such as the Gulf War although having similar consequences on tourist traffic movement as an economic factor such as recession, asks for a different action to be taken by NTOs. The former is better approached by the lobbying of important people to reassure security to travellers against terrorism threats, whereas the latter, a question of affordability, is better coped by raising additional non-government funding and by reinforcing and redirecting promotion in terms of good value offers.

Before allocating the promotion budget to the foreign markets, NTO's managers should decide on how much of the budget should be reserved for maintenance purposes (maintenance budget), and what share should be devoted for expansion (expansion budget).

Finally, the budget allocation decision will fall within the following framework of possible solution categories:

- Expand Budget;
- Maintain Budget;
- Reduce Budget;
- Close Down Offices;
- Open New Offices.

CONCLUSIONS

This paper has analysed and discussed the findings generated from interviews undertaken with a sample of European National Tourist Offices. These in-depth interviews were carried out as part of an overall research methodology which also involves a worldwide mail survey questionnaire, and that underlies the knowledge acquisition process to build TOUREX, an expert system aimed at helping NTOs in the allocation of promotion budget sums to international travel markets.

The fieldwork interviews produced a number of useful results whereby the particular model and demonstration system could be enhanced. The findings suggested that some factors could be cut out, and replaced by new ones. In addition, the results provided some important if-then rules/criteria and what-if scenarios to be included in the knowledge base.

The end benefits are that NTO's managers improve understanding of the way the knowledge is used for decision making by being prompted to consider key factors, relationships and inference procedures that they might otherwise overlook. Managers can also greatly enhance their managerial performance by having the opportunity to access expert advice at any time, the ability to query the expert's reasoning, the possibility of having an "aide-memoire," and the ability to obtain consistent advice.

REFERENCES

Basu, A. and Batra R. (1988). ADSPLIT: A Multi-Brand Advertising Budget Allocation Model. *Journal of Advertising*, 17(2), 44-51.
Birks, D. and Southan J. (1990). The Potential of Marketing Information Systems in Charitable Organisations. *Marketing Intelligence and Planning*, 8(4), 15-20.
Broadbent, S. (1988) Advertising Effectiveness: Wait And Measure. *Marketing* (September 22), 22-23.
Crouch, G. (1991). Expert Computer Systems In Tourism: Emerging Possibilities. *Journal of Travel Research* (Winter), 29(3), 3-10.
Day, G. (1984). Strategic Market Analysis and Definition: An Integrated Approach. In B. Weitz and R. Wensley (Ed.) *Strategic Marketing Planning, Implementation and Control*. Boston: Kent Publishing Company.
Hawkins, D. and Ritchie B. (1991). *World Travel and Tourism Review: Indicators, Trends and Forecasts*. Oxford: C.A.B. International.
Heneghan, P. (1976). *Resource Allocation in Tourism*. London: Tourism International Press, London.
Henshall, R. and Roberts R. (1985). Comparative Assessment of Tourist Generating Markets for New Zealand. *Annals of Tourism Research*, 12(2), 219-238.
Jefferson, A. (1990). Marketing in National Tourist Offices. In C. Cooper (Ed.) *Progress On Tourism And Hospitality Management* (pp. 82-95). Guildford: University of Surrey.
Kotler, P. (1988). *Marketing Management: Analysis, Planning, Implementation, and Control*. New Jersey: Prentice Hall.
Mazanec, J. (1986). Allocating an Advertising Budget to International Travel Markets. *Annals of Tourism Research*, 13(3), 609-634.
McElnea, J. (1991). We've Reached The Crossroads: Which Path Will We Take? *Marketing News* (April), 25(8), 22.
McQueen, J. and Miller K. (1985). Target Market Selection of Tourists: A Comparison of Approaches. *Journal of Travel Research* (Summer), 24, 2-6.
Olson, J. and Rueter H. (1987). Extracting Expertise from Experts: Methods for Knowledge Acquisition. *Expert Systems*, 4(3), 152-168.
Rita, P. (1991a). An Expert System for Resource Allocation Decisions in National Tourism Organizations: Knowledge Acquisition Issues. In *Principles And Practices In Economic And Business Research Methods* (pp. 137-151). Colloquium held at the University of Wales, Cardiff, United Kingdom, (October).
Rita, P. (1991b). An Expert Support System for Promotional Budget Allocation in National Tourist Offices. In L. Moutinho (Ed.) *The Services Manufacturing Divide: Synergies and Dilemmas*. Conference held at the University of Wales, Cardiff, UK, (September 26-27).
Rosenthal, A. (1991). Tough Times Give Incentives New Muscle. *Business Marketing* (March), 76(3), T1, T6.
Vaughan, R. (1988). Expert Systems Come Out of Their Shells. *Systems International* (March), 16(3), 35-40.
Vavrik, U. and Mazanec J. (1990). A Priori and a Posteriori Travel Market Segmentation: Tailoring Automatic Interaction Detection and Cluster Analysis for

Tourism Marketing. *Cahiers du Tourisme*, Serie C, No.62, Centre des Hautes Etudes Touristiques.

White, A. (1991). Press Releases: Don't Keep a Dog and Then Do Your Own Barking. *Business Marketing Digest*, 16(1), 111-114.

Wind, Y. and Douglas S. (1972). International Market Segmentation. *European Journal of Marketing*, 6(1), 17-25.

Wynegar, D. (1989). Back to Basics: Evaluation Research Pragmatism vs. Precision? In *Twenty Years of Travel and Marketing Research Revisited*. Conference held at the Sheraton Waikiki Hotel, Honolulu, Hawaii, (June 11-15).

Zentner R. (1982). Scenarios: Past, Present and Future. *Long Range Planning*, 15(3), 12-20.

Cross-Cultural Tourism Marketing Research: An Assessment and Recommendations for Future Studies

Frédéric Dimanche

SUMMARY. An examination of tourism literature shows little cross-cultural research, particularly in the contexts of tourist behavior and marketing. The rapid globalization of the tourism phenomenon and its international nature should generate more interest for cross-cultural research. This paper examines some of the reasons why cross-cultural tourism research has been limited, and presents some arguments in favor of this type of research. Methodological guidelines regarding the translation of instruments, the equivalence of similar concepts in different cultures, and measurement equivalence are considered. More cross-cultural research is warranted in tourism marketing for a better understanding of the "global tourist."

INTRODUCTION

No one would challenge the fact that tourism has become an international phenomenon of global consequence. However, tourism researchers seem to be extremely slow in recognizing this fact given the small number

Frédéric Dimanche is affiliated with the School of Hotel, Restaurant, and Tourism Administration, University of New Orleans, New Orleans, LA 70148.

[Haworth co-indexing entry note]: "Cross-Cultural Tourism Marketing Research: An Assessment and Recommendations for Future Studies." Dimanche, Frédéric. Co-published simultaneously in *Journal of International Consumer Marketing* (The Haworth Press, Inc.) Vol. 6, No. 3/4, 1994, pp. 123-134; and: *Global Tourist Behavior* (ed: Muzaffer Uysal) The Haworth Press, Inc., 1994, pp. 123-134. Multiple copies of this article/chapter may be purchased from The Haworth Document Delivery Center [1-800-3-HAWORTH; 9:00 a.m. - 5:00 p.m. (EST)].

123

of cross-cultural research publications. An overview of the tourism literature shows the paucity of cross-cultural and international research, particularly in consumer behavior and marketing. Burnett, Uysal, and Jamrozy
(1991, p. 49) indicated that "serious study of travel and tourism eventually
involves detailed consideration of international concern," but they showed
that a leading North American tourism research journal rarely published
articles of international nature. Another indication of this tendency can be
found in examining the *Travel Tourism and Hospitality Research* handbook edited by Ritchie and Goeldner (1987). Despite the inclusion of a
chapter dedicated to estimating the potential of international markets, no
information is given about cross-cultural research methods in this otherwise in-depth survey of tourism research methods and practices. Clearly,
tourism researchers need to adopt a cross-cultural and international perspective, one that includes a global approach to tourist behavior and marketing research, as well as to learn the necessary cross-cultural research
methods. The term "cross-cultural" will be used in this paper because it is
broader and because it "reflects more possible differences in consumer
behavior than 'cross-national'" (van Raaij, 1978, p. 693).

The purpose of this paper is twofold: (1) To review the existing cross-
cultural tourism marketing literature and to identify factors that may prevent
researchers from doing such research, and (2) to provide cross-cultural
research methodological recommendations that would help understand the
problems posed by cross-cultural studies.

REVIEW OF EXISTING CROSS-CULTURAL TOURISM MARKETING LITERATURE

Conducting research in intercultural and international settings leads to
obvious problems related to cultural and language differences. Due to
these problems, very few cross-cultural studies exist in tourism research.
Plog (1990, p. 43) noted that "cross-cultural research, particularly related
to travel behavior, is quite rare." Richards (cited in Brislin, 1980, p. 426)
asserted that translation is "probably the most complex type of event yet
produced in the evolution of the cosmos." Often, when faced with the task
of ensuring proper equivalence of a research instrument across cultures
and languages, researchers tend to deny the problem and pursue their
research goals in a single language, English. For example, Albaum, Erickson, and Strandskov (1990) recently studied the question "whether
translation is necessary and even desirable when a population understands,
to a greater or lesser degree, the language of the researcher" (p. 10). The
"all English" approach has often been used in consumer behavior or

tourism research. For example, Zaichkowsky and Sood (1989), doing cross-cultural research on consumer involvement, simply used their English instrument in 15 different countries, assuming that the educated respondents would have sufficient knowledge of English to understand all the items: "It is assumed that this (the questionnaires being prepared in English) will have little bias effect on the responses" (p. 24). However, McQuarrie and Munson's (1987) critique of the Zaichkowsky's (1985) instrument concerning some difficult to understand items raises questions regarding Zaichkowsky and Sood's assumption.

In a tourism marketing study, Moschis and Bello (1987) used a questionnaire written in English to survey travelers from 28 different countries on their travel behavior. They indicated as a limitation of their study that "although English is the international language and many citizens of other language speak English, one cannot guard against different levels of ability to read and understand the questions" (p. 87). An examination of Moschis and Bello's (1987, pp. 88-89) items shows that indeed, they did not use the most familiar vocabulary. One can be skeptical about the proper understanding of their items by non-English speakers. This can also be said of Ahmed's (1989) English questionnaire which was used to survey Sri Lankans and English, French, and German tourists to compare their psychological profiles. Ahmed (p. 355) acknowledged that the non-English participants' responses "may be subject to response biases."

Thus, questions abound regarding international respondents' understanding of the questionnaires used in much contemporary research. Assuming the understanding "to a lesser degree" (Albaum et al., 1990) of the researcher's language by foreign subjects should not be a reason for conducting cross-cultural research in that language. Translating the questionnaires into the subjects' native language should then be the preferred methodology. This is also true in cross-cultural research within one single country. For example, for the purpose of studying native Americans, Hispanics, or Asians in the USA, one should show extreme concern about cultural meaning differentials and use the primary language spoken by these populations. Often, even English words and phrases have different meanings according to the cultural group.

In addition to the relative scarcity of cross-cultural studies reported in the tourism literature, most of those using translated instruments tend to lack sufficient information concerning the validity and reliability of the question items in the various cultures, therefore making the results suspect. For example, Richardson and Crompton (1988) did not mention translation procedures in their use of secondary data for a study of French- and English-speaking Canadians. An example of cross-cultural research conducted in tourism contexts with a translated instrument is the study of foodservice preferences in vacation destinations conducted by Sheldon and Fox (1988) with Canadians, Americans, and Japanese. A questionnaire was translated into Japanese and administered in Japan, but the authors did not give any information regarding the translation and the cultural equivalence of the research instrument nor did they address reliability issues. This lack of information causes the reader to question the results of studies indicating "cultural differences." For example, differences found may simply be due to the misunderstanding of some parts of the questionnaire by the subjects. This misunderstanding may, in effect, be related to vocabulary problems or to the Japanese's lack of certain food-related concepts existing in the USA. More recently, in a controversial test of Plog's (1974) allocentric/psychocentric model, Smith (1990) did not give any information about translation and other cultural equivalence problems in reporting the results of a survey administered to travelers from seven European and Asian countries. In light of these shortcomings, the following section will examine some of the factors that may be hindering cross-cultural tourism marketing research.

FACTORS IMPEDING CROSS-CULTURAL RESEARCH

Misunderstanding the value of cross-cultural research. The first factor limiting the use of cross-cultural research may simply be a misunderstanding of its value and potential benefits. Triandis, Vassiliou, Vassiliou, Tanaka, and Shanmugam (1972) reported several reasons for doing cross-cultural research, outlined here in the context of tourist behavior and marketing research: A primary purpose of cross-cultural research would be to test a touristic phenomenon or construct in various cultural environments, therefore providing different conditions needed to test that phenomenon or construct. The variations issued from the cultural differences are likely to provide a better understanding of the construct or phenomenon in question.

Most of our research has one main limitation in that it is culture-specific. Then, a second purpose would be to test tourist behavior and marketing theories in international settings, in order to learn whether the theories can be generalizable or whether they are culture-specific. The cross-cultural psychology literature suggests that it is unlikely that theories be generalizable across cultures. Indeed, in tourism contexts, behavior and vacation patterns are often culture-specific. However, recognizing differences between cultures and understanding them through research appears important.

A third purpose of doing cross-cultural research is to explore other cultures, learn about them, and to test cultural differences in tourism marketing contexts. This responds to a marketing approach where practitioners have to understand people's various needs in order to better target and satisfy them. Tourism researchers could investigate tourists' behavioral and attitudinal differences in several international markets. Although the number of international visitors to the USA has greatly grown in the last five years (Shields, 1992), and although many cities and states are targeting foreign markets, we should realize that we know very little about international travelers. O'Halloran and Hensarling (1991, p. 170) indicated that the U.S. hospitality and tourism industries are putting "little effort into exploring the cultures and the work ethic of the countries that they are seeking to attract to their businesses." We have much to learn about international tourists and the differences they show in terms of behavior, attitudes toward destinations, spending patterns, motivations, satisfaction levels, etc.

In addition, a growing body of tourism literature mainly coming from anthropology examines the relationships between hosts and guests (e.g., Evans, 1976; Smith, 1989). Researchers in consumer behavior and marketing could learn from anthropologists' work and start examining the impact of cultural differences on the quality of cross-cultural interactions between tourists and locals working in the tourism industry or not. Brislin (1981) provides a basis for the study of these cross-cultural encounters by summarizing the existing literature dealing with these issues, while recognizing the complexity of such a study area.

Ethnocentrism. The little interest in cross-cultural research shown by researchers may not only be due to a lack of understanding of its importance but could also be due to ethnocentrism, as Burnett et al. (1991) suggested. Because most tourist behavior research is being conducted in the USA, the theories and practices that are developed are limited to the white middle-class American culture and lack either generalization or specific applications to other cultural settings. As indicated earlier, general cross-cultural theories of tourist behavior taking into consideration the "global tourist" may not always be relevant because of the culture-specificity of tourist behavior. This means that researchers need to go beyond the centrality of their culture (i.e., ethnocentrism) which is affecting the assumptions and values that are the basis for their research. Ethnocentrism and ignorance about other cultures "obstruct the development of objective assessment of cultural differences" (Stewart & Bennett, 1991, p. 164). These authors added that because of ethnocentrism, "The patterns of other cultures may be ignored in deference to the naturalness of the reference culture. Or the other cultures may simply be treated as deviations from reality or normality rather than as variations" (p. 161). At the very least, we need to acknowledge our cultural biases and learn to interpret them in the studies we conduct. At best, we need to educate ourselves to cultural diversity and learn to discard the lack of interest in or the stereotypes of the "other." Cateora and Keaveney (1987) indicated that the most important step in the marketing research process involves correctly defining the problem, and pointed to the difficulty of such a task in international contexts because of the "self-reference criterion." The self-reference criterion has to be identified by the marketing researchers so that they can avoid being led into error by cultural differences.

Lack of resources. International research often requires extensive funding or/and some cooperative colleagues abroad sharing the same research interests. Of course, the lack of financial resources may be due to ethnocentrism. Monies may not be allocated to research projects that are deemed unimportant because of a lack of sensitivity to cross-cultural issues. Mayer (1978, p. 77) purported that "research budgets are generally controlled at the national level and, at that level, the concern about comparability across nations is not strongly felt." A possible way to relieve budget constraints is to cooperate with a colleague in the target culture. Also, having a colleague in the other culture will help for translation and cultural equivalence issues. It might also be critical in alleviating the suspicions that are often expressed by minorities vis-à-vis Caucasian researchers. This should help contribute to better validity and possibly higher response rates.

An asset that may also be lacking is our knowledge of cross-cultural research methods. We, as researchers, have not been educated to conduct cross-cultural research. We tend to be afraid of studying populations that are very different from what we are. Most of the research conducted in travel and tourism deals with middle-class Caucasian samples because we don't have the necessary background to study other populations whether it be in our own country or internationally.

Language and cross-cultural skills. The greatest barrier researchers face before conducting sound cross-cultural research is, of course, language and cultural differences and their effects. These problems are often seen as the main reason why very few cross-cultural consumer behavior research studies exist (Zaichkowsky & Sood, 1989). In fact, Alden, Hoyer, and Wechasara (1989) reported the apparent non-existence of cross-cultural consumer studies of affective, cognitive, or heuristic components of decision-making in the consumer behavior literature. Cateora and Keaveney (1987) warned their readers about translation problems in marketing, and also indicated the danger of miscommunicating even in countries sharing the same language.

American researchers seem to be intimidated by foreign languages and rarely do they have the required knowledge base to effectively conduct research in another language. However, it is critical to have a minimum understanding of a foreign language because a language is the necessary key to properly perceiving another culture. Knowing a language broadens the horizon of the researcher and helps her/him understand the problem under study from a different cultural perspective. Also, it contributes to a better comprehension of the methodological problems of cultural and translation equivalence. If the importance of cross-cultural research is recognized in tourism studies, academicians probably will have to change the function of language learning in curricula and realize that computer and statistical skills, often required in doctoral programs, should be complemented by the understanding of a foreign language.

Clearly, the potential exists to conduct cross-cultural studies in tourist behavior and tourism marketing research. Addressing the aforementioned issues appears necessary if the research literature is to grow in that domain. Learning from existing methods in cross-cultural research would allow tourism researchers to use the proper tools that are necessary to engage in fruitful research. It is essential for tourism researchers to improve their crosscultural methodological skills and to pay more attention to language and cultural equivalence issues in order to improve the quality of the studies conducted. There is a need to learn from the methodologies that have been developed by cross-cultural psychologists which can be applied in tourism marketing studies. The following section attempts to summarize some of the main methodological considerations issued from the cross-cultural psychology literature. For further information on these problems, the reader is referred to Brislin (1970, 1976, 1980) and Hui and Triandis (1985), as well as Green and White (1976) or Mayer (1978) who considered methodological problems in multinational marketing and consumer research.

METHODOLOGICAL GUIDELINES
FOR CROSS-CULTURAL RESEARCH

Language. The major problem in cross-cultural research is to determine whether or not the translation is equivalent to the original language. Cross-cultural researchers have indicated the difficulties of translating and evaluating the quality of the translations (Brislin, 1970, 1980; Sechrest, Fay, &

Zaidi, 1972). There are various types of problems in translation, and this short review will not consider all of them in detail.

Brislin (1970, 1980) indicated four basic translation methods and recommended that various combinations may be appropriate, depending upon the needs of specific research projects: (a) back-translation; (b) the bilingual technique; (c) the committee approach; and (d) pre-test procedures. Back-translation refers to the use of two bilinguals. The first person translates the material from the source language to the target language, and the second person translates back from the target to the source without having knowledge of the original material. The researcher can then, without having knowledge of the target language, make a judgement about the quality of the translation by comparing the two materials in the original language. The bilingual technique uses bilinguals who take the test in the two languages. The items yielding different responses can then be identified. In the committee approach, a bilingual group translates from the source to the target language. This method permits members of the committee can correct each other. Finally, the pretest procedure consists of field-testing the translation to ensure complete comprehension of the text by subjects. Brislin (1970) indicated that too often, little if any information is given in research reports to demonstrate the equivalence of the source language form and the translated form. An effort to use back translation and the committee approach was reported by Dimanche (1990) and Dimanche, Havitz, and Howard (1991), for the translation of a scale from French into English in a study of involvement in touristic contexts.

Experiential and conceptual equivalence. Sechrest et al. (1972) identified several kinds of equivalence that have different effects in translation: (a) vocabulary equivalence; (b) idiomatic equivalence; (c) grammatical-syntactical equivalence; (d) experiential equivalence; and (e) conceptual equivalence. The first three problems involve linguistic considerations and will not be presented in this paper.

Experiential equivalence refers to the idea that "in order for translations to be successful from one culture to another, they must utilize terms referring to real things and real experiences which are familiar in both cultures, if not exactly equally familiar" (Sechrest et al., 1972, p. 47). This equivalence also called cultural translation, refers to the fact that, for instance, an item of a questionnaire must have the same cultural meaning in the two languages. Sechrest et al. (1972) indicated the word "feminine" ("Maria is more feminine than Elena") as an example of a difficult word to translate in the culture they were studying. Przeworski and Teune (cited in Sechrest et al., 1972) indicated that "an instrument is equivalent across systems to the extent that the results provided by the instrument reliably describe with (nearly) the same validity a particular phenomenon in different social systems." Similarity of factorial structure is recommended by these authors as well as Hui and Triandis (1985) to assess the structural similarity of a construct across cultures. If a construct is the same in two different cultures, it should have the same internal structure in these cultures. Factor analysis is the most popular method in assessing cross-cultural equivalence by examining the internal structure of a construct (Hui & Triandis, 1985). In the marketing literature, Davis, Douglas, and Silk (1981) recommended the use of confirmatory and structural equation methods to conduct tests of the equivalence of factor structures across different samples in cross-national studies.

Conceptual equivalence which is similar to the aforementioned equivalence refers to the degree that two concepts are equivalent in the cultures under study. For example, Dimanche (1990) in a study of involvement in touristic context indicated that this construct was equivalent between France and the USA. A second aspect of conceptual equivalence is that a commonly used and understood concept in a culture might just be absent in another culture. Sechrest et al. (1972) reported difficulty finding a concept in the Philippines which had the same connotations as the concept of homosexuality in the USA These equivalence problems will affect the definition of the problem to be studied in each cultural environment (Mayer, 1978).

Measurement equivalence. To the conceptual equivalence discussed above, Hui and Triandis (1985) added three types of measurement equivalence: (a) equivalence in construct operationalization; (b) item equivalence; and (c) scalar equivalence. Operationalization is defined as the transition from theory to measurement. A construct must be operationalized in the same way in different cultures so that the instrument may be qualified as equivalent in construct operationalization across cultures. Item equivalence presupposes conceptual and operational equivalence. Then, the construct has to be measured in the different cultures by the same instrument. The items used have to be identical in the different cultures; each item should have the same meaning to people in both cultures. Item equivalence is a condition for direct comparison of test scores in two cultures. "A psychological test that lacks item equivalence is in effect two separate tests, one for each culture. If this happens, direct comparison of test scores is misleading and illegitimate" (Hui & Triandis, 1985, p. 135).

Finally, an instrument has scalar equivalence for two cultures if the other types of equivalence are present and if "it can be demonstrated that the construct is measured on the same metric" (p. 135). A value on a scale should refer to the same degree of the construct regardless of the population. Hui and Triandis noted that this equivalence is the most difficult to achieve. This difficulty can be avoided with the use of standardized instruments employing Likert scales. Munson and McIntyre (1979) suggested that the Likert type of rating approach would be beneficial to researchers engaged in cross-cultural marketing.

Davis et al. found that cross-national studies may be producing problems in the reliability of measurements. They indicated that "significant between sample reliability differentials can arise for the types of measures commonly collected in cross-national surveys employing instruments developed through the use of simply but routinely used back translation procedures that attempt to achieve linguistic and conceptual equivalence" (p. 107). Careful attention to translation and conceptual equivalence may not totally preclude validity and reliability problems; however, researchers need to address these issues because of the potential for the decrease in the power of statistical tests.

CONCLUSION

The challenge of conducting cross-cultural research in tourism marketing and tourist behavior is great, but the potential benefits for the advancement of knowledge in tourism gained from such studies should outweigh the costs. Since cross-cultural tourism marketing research is affected by numerous environmental and methodological problems, the purpose of this paper was to draw tourism researchers' attention to them. Therefore, these issues have only received here a cursory treatment. It is hoped, however, that this paper will contribute to understanding, if not breaking down, some of the methodological barriers that may have prevented tourism researchers from investigating cross-cultural issues and problems. It becomes more important for academicians and practitioners to understand how research can be conducted, interpreted, and transmitted in cross-cultural settings. If we are to better understand tourists' behavior and to find relevant theories to improve our international marketing practices, conducting crosscultural research with the appropriate methods becomes necessary.

REFERENCES

Ahmed, S. A. (1989). Psychological profiles of Sri Lankans versus tourists. *Annals of Tourism Research 16*(3), 345-359.
Albaum, G., Erickson, R., & Strandskov, J. (1990). Questionnaire design in international and cross-cultural research: Is translation necessary? In: M. P.

Gardner (Ed.), *Proceedings of the Society for Consumer Psychology* (pp. 10-15). St Louis, MO: University of Missouri.

Alden, D. L., Moyer, W. D., & Wechasara, G. (1989). Choice strategies and involvement: A cross-cultural analysis. *Advances in Consumer Research, 16* 119-126.

Brislin, R. W. (1970). Back-translation for cross-cultural research. *Journal of Cross-Cultural Psychology 1*(3), 185-216.

Brislin, R. W. (Ed.). (1976). *Translation: Applications and research.* New York: Wiley/Halsted.

Brislin, R. W. (1980). Translation and content analysis of oral and written material. In H. C. Triandis & J. w. Berry (Eds.), *Handbook of CrossCultural Psychology: Vol. 2. Methodology.* Boston: Allyn & Bacon.

Brislin, R. W. (1981). *Cross-cultural encounters.* New York: Pergamon.

Brislin, R. W., Lonner, W. J., & Thorndike, R. M. (1973). *Cross-cultural research methods.* New York: Wiley.

Burnett, G. W., Uysal, M, & Jamrozy, U. (1991). Articles on international themes in the Journal of Travel Research. *Journal of Travel Research 29*(3), 47-50.

Cateora, P. R. & Keaveney, S. (1987). *Marketing: An international perspective.* Homewood, IL: Irwin.

Davis, H. L., Douglas, S. P., & Silk, A. J. (1981). Measure unreliability: A hidden threat to cross-national marketing research? *Journal of Marketing 45*(Spring), 98-109.

Dimanche, F. (1990). Measuring involvement in recreational and touristic contexts with the Involvement Profile scale. *Dissertation Abstracts International.*

Dimanche, F., Havits, M. E., & Howard, D. R. (1991). Testing the Involvement Profile (IP) scale in the context of selected recreational and touristic activities. *Journal of Leisure Research 23*(1), 51-66.

Evans, N. H. (1976). Tourism and cross-cultural communication. *Annals of Tourism Research,* 3(4), 189-198.

Green, R. T. & White, P. D. (1976). Methodological considerations in cross-national consumer research. *Journal of International Business Studies, 7*(2), 81-87.

Hui, C. H., & Triandis, H. C. (1985). Measurement in cross-cultural psychology: A review and comparison of strategies. *Journal of CrossCultural Psychology, 16*(2), 131-152.

Mayer, C. S. (1978). Multinational marketing research: The magnifying glass of methodological problems. *European Research 6*(2), 77-84.

McQuarrie, E. F., & Munson, J. M. (1987). The Zaichkowsky Personal Involvement Inventory: Modification and extension. *Advances in Consumer Research 14* 36-40.

Moschis, G. P., & Bello, D. C. (1987). Decision-making patterns among international vacationers: A cross-cultural perspective. *Psychology and Marketing 4*(1), 75-89.

Munson, J. M., & Mcintyre, S. H. (1979). Developing practical procedures for the measurement of personal values in cross-cultural marketing. *Journal of Marketing Research 16*, 48-52.

O'Halloran, R. M., & Hensarling, D. M. (1991). Catering to foreign visitors: what is service anyway? *International Journal of Hospitality Management 10*(2), 169-171.

Plog, S. C. (1974). Why destinations areas rise and fall in popularity. *Cornell Hotel and Restaurant Administration Quarterly 14*(4), 55-58.

Plog, S. C. (1990). A carpenter's tools: An answer to Stephen L. J. Smith's review of Psychocentrism/Allocentrism. *Journal of Travel Research 28*(4), 43-45.

Richardson, S. L., & Crompton, J. L. (1988). Latent demand for vacation travel: A cross-cultural analysis of French- and English-speaking residents of Ontario and Quebec. *Leisure Sciences 10*(1), 17-26.

Ritchie, J. R. B., & Goeldner, C. R. (Eds.). (1987). *Travel, tourism, and hospitality research: A handbook for managers and researchers.* New York: Wiley.

Sechrest, L., Fay, T. L., & Zaidi, S. M. H. (1972). Problems of translation in cross-cultural research. *Journal of Cross-Cultural Psychology 3*(1), 41-56.

Sheldon, P. J., & Fox, M. (1988). The role of foodservice in vacation choice and experience: A cross-cultural analysis. *Journal of Travel Research, 27*(2) 9-15.

Shields, H. M. (1992). 1992 outlook for international travel. *1992 outlook for travel and tourism: Proceedings of the U.S. Travel Data Center's Seventeenth Annual Travel Outlook Forum.* Washington, D. C.: U.S. Travel Data Center.

Smith, S. L. J. (1990). A test of Plog's allocentric/psychocentric model: Evidence from seven nations. *Journal of Travel Research 28*(4), 40-43.

Smith, V. L. (Ed.). (1989). *Hosts and guests: The anthropology of tourism* (2nd ed.). Philadelphia: University of Pennsylvania Press.

Stewart, E. C., & Bennett, M. J. (1991). *American cultural patterns: A cross-cultural perspective* (Revised Edition). Yarmouth, ME: Intercultural Press.

Triandis, H., Vassiliou, V., Vassiliou, G., Tanaka, Y., & Shanmugam, A. (1972). *The analysis of subjective culture.* New York: Wiley.

van Raaij, W. F. (1978). Cross-cultural research methodology as a case of construct validity. *Advances in Consumer Research 5*, 693-701.

Zaichkowsky, J. L., & Sood, J. H. (1989). A global look at consumer involvement and use of products. *International Marketing Review. 6*(1), 20-34.

Zaichkowsky, J. L. (1985). Measuring the involvement construct. *Journal of Consumer Research 12*(December), 341-352.

Travel Motivation Variations of Overseas German Visitors

Ute Jamrozy
Muzaffer Uysal

SUMMARY. Motivations have been researched extensively in leisure and travel studies. However, little has been done to delineate the role and variations of these salient dimensions of travel and leisure behavior on travel groups. This research then identifies five travel groups and relates them to delineated factor groupings of motivational push and pull forces. Results indicate that overseas travellers from Germany, to a large extent, display variations in push motivations while traveling alone and in friendship groups, as opposed to families, couples and tour groups. Marketing implications suggest to use travel units as target segments and design travel products according to those varied needs of the overseas visitors.

INTRODUCTION

International tourism, the movement across international boundaries, has increased dramatically over the last two decades. Technology and information, the emergence of a large number and variety of travel des-

Ute Jamrozy is a doctoral candidate in the Department of Parks, Recreation and Tourism Management, Clemson University, Clemson, SC. Muzaffer Uysal is Professor of Travel and Tourism, Department of Hospitality and Tourism Management, Virginia Polytechnic Institute and State University.

[Haworth co-indexing entry note]: "Travel Motivation Variations of Overseas German Visitors." Jamrozy, Ute, and Muzaffer Uysal. Co-published simultaneously in *Journal of International Consumer Marketing* (The Haworth Press, Inc.) Vol. 6, No. 3/4, 1994, pp. 135-160; and: *Global Tourist Behavior* (ed: Muzaffer Uysal) The Haworth Press, Inc., 1994, pp. 135-160. Multiple copies of this article/chapter may be purchased from The Haworth Document Delivery Center [1-800-3-HAWORTH; 9:00 a.m. - 5:00 p.m. (EST)].

tinations, and decreasing costs, gave birth to a highly competitive industry. More countries than ever hope to generate tourism dollars by attracting lucrative markets from all over the world. Germans[1] have been considered as the 'world champions of travel.' The Economic Intelligence Unit describes in its 1989 Market Segment Study:

> The West-German outbound market is the world's largest and has great underlying strength. In terms of future development, however, the scope for increasing the number of leisure travellers is limited by the basic maturity of the market and those concerned with marketing travel to West Germany in the future have to deal with an increasingly sophisticated and discerning clientele. . . . Growth will come from changing travel patterns—more short breaks, more holidays per annum but of shorter duration, greater use of regional airports, greater market segmentation, and the development of new destinations. (p. 1)

In 1990, the U.S. Travel and Tourism Administration (USTTA) and Tourism Canada estimated a target market size for potential overseas visitors as 24 percent of the total adult population which are 11.2 million people. Fifty-six percent of these travellers have actually taken a long haul vacation in the last three years and are potential repeat travellers. The remaining 44 percent plan to take a trip in the next two years. There lies a tremendous potential in this population, but interested branches of the industry need to know why Germans travel and what underlying variations occur within their behavior and the market. Travellers cannot be treated as homogeneous groups. Travel providers should have knowledge about the behavior and attitudes, psychological needs, and expectations of travellers in order to recognize segments and serve effectively the different types and groups of visitors. Psychologists try to explain why people travel and try to understand travel related decisions and those factors that influence the behavior (Mayo and Jarvis,1981). They focus on the individual traveller who is motivated by psychological forces. Marketers view tourists as consumers and motivated individuals who make buying decisions. Behavior models suggest that behavior choices are determined by psychological factors like motivation, perception, learning, beliefs, attitudes, and these by personality, society, and culture (Kotler, 1984; Moutinho, 1987).

Concepts like motivations have been researched extensively in recreation and leisure; "the experiences derived from participation in recreation activities have been subject to a variety of terminology including 'motivation,' 'satisfaction,' 'psychological outcomes,' and 'experience expectations'" (Manning, 1985). A motive is considered to be an internal factor that arouses, directs, and integrates a person's behavior (Murray, 1964).

In tourism, several theories and concepts about motivations have been applied: Maslow's Hierarchy of Needs (1954); Dann (1977) describe seven approaches towards motivation in terms of individuals and their cultural conditioning. Mayo and Jarvis (1981) explain the need for consistency and complexity, people seek harmony and balance. Tension occurs when some need arises, and a person in disequilibrium will initiate some course of action to restore equilibrium. MacCannel (1976) and Cohen (1978, 1979) explore the sociological background of tourist behavior, while Crompton (1979) defines sociopsychological and cultural motives.

The interdisciplinary nature of motivation theories is easily observable, yet, the interrelationship of the individual with his/her environment is subject of social psychology. As Iso Ahola (1980) points out, that social influence, which is the key concept in social psychological analysis, is said to occur whenever one individual responds to the actual, imagined, or implied presence of one or more others. The social group variable is included in leisure theory while explaining behavior, since people's behavior is influenced by their social environment. Field and O'Leary (1973) added the social group variable to their more traditional social aggregate variables to increase the amount of variance explained with regard to frequency in participation:

> Not only is the social unit with which one predominantly participates an important predictor of recreation behavior, the literature suggests that meanings attached to participation in a particular activity may vary in accordance with the social unit of participation. (Allen and Donnelly, 1985; Buchanan et al., 1980; Field et al., 1973; Burch, 1969)

Research reveals some influence of the participant group on the individuals' behavior. However, little has been done to delineate the role and variation of these salient dimensions of leisure behavior on travel groups. Pearce (1982) stresses that studies of tourist motivations are considered from a long-term, multimotive, nondeterministic view for particular travel groups. Does the alone-traveller want to explore a foreign country and culture on her/his own; does a couple want to get away from its everyday obligations in order to finally be pampered at a resort? Travel behavior, as the stimulating forces behind it or the actual conduct, varies for most individuals, but does it for different types of groups? Should those, who promote recreation, leisure, and tourism, and those, who manage and market the supply side of the industry, focus their attention and efforts on travel groups as a unit of analysis in tourism research? This study focused on German tourists traveling overseas for pleasure, who have taken a trip

by plane in the last four years, in company or by themselves for a variety
of reasons. It is hypothesized that variations in travel motivations occur for
different travel groups.

RELATED LITERATURE

People give several reasons why they travel: in general, to see different
places, to visit friends and relatives, to get away from the daily routine, to
relax and enjoy, for sports and educational purposes. But for the researcher
exploring people's behavior, these answers do not reveal deeper causes of
why, specifically, people want to see the world, get away from it all, or fly
thousand of miles to lie out in the sun. Lundberg (1976) points out that
what travelers call their motivations "maybe only reflections of deeper
needs, needs which he himself does not understand, may not be aware of,
or may not wish to articulate." Therefore, besides the cognitions of the
travelers themselves, researchers in sociology, anthropology, psychology,
and consumer behavior, need to explore the underlying dimensions of
expressed reasons for leisure travel behavior.

The critical conditions for the experience of leisure are identified as
perceived freedom and intrinsic motivation. It appears that intrinsic motives for stimulation and activity are innate, with learning playing only a
secondary role (Murray, 1964). To view leisure as a state of mind has its
roots in psychological studies, while sociologists to a large extent objec-
tively conceptualize leisure as an institution beyond the time spent for
work and subsistence. Moutinho (1987) explains in "Consumer Behavior
in Tourism" the interaction of elements in the psychological field of the
consumer that influence behavior: At the arousal stage, needs and motivations are forces that activate goal-oriented behavior. This behavior is influenced by consumer perceptions of alternatives, which take into account
psychological influences, learning experiences, attitudes, beliefs, personality and self-image. The psychological influences are partially condi-
tioned by cultural and social influences. These concepts are often interre-
lated.

Crandall (1979) argues that (a) social interaction is an important leisure
activity. As a component of any leisure activity it is significant for motivation for participation and satisfaction in chosen activities; and (b) individual attitudes are more important for understanding leisure behavior than
traditional measures like expenditures, duration, and social class. Social
interaction as a motivator for leisure can fulfill several needs, like a need
for affiliation, safety needs, or even the need to escape; which are often not
recognized as being social. Most of these needs and motivations for leisure

participation and social interaction can be found in travel studies. Crompton (1979) in his work about motivations for pleasure vacation identifies seven sociopsychological needs which are all determined by the social surroundings. He emphasizes social influence while determining motivations. Crandall (1979) proposes a social to nonsocial continuum for a conceptualization of leisure activities: "People's feelings about activities and their reasons for participation should be more important than simple information about what they do for leisure." However, Crandall does *not* want to "suggest that only social reasons are important for leisure," but proposes to further study the role of social contact in leisure.

Iso Ahola (1990) elaborates on the intrinsically motivated leisure behavior. Leisure consists of self-determined, competence-elevating behavior and the avoidance, escape behavior. People are seeking or avoiding intrinsic rewards. The person at leisure can in fact try to escape personal environments (problems, stress), escape interpersonal environments (boss, family), seek personal rewards (self discovery), and seek interpersonal rewards (visit friends, meet new people). Where we are on this continuum depends on "person, situation, and time," and maybe these motivations are different depending on the people with whom we participate.

The social group variable has been studied widely within the context of leisure behavior. Cheek and Burch (1976) point out that during work, behavior is influenced by individual factors while leisure behavior occurs in groups. Field (1971) argues that regardless of leisure settings, participation within groups dominates. He researched leisure participation using group categories like "alone," "with friends," "family," "family and friends." Within all types of social groups, "family" seems to be the most common unit for leisure participation, while they even participate in similar activities in different settings. Burch (1969) developed the idea of "personal communities"; while studying campers, he found that familiarity and compensatory desires both influence behavioral choices and that small circles of workmates, family, and friends shape their free time. Buchanan et al. (1981) explored experience preferences for different social groups, which were family groups, friendship groups, and family/friendship groups, and for different activities, which were power boating, boat fishing and swimming. Applying discriminant analysis and discriminant functions, they found out that family groups scored highest on equipment and fishing, while friendship groups scored highest on risk-taking, being with friends, learning and discovery, creativity, escaping family, and meeting and observing others. Depending on the leisure activity, preferences varied for social groups. Heyward (1987) studied motivations for river running and the variations for different social groups, primary friend or family groups, some members unknown, all other members unknown. He clustered 36 motivations into change (escape routine and scenery), quiet and escape, group adventure, and adventure in general, and found out that smaller primary groups preferred quiet and escape while strangers preferred group adventures. Allen and Donnelly (1985) researched predominant social units and whether a relationship exists between participating in and reasons for the most enjoyable activities. They proposed that human behavior and specifically leisure behavior may be partially explained by understanding the social groups with which an individual predominantly participates. It was concluded that social interaction varies with social unit, but that primary reasons for participation remained stable regardless of social unit. In most of the studies it has been pointed out that the meaning an individual assigns to a leisure activity determines motivation and participation; and this might be influenced by the group with which to participate.

Recreation choice behavior depends on activities, settings and companions (Williams, 1984). According to Williams, the consumer of a recreation product has some influence on where, with whom and in what to participate, while one of these factors can dominate and have an effect on the others. Activities may be subordinate to the social meaning of the participation (with whom we participate may be more important in the decision to recreate than what activity we select) (O'Leary et al., 1974; Williams, 1984). For one group, two destinations may be equally desirable to visit, while for another group different settings and activities are important. This all depends on needs, distinctive to the group. It has often been suggested that social motives themselves may be among the most important reasons for recreation participation. Social dynamics may do much to mask the link between motive and environment/behavior (Schreyer, Knopf, Williams, 1984). Some individuals participate in an activity more because of sociocultural values and because friends and family are engaged in it, the social needs become more important than other individual psychological needs.

Role expectations and social norms within leisure participation has also been applied in studies about travel behavior across the life span. It can be expected that some social units are more dominant through different phases of the life cycle and that, for example, the motivation to escape is different for a family, a friend's unit, or a couple. Hill, McDonald and Uysal (1990) researched motivational differences for visiting a resort for four different life cycles, with groups similar to studied social units. No significant differences were found for relaxation, escape, novelty, education, and prestige. However, kinship relationships are more important to those who are married, and health and social motivations are more important to single vacationers.

Leisure behavior studies have extensively dealt with the social element in participation. First, because many of the activities require the presence of others, many are the primary social motive for participation and some social units influence behavior. One of the few studies examining this problem specifically for travel behavior is Crompton's work about the "Dimensions of the Social Group Role in Pleasure Vacation" (1981). In his qualitative study participants were asked about their interpersonal associations in vacations. Crompton followed Mead's interactionist's approach that individuals derive their very psychic skeleton from the social environment in which they live and grow. The group exerts social influences on the individual's decisions. In relation to past travel motivation studies, Crompton states specifically "social groups may serve to reinforce or modify biogenic or psychogenic tension states," which occurs in four different ways: (1) direct group influence on destination selection, (2) the normative influence of social groups, (3) the long-term influence of social groups, and (4) the locational influence of social groups. Further, the composition of the group (e.g., social unit) is important and the positive implications of a social group for a pleasure vacation should be considered. The first proposed influence deals with the initial choice to go. Motivated behavior towards taking a vacation is initiated through word of mouth communication: interaction and a shared meaning of a vacation occur. Normative influences are exerted when images and preferences are formed, there are norms and role expectations within the group who may determine what we are looking for in a vacation. The long-term influence is derived from the socialization process, what attitudes towards traveling are cultural, and what meanings about traveling are communicated through the family. The final impact can be discovered from direct social interaction as the activity: Visiting friends and family, the seeking of interpersonal relationships (Iso Ahola, 1990). The composition of the social unit, if "alone," "a couple," "a family," "friends," or "a tour group" should exert some varying influence on motivations, preferences, and activities. "The answer to the question, 'Why do people go on vacation or go to a particular destination?' is sociological as well as psychological, for the social group reinforces, modifies, and molds the motivations of its members" (Crompton, 1981). Thus, the purpose of this study is to test empirically if these influences are different for different travel units.

DATA SOURCES AND ANALYSIS

The investigation of travel behavior variation of German overseas visitors used data from a research study sponsored jointly by the U.S. Travel and Tourism Administration (USTTA) and Tourism Canada prepared by Market Facts Limited. An interest in overseas countries and their potential travel markets has led to a five-year agreement during which approximately four countries are to be studied each year. In 1989, the same countries, including France, Germany, United Kingdom, and Japan, as in 1986, were surveyed and examined.[2]

A total of 1,212 personal interviews were conducted with international travelers who met the following target qualifications; those who were (1) 18 years of age or over, and (2) took a vacation trip of four nights or longer by plane outside of Europe and the Mediterranean in the past three years or intended to take such a trip in the next two years. Personal in-home interviews were conducted throughout West Germany where interviewers followed predetermined walk patterns from a total of 315 computer selected starting points. In screened households with more than one qualified respondent a random selection was made using the next birthday method. The incidence of qualified respondents was determined by recording the results of these screening procedures (*Pleasure Travel Markets to North America: Germany* 1989). The survey instrument used by the interviewers is a questionnaire, which takes about an hour to complete. It consists of an interrogation concerning market size, travel behavior, likely vacation destinations, sociodemographic data, perception of Canada and the United States; and it also includes segmentation by product, philosophy, and benefit statements.

This study focuses on a subsample (n = 609) drawn from the entire sample of 1,212 respondents. The subsample was further refined by selecting respondents who actually took a vacation trip overseas for four nights or longer in the past three years and who could be assigned to one of the five mutually exclusive travel groups: alone-travelers (36.8%); persons who traveled either with their wife/husband/girlfriend/boyfriend as couples (44.3%); family group (6.1%); friendship group (9.2%); and organized group (3.1%). These travel groups were then examined regarding the variation of "push" and "pull" travel motivational forces in planning overseas vacation trips.[3]

Thirty motivational push forces and fifty-three pull forces were measured on a four-point Likert-type scale (1 = very important; 2 = somewhat important; 3 = not very important; and 4 = not at all important). The respondents were asked to indicate the importance of motivations in deciding to take an overseas vacation destination.[4]

The analysis of the study consisted of two distinct stages. First, once the five travel groups were identified, thirty push and fifty-three pull motivational items were factor analyzed to delineate the underlying dimensions that were associated with leisure travel behavior. In extracting the factors common factorial criteria were used: all factors had eigenvalues greater than one, and together they explained a substantial share of total variance in the push and pull motivational items. In addition, only factor loadings greater than .35 were calculated for each factor grouping. Second, analysis of variance was used to see if differences existed between the five travel groups with respect to delineated factor groupings of motivational push and pull factors. If differences between the five groups were detected at the 5 percent or better probability level (p = .05), the Duncan Range Test was employed to further specify possible variations.

RESULTS AND DISCUSSION

Variations in travel behavior between different travel groups can be discovered in a sequence of analyses. The dependent variables of push and pull variations are ranked and organized into factors. Table 1 describes travellers in terms of their travel party characteristics, resulting in five mutually exclusive groups.

The study revealed that a large percentage (36.8%) of overseas travellers initially traveled alone. However, the largest group (44.3%) went on vacation overseas with either the wife, husband, girlfriend, or boyfriend ("WHGB," couple). Only a few traveled overseas in friendship (9.2%), family (6.1%), and organized tour groups (3.6%). The large number of alone-travellers is an important issue while explaining and possibly predicting travel behavior.

Table 2 shows the importance rankings of selected motivational push forces. Motivational push forces are considered to come from within the traveller, giving the tourist the initial push to go and travel. The items

TABLE 1. Travel Groups

Travel Group:	n	%
Alone ("alone")	224	36.8
Wife/husband/girlfriend/boyfriend ("WHGB")	270	44.3
Family ("family")	37	6.1
Friends ("friends")	56	9.2
Organized tour group ("organ.")	22	3.6
Total	609	100.0

TABLE 2. Importance Rankings of Motivational Push Forces

Five most important push forces	Mean Score
Experiencing new and different life styles	1.70
Seeing and experiencing a foreign destination	1.72
Being free to act the way I feel	1.74
Finding thrills and excitement	1.79
Getting a change from a busy job	1.80
Five least important push forces	
Participating in sport	2.82
Roughing it	2.93
Reliving past good times	3.02
Watching sporting events	3.20
Visiting places my family came from	3.26

Note: Importance Rankings are based on mean scores measured on a Likert type scale from 1-4 (1 = very important, 2 = somewhat important, 3 = not very important, 4 = not at all important).

presented revealed possible benefits of traveling and the tourist responded by expressing how important each one of these motivational forces were to her/him. Most of the 30 items were viewed as quite important to the whole sample. Only 5 statements had a mean score of above 2.80; half of them are perceived as important ($\bar{x} < 2.20$). The most important items were "experiencing a new life-style" ($\bar{x} = 1.70$), "seeing and experiencing a foreign destination" ($\bar{x} = 1.72$), "being free to act the way I feel" ($\bar{x} = 1.74$), "finding thrills and excitement" ($\bar{x} = 1.79$), and "getting a change from a busy job" ($\bar{x} = 1.80$). Approaching the new and escaping the ordinary were important travel motivators. Less popular were "reliving past good times" ($\bar{x} = 3.02$), "watching sporting events" ($\bar{x} = 3.20$), and "visiting places my family came from" ($\bar{x} = 3.26$).

Table 3 represents the five most important and least important pull forces. Almost fifty percent of the items were expressively important ($\bar{x} < 2.20$) and only 15 items were less significant ($\bar{x} > 2.80$). The top five items were "interesting and friendly local people" ($\bar{x} = 1.61$), "outstanding scenery" ($\bar{x} = 1.68$), "warm welcome for tourists" ($\bar{x} = 1.70$), "warm and sunny climate" ($\bar{x} = 1.70$), and "environmental quality of air, water, and soil" ($\bar{x} = 1.72$). Interestingly, five possible leisure activities were the

TABLE 3. Importance Rankings of Motivational Pull Forces

Five most important pull forces

Interesting and friendly local people	1.61
Outstanding scenery	1.68
Warm welcome for tourists	1.70
Warm and sunny climate	1.70
Environmental quality of air, water, and soil	1.72

Five least important pull forces

Golf and tennis	3.32
Casinos and gambling	3.36
Fishing	3.40
Snow skiing, downhill, cross country	3.41
Hunting	3.52

Note: Importance Rankings are based on mean scores measured on a Likert type scale from 1-4 (1 = very important, 2 = somewhat important, 3 = not very important, 4 = not at all important).

least pulling elements in planning an overseas trip. These activities included golf and tennis, casinos and gambling, fishing, snow skiing, and hunting. While general atmosphere seemed to be an important pulling factor, general leisure activities were less important.

FACTOR GROUPINGS OF PUSH AND PULL MOTIVATIONS

Motivational push forces are the needs and desires within the travelers which activate them to move (in their preferred way) towards a destination. Basic and higher needs cause the primary demand to travel (push), while the secondary motives are considered as pull forces of the destination. The factor analysis of thirty individual motives resulted in eight factor groupings, and accounted for almost 58 percent of the motivation variance (Table 4).

Factor 1 was labeled the "escape" factor. This was one of the most important motivators to travel and explained 15.0 percent of the variance (reliability coefficient = .77). All five motives that made up this factor grouping reflected the desire to get away and experience a change from the

TABLE 4. Motivational Push Factors

Push Factor Groupings	Statistics		
	Eigen-value	Variance explained (%)	Reliability Coefficient
Factor 1: Escape	4.49	15.0	.77
Factor 2: Novelty, experience	3.46	11.5	.73
Factor 3: Family, friends togetherness	2.78	7.5	.72
Factor 4: Sports activities	2.10	7.0	.75
Factor 5: Adventure, excitement	1.50	5.0	.61
Factor 6: Familiar environment	1.23	4.1	.58
Factor 7: Luxury, doing nothing	1.20	4.0	.47
Factor 8: Prestige	1.08	3.6	.58
Total Variance explained		57.6	

old. Factor 2 reveals that as people approach differences, they wish to experience novelty. Learning, trying, and experiencing something new, foreign, or different was the main concern of people who showed high agreement on this factor. This described approach behavior explained 11.5 percent of the variance and had a reliability coefficient of .75. This factor had the lowest mean score for the overall sample, reinforcing the importance agreement of this frequently cited push motivator. Factor 3, labeled "family, friends togetherness" explained 7.5 percent of the variance with a reliability coefficient of .72. It demonstrated the importance of social interaction or the connectiveness as a group. People seek interpersonal rewards (Iso Ahola, 1990). However, this push factor had a higher mean score, assigning less importance to the family factor. Factor 4 was concerned with sports activities with 7 percent variation explained (reliability coefficient = .75). A mean score of 2.89 for the factor, and, for example, a 3.20 high score for watching sporting events signified a low motivational push for sports activities during an overseas vacation. On the other hand people were looking for "adventure and excitement"; factor 5 explained 5 percent of the variance (reliability coefficient = .61): seeking adventure, different experiences, had a factor mean score of 2.03. Factor 6 indicated the desire to travel in familiar environments. Meeting people with similar interests and feeling at home away from home was fairly important to overseas travellers. Factor 7 "luxury, doing nothing" had a considerable low importance score of 2.35; this factor explained 4.0 percent of the variance with a reliability coefficient of .47. Slightly more important for overseas travellers was factor 8, "prestige" ($\bar{x}$ = 2.25). However, it explained only 3.6 percent of the variance with a reliability coefficient of .59. Overall, the factors "escape" and "novelty, experience" captured 26.5 percent of the variance and were considered as the most important motivational push to go on an overseas vacation for German travellers. Both of the factors are experiential in nature; the escape factor demonstrates avoidance behavior and the novelty, experience factor shows that the tourists actively approach or seek, initiated by their basic needs, different environments.

The 53 motivational pull forces resulted in eleven factor groupings. Table 5 summarizes the results of factor analysis with their associated statistics. Factor 1 was concerned with people's importance ratings of an active sports environment. In general, people were not that much interested in activities like hunting, fishing, spectator events, water sports, and skiing which received low ratings. Overall this factor had a mean score of 3.28 and explained 14.1 percent of the variance with a reliability coefficient of .80. Factor 2 was labeled as "unique natural environment," had a low mean score of 1.96, indicating an important motivational pull factor.

TABLE 5. Motivational Pull Factors

Pull Factor Groupings	Statistics		
	Eigen-value	Variance explained (%)	Reliability Coefficient
Factor 1: Active sports environment	7.49	14.1	.80
Factor 2: Unique natural environment	5.31	10.0	.81
Factor 3: Clean safe environment	4.42	8.3	.71
Factor 4: Sunshine environment	2.49	4.7	.78
Factor 5: Inexpensive environment	2.08	3.9	.64
Factor 6: Cultural activities	1.69	3.2	.65
Factor 7: Entertainment	1.51	2.8	.68
Factor 8: Sightseeing	1.32	2.5	.54
Factor 9: Local culture	1.24	2.3	.56
Factor 10: Different culture and cuisine	1.06	2.0	.56
Factor 11: Small towns, villages, and mountains	1.03	1.9	.56
Total Variance explained		55.9	

This factor grouping included natural environments like National Parks and Forests, as well as unique cultural attractions and experiential, educational settings. The factor had an Eigenvalue of 5.31 and explained 10 percent of the variance with a reliability coefficient of .81. Factor 3 referred to the hospitality of an environment. This factor, "a clean, safe, and friendly environment," had an overall mean score of 2.06, with some differences in individual ratings of "interesting and friendly local people," "personal safety when traveling alone," and "first class hotels." This factor explained 8.3 percent of the variance with a reliability coefficient of .71. Six items could be included in the fourth factor, "sunshine environment." Beaches and nice weather as well as environmental quality accounted for 4.7 percent of the variance with a reliability coefficient of .78. With an overall mean score of 1.96, the factor seemed to be very important. Factor 5, an "inexpensive environment," was also fairly important with a mean score of 2.23. This factor, however, explained only 3.9 percent of the variance and had a reliability coefficient of .64. Factor 6, "cultural activities," had a mean score of 2.53, an Eigenvalue of 1.69, 3.2 percent of the variance was explained and its reliability coefficient was .65. Factor 7, "entertainment," was a fairly unimportant motivational pull factor with a 3.02 mean score, including nightlife, gambling, and big cities (Eigenvalue = 1.51, 2.8 percent of variance explained, and reliability coefficient = .68). "Sightseeing," Factor 8, had a mean score of 2.29 with a reliability coefficient = .54. Factor 9 was labeled as "local culture"–local festivals, crafts, and theme parks–and had a mean factor score of 2.59 (Eigenvalue 1.24, 2.3 percent variance explained, and reliability coefficient = .56). The last two factors, "different culture and cuisine" and "small towns, villages, and mountains," explained almost 4 percent of the variance with a relatively high reliability coefficient of .56 each. Combined, the eleven factors of 53 motivational pull forces explained approximately 56 percent of the variance.

All statements could be included in the Factor Analysis, meaningfully assigned to one of the factors. Items like novelty, experience, and excitement received low scores, which signified their overall importance. German overseas travellers liked to experience different and new environments on their overseas vacation rather than spending it with visiting friends and relatives.

COMPARISONS BETWEEN THE FIVE TRAVEL GROUPS

In the final step of the study, analysis of variance (ANOVA) was performed for the resulting factors in order to determine if variations in motivational push and pull factors occurred for different travel groups.

Differences in mean scores were analyzed for all factors for the 5 different travel groups: "alone," "wife/husband/girlfriend/boyfriend," "family," "friends," and "organized groups." Tables 6 and 7 present individual and overall mean scores and the F values. An (*) signifies a statistically significant F value, p ≤ .05. For motivational push factors these were escape, family and friends togetherness, activities and sports, adventures and excitement, and luxury and doing nothing. Some differences could be found for pull factors like in clean, safe and friendly environment and a sunshine environment. Interestingly almost all motivational push factors presented significant differences while hardly any pull factors showed variations in importance rankings. In order to identify where differences occurred, the Duncan Multiple Range test was performed. Values with (*) are significantly different from others, presented underlined in the table (Duncan multiple range test, p ≤ .05).

The escape factor can be interpreted as avoidance behavior from personal and interpersonal environments. Escaping is significantly less important for organized groups than it is for friends, alone-travellers, and wife/husband/girlfriend/boyfriend groups. Although the overall score signified high importance, organized tour groups did not express such a strong need to get away from everything; their more important need was a desire for novelty and experience. The demands and expectations within an organized, and possibly unknown, tour group were less threatening or restricting to these people; they did not avoid but rather sought the company of others with similar interests.

"Novelty and Experience," the approach behavior towards foreign environments was equally important for all groups, and this motivator can be treated as an important and interesting result for travel researchers. It appears as if the personality of German overseas travellers in general pushed them to seek new experiences overseas. No matter with whom they traveled, the main purpose was being in and taking part in a foreign life.

"Family and friends togetherness" in general, was not considered as an important push factor for overseas travellers, because if people want to visit friends and relatives, or just spend some time with their friends as a main need for their vacation, they do not necessarily need to travel overseas. However, significant differences occurred for the least interested travel groups, organized groups and friends, as compared to couples. It appears that affiliation is stronger for couples and families, and interpersonal relationships within those affiliated groups is important on a vacation. "Activities/Sports" are much more important for friends groups than for the other groups who are in general not very motivated by this factor.

TABLE 6. Comparison of Push Factors for Different Travel Groups

Travel Groups:	Mean Scores						Significance of F-Test
	All	Alone	WHGB	Family	Friends	Organ.	
Push Factor Groupings:							
1. Escape	1.94	1.94	1.91	2.07	1.85	2.26*	.037*
2. Novelty, experience	1.87	1.86	1.88	2.02	1.76	1.83	.148
3. Family, friends togetherness	2.95	2.99	2.86*	2.97	3.11	3.30	.010*
4. Activities, sports	2.89	2.87	2.91	3.10	2.65*	3.08	.016*
5. Adventures, excitement	2.03	1.96*	2.09	2.28	1.86	1.99	.002*
6. Familiar environment	2.15	2.15	2.15	2.15	2.21	2.05	.852
7. Luxury and doing nothing	2.35	2.42	2.23*	2.30*	2.64	2.47	.000*
8. Prestige	2.25	2.29	2.21	2.42	2.06*	2.52	.056

Note: * presents significant difference at the 5 percent or better probability level for F (ANOVA). For the groups, . . . * are significantly different from ____ scores (Duncan Range Test). All = all travel groups; alone = alone-travellers; WHGB = wife/husband/girlfriend/boyfriend (couples); family = families; friends = friendship groups; organ. = organized tour groups.

TABLE 7. Comparison of Pull Factors for Different Travel Groups

Travel Groups:	Mean Scores						Significance of F-Test
	All	Alone	WHGB	Family	Friends	Organ.	
Pull Factor Groupings:							
1. Active sports	3.28	3.31	3.23	3.40	3.21	3.46	.127
2. Unique natural environment	1.96	1.96	1.94	2.09	1.92	2.08	.272
3. Clean, safe, and friendly environment	2.06	2.11	1.97*	2.01	2.27	2.14	.000*
4. Sunshine environment	1.96	2.03	1.89*	1.93	1.96	2.14	.031*
5. Inexpensive	2.33	2.34	2.34	2.37	2.24	2.24	.649
6. Cultural	2.53	2.53	2.52	2.50	2.64	2.55	.770
7. Entertaining	3.02	2.97	3.06	3.08	3.03	2.91	.540
8. Sightseeing	2.29	2.33	2.22	2.44	2.36	2.30	.102
9. Local culture	2.59	2.62	2.55	2.69	2.54	2.76	.405
10. Different culture, cuisine	1.80	1.80	1.78	1.93	1.80	1.91	.567
11. Small towns, villages, mountains	2.48	2.53	2.44	2.51	2.38	2.74	.068

Note: * presents significant difference at the 5 percent probability level for F (ANOVA). For the groups, . . . * are significantly different from ____ scores (Duncan Range Test). All = all travel groups; alone = alone-travellers; WHGB = wife/husband/girlfriend/boyfriend (couples); family = families; friends = friendship groups; organ. = organized tour groups.

The results showed again that leisure and sports activities were mostly engaged in within larger friendship groups than others. Even when traveling overseas, while needs might differ from the usual leisure wants as sports activities, friendship groups are pushed by more active motivators. Friends and alone-travellers seek adventures while traveling overseas. In comparison to families, alone-travellers wanted significantly more excitement. Again to go out and experience something different was most important to these groups, while families had a need for less risky, more secure vacations. Although German travellers seek cultural experiences and novelty, to some extent all travel groups have a need for a comforting, familiar "care free" environment. This need was fulfilled to the extreme by luxury or laziness, and significant differences occurred for couples and families as opposed to others. Especially, the more intimate wife/husband/girlfriend/boyfriend groups had a need for doing nothing and just being with each other, while a group of friends would become rather restless and unsatisfied during such a vacation, looking more for a variety of experiences. The prestige factor was much more important to friendship groups than to families and organized tour groups. While families were rather guided by their closer social circles, friendship groups were more outward directed towards people not in the immediate travel group. They consider more the opinion of friends staying at home and, also, are concerned with the prestigious value of the vacation. Taking part in an organized tour group is less popular among Germans and these tours, unless to remote destinations or otherwise unusual, were not satisfying any need for prestige. A significant amount of differences were found in the initial motivational push factors, while secondary pull motives present the reasons why certain environments and destinations are chosen over the others.

Differences in motivational pull and choice factors and the individual mean scores for each travel unit are presented in Table 7. Significant differences occurred for a "clean, safe, and friendly environment" which was significantly more a pulling factor for couples (wife/husband/ girlfriend/boyfriend), than for alone-travellers. Again, as indicated while discussing motivational push factors, also, as a predictable choice factor, a predictable safe and friendly vacation was important for couples, while the more adventurous alone-travellers and friendship groups placed less importance on this factor while choosing a destination. They were less threatened by surprises and were willing to take more risks.

A "sunshine" environment was significantly less a pulling factor for alone-travellers than for couples. Alone-travellers placed less importance on beaches than couples did, who were more inclined to spend time together in just warm climatic conditions. The need factor of interpersonal togetherness and luxurious, lazy vacations were expressed, while alone-travellers more decisively found unique, natural environments and different cultures as important motivational pull factors.

MARKETING IMPLICATIONS

Germans are experienced travellers since the early 19th century, with the elite population, the middle classes, and finally all classes and social groups traveling for pleasure. This study focused on overseas travellers since the outbound market for Germany is significantly larger than the inbound market. In response to the increasing demand, more and more suppliers of the tourism industry hope to generate tourism dollars by attracting travellers from all over the world. With an increasing sophistication of tourists' wishes and needs and more diversified tourism products, more specific marketing techniques and approaches are required to serve the population's needs, manage the destinations and facilities and develop diversified travel products.

This study focused on motivations for an improved understanding of German travel behavior and selects travel groups as a possible segmentation basis for overseas pleasure vacationers. Descriptive rankings provided insights of what Germans feel as important on their overseas vacation trip. Travelling and vacationing is a psychological experience; the provided travel service is intangible–it can neither be seen, touched, or taken home, except for, as symbolic, items like pictures, rocks, or other collectibles. The motivational push forces were all perceived as very important, supporting findings in the literature so there are multidimensional reasons of why people feel an initial need to go on vacation. Dann (1977) suggests focusing on these initial, primary push forces, because the actual decision to visit a destination is consequent to the prior need for travel and the question, 'What makes people travel?' is not easily answered by destination attributes, which are requirements of the "pull" factors. Marketers have to research the causally primary needs and then look at a secondary specific needs as choice factors (what pulls the travellers to a certain environment). The marketer has to understand primary and secondary needs while making a decision, and know, if at all possible, how to satisfy these needs within a specific destination. Results show that the most important push forces were experiential in nature. German travellers had an initial need to experience a new and different world, as in lifestyle and environment, and "being free to act the way I feel." The change from the usual surroundings over a longer period of time and the desire to experi-

ence foreign life were perceived as much more important push forces than
"feeling at home away from home," visiting relatives, feeling safe and
secure, or indulging in luxury. In general, managers and marketers have to
provide an environment where travellers learn and experience what is
unique to that specific culture or destination rather than focusing on providing similar hospitality services that travellers are accustomed to at
home.

The secondary influential choice factors, the pull motivations, were
unique and different environmental attributes such as a "warm and sunny
climate," and outstanding scenery and environmental quality. The least
important pull motivators were sporting events and facilities, fast food
restaurants or First Class Hotels, so managers and marketers should focus
on natural and cultural environmental qualities when developing and promoting their travel products to Germans.

TRAVEL BEHAVIOR VARIATIONS

In response to the multitude of various motivations, factor analysis
provided some underlying dimensions about these forces of travel behavior. Push and pull factors demonstrated different domains of behavior
which have important marketing implications. The motivational push
factors showed that "escape," "novelty and experience" and "adventure and excitement" are the most agreed upon travel domains for German overseas vacationers. "Family togetherness" and "sports activities" were less important. Therefore the travellers were looking mostly
for different culture and cuisine, unique natural environments, sunshine,
and a clean, safe, and friendly environment. Cultural activities, sightseeing, and an inexpensive destination were less important pull factors,
while entertainment and an active sports environment were the least
important decision making factors as pull forces to travel. This summarizes the need to focus on a unique and different environment rather than
on provided amenities and services when marketing to overseas German
pleasure vacationers.

However, the nationality does not mean that Germans were one homogeneous group of travellers. The marketer had to identify possible market
segments to potentially target those segments. The purpose of this study
was to explore if there were differences in motivations for different travel
groups. The results showed that most Germans traveled overseas as alone-
travellers or with wife/husband/girlfriend/boyfriend. Their needs were especially important but also the needs of other travel groups should not be
neglected as potential travel markets. As Krippendorf (1987) points out,

"the motivation of the individual person to travel, to look outside for what he cannot find inside, is produced not so much by an innate impulse, but develops primarily under the influence of the social environment, from which every individual draws his norms" (p. 17). Although there are very innate, intrinsic motivations, some motivations have sociopsychological character, implying that the behavior is also influenced by the presence of others. Pearce (1982) suggests that the following factors warrant attention: the way tourists perceive their role while traveling, their motivations, their preferred amount of contact with the local people and fellow travellers and the environmental setting they seek to visit. He asks for research, which is obtaining a social-psychological profile of tourists which links roles, motivations, and social and environmental preferences.

According to the literature reviewed, the reasons why people are participating with others in leisure and recreation activities was influenced by motivations and resulted in different behavior. This study focuses on the travel units as the determining, influencing factor of travel behavior variations. The results provided evidence that there *are* differences, especially in the initial push factors, which should be accounted for in marketing and management of tourism experiences and services. Alone-travellers and friends, couples or families, or organized tour groups have different motivations that push them to travel, and pull them to certain environments, which could be choice factors for destinations.

For an organization, agency, or destination within the global market, this means that marketing efforts should be differentiated according to those needs. Certainly, the escape, novelty and experience factors are important to all groups and should be emphasized in most promotional material, but for organized tour groups this factor has significantly less weight; otherwise, travellers who "need to get away from it all" probably would not join a rather restricted travel unit with group norms and decisions. More than any other group, the organized tour groups prefer a comforting, unthreatening environment. They also want to learn and experience something new, but within a predictable manner with travel companions having the same interests. Friendship groups appear to be more adventurous and, therefore, marketing efforts should point out the experiential part of their vacation. They also presented the group who is most likely to be pushed by the desire to see or participate in sports activities; these motivators were, for example, emphasized in club or resort vacations. Family togetherness was hardly a motivational push factor for overseas vacationers and should not be emphasized in destination promotion, however, some luxury, lazy and pampered vacations were important for all couples and some family groups. On the other hand, a family friendly environment would certainly pull parents with their children to the destination if child activities were offered, and parents had the opportunity to participate with their children and enjoy family life or get away from them for a while. Couples often had the desire to stay within their travel unit, the comforting, predictable environment being much more important than adventure. The alone-travellers on the other side, were definitely looking for novelty, experience, and adventure. They were the least inclined to look for a safe and friendly environment as pull factors and they would be less impressed by a sunshine environment, but more by exciting cultural and learning opportunities within a foreign destination. In accordance with Iso-Ahola (1990), the alone-travellers were seeking personal rewards, although even as alone-travellers they might have been looking for contact with other travellers or the host population, but they also escaped their own personal environment. Friendship groups to the largest extent sought interpersonal rewards and also to a large extent personal rewards. Tour groups sought personal rewards as learning experiences and escaping their own personal environments, but seeking to meet other people with the same interests. Couples and families escaped their wider interpersonal environments but stayed within their close personal environments with a lesser extent seeking interpersonal rewards. These sociopsychological dimensions have to be considered when designing a travel product specifically to the targeted travel unit in order to satisfy their needs and avoid conflict.

Booms and Bitner (1980) pointed out that in a tourism service industry, where marketers in general promote an experience, besides the four traditional elements of the marketing mix, product, price, place, and promotion, new variables like participants, physical evidence, and process of service assembly have to be included. This means, because of the definite need for experience, and the feature of an intangible vacation, the personal and interpersonal environments of participants (such as hosts and other travellers) have to be managed accordingly. Depending on motivations and whom they travel with, tourists expect certain experiences, and the travel product should be designed accordingly. If incompatible market segments are targeted at the same time, a clear and focused image of the destination or travel product cannot be conveyed and conflict might arise if travellers come in with different expectations. A group of friends looks for excitement and adventure and a couple looks for a comforting, more intimate environment; if both segments are targeted with the same travel product, at least one group's expectations will not be met and dissatisfaction will occur. If the product offers something for everybody, it is more than likely that efforts are not focused enough and the quality of the experience will suffer. The competitive environment of today's overseas travel market wishing to attract an experienced German travel market needs to offer quality travel products in environments with experiential opportunities targeted at specific market segments, as it could be at different travel units.

In a competitive global tourism industry it is important to understand the travellers and their behavior. This study focused on an experienced travel nation, Germany. Results showed that they have distinct needs; besides escaping their usual surroundings, the majority of Germans seek experiences, new and different cultures, lifestyles and natural surroundings.

However, a consumer oriented marketing approach is not just trying to explain or predict behavior, but also attempts to find bases for segmentation. The results indicated that travel groups are distinctive market segments. Adventure trips, culturally distinct accommodations and restaurants, and natural surroundings attract more friendship groups. While for families and couples planning their trips in terms of facilities, predictability, safety, and comfort is of high importance, friends like to travel with some uncertainty. Organized tour groups want to experience important attractions; they do not want to worry about planning, but need to travel with people with similar interests. Adventure and active participation should be the main component in travel products for friendship groups and alone-travellers. Promotional materials should always stress the escape dimensions and experience motivators, but the distinct needs of every travel unit have to be emphasized. Also, while designing and managing the product or destination, targeted travel groups should be compatible, specific quality expectations should be met and pricing strategies adjusted to the market segment. This compares with the societal marketing approach, which identifies the markets, consumer and competition, and designs the product consistent with the opportunities of an environment (Ryan, 1991). This can be applied to physical and social-psychological environments.

So far, sociopsychological components of travel behavior have been neglected in tourism research. More studies have to be conducted to explain and predict behavior of tourists relating to their interdependence with each other when traveling together, other tourists, and residents of the host communities. Extended research could include how the tourists can be reached and what information sources do they use. How can travel products and activities more specifically be designed to meet the distinct needs of the target segment(s)? Do different nations have similar segmentation bases? The opportunities in this area of research are wide open and important since the demand for global travel is increasing.

NOTES

1. Throughout this work the study population is called "Germans," although it is drawn from the West German (1989) population. The authors show their appreciation for Tourism Canada and the United States Travel and Tourism Administration (USTTA) for providing the "Pleasure Travel Markets to North America" study data set and information on German travel behavior.

2. The purpose of USTTA and Tourism Canada's studies has been identified:

> By combining resources the national tourism organizations of the two countries will be able to produce better market information than either could have done by work alone. As a result, agencies marketing Canada, the United States or both will be able to select their target markets with a good deal more precision than has been possible in the past. In addition, agencies responsible for developing the tourism products of both countries will have a clear idea of what their strengths and weaknesses are in the mind of the consumer. They would then be able to develop a better tourism product and one that will have a strong appeal to consumers in a variety of overseas countries. (Pleasure Travel Markets to North America-West Germany, 1989)

3. The literature on tourist motivation indicates that the examination of motivations based on the concept of push and pull factors has been generally accepted (see for example: Dann, 1977; Crompton, 1979; Yuan and McDonald, 1990). Push factors are considered to be the sociopsychological constructs of the tourists and their environments that predispose the individual to travel and help explain the desire to travel. Pull factors, on the other hand, may be destination attributes that respond to and reinforce push factors of motivations. Destination attributes can either be tangible resources or the perceptions and expectations of the traveller (Uysal and Hagan, 1993). In this study, push and pull motivational factors are not necessarily mutually exclusive, but rather they complement each other.

4. Some caution is in order when examining these push and pull motivations. First, the specific motivational components were preselected by the data collectors, and motivational was inferred from "attitude measurement scales." These motivations did not come from open-ended questioning. Second, motivations dealing with self-actualization and the consistency-complexity continuum were absent. Therefore, the list of travel motivations may not be exhaustive. However, the study assumes that a significant number of push and pull motivators included in the travel and tourism literature have been included.

REFERENCES

Allen, L. R., Donnelly, M. A. (1985). An Analysis of the Social Unit of Participation and the Perceived Psychological Outcomes Associated With Most Enjoyable Recreation Activities. *Leisure Sciences*, 7(4): 421-441.

Booms, B. H. and M. J. Bitner. (1980). New Management Tools for the Successful Tourism Manager. *Annals of Tourism Research*, 7(3): 337-352.

Buchanan, T., J. Christensen, and R. Burdge. (1980). Social Groups and Meanings of Outdoor Recreation Activities. Research Paper No. 321. Champaign-Urbana: University of Illinois.

Burch, W. R.(1969). The Social Circles of Leisure: Competing Explanations. *Journal of Leisure Research,* 8(2): 112-122.

Cheek, N. H. and W. R. Burch. (1976). *The Social Organization of Leisure in Human Society.* New York: Harper & Row.

Cohen, E. (1978). The Impact of Tourism on the Physical Environment. *Annals of Tourism Research,* 5(2): 215-237.

Cohen, E. (1979). Rethinking the Sociology of Tourism. *Annals of Tourism Research,* 6(1): 18-35.

Crandall, R. (1979). Social Interaction, Affect and Leisure. *Journal of Leisure Research,* 11(3): 165-181.

Crandall, R., (1980). Motivations for Leisure. *Journal of Leisure Research,* 12(1): 45-54.

Crompton, J. L. (1979). Motivations of Pleasure Vacation. *Annals of Tourism Research,* 6(4): 408-424.

Crompton, J. L. (1981). Dimensions of the Social Group Role in Pleasure Vacations. *Annals of Tourism Research,* 6(4): 408-424.

Dann, G. (1977). Anomie, Ego-Enhancement and Tourism. *Annals of Tourism Research,* 4(4): 184-194.

Economic Intelligence Unit. (1989). West Germany Outbound. *Travel and Tourism Analyst,* (4): 38-59.

Field, D. R. (1971). Interchangeability of Parks With Other Leisure Settings. Paper presented at the AAAS Symposium, Philadelphia, PA, December 26-31.

Field, D. R. and J. T. O'Leary. (1973). Social Groups as a Basis for Assessing Participation in Selected Water Activities. *Journal of Leisure Research,* 5(1): 16-25.

Heyward, J. L. (1987). Experience Preferences of Participants in Different Types of River Recreation Groups. *Journal of Leisure Research,* 19(1): 1-12.

Hill, J. B., C. D. McDonald and M. Uysal. (1990). Resort Motivations for Different Life Cycle Stages. *Visions in Leisure and Business,* 8(4): 18-27.

Iso-Ahola, S. E. (1980). *The Social Psychology of Leisure and Recreation.* Dubuque, Iowa: W.C. Brown Company.

Iso-Ahola, S. E. (1990). Motivation for Leisure. In Jackson and Burton (ed.) *Understanding Leisure and Recreation.* State College, PA: Venture Publ., Inc.

Kotler, P. (1984). *Marketing Management: Analysis, Planning, and Control* (5th ed.) Englewood Cliffs, NJ: Prentice Hall.

Kotler, P. (1987). *Strategic Marketing for Nonprofit Organizations* (3rd ed.). Englewood Cliffs, New Jersey: Prentice Hall.

Krippendorf, J. (1987). *The Holiday Makers: Understanding the Impact of Leisure and Travel.* Heinemann Professional Publishing, Redwood Burn, Ltd., Trowbridge, Wildshire, England.

Lundberg, D. E. (1976). *The Tourist Business.* Boston: CBI Publishing Company, Inc.

Manning, R. E. (1985). *Studies in Outdoor Recreation.* Corvallis, OR: Oregon State University Press.

Maslow, A. H. (1954). *Motivation and Personality.* New York: Harper & Row.

Mayo, E. J., Jr. and L. P. Jarvis. (1981). *The Psychology of Leisure Travel.* Boston: CBI Publishing Company, Inc.

MacCannel, D. (1976). *The Tourist.* New York: Schocken.

Mountinho, L. (1987). Consumer Behavior in Tourism. *European Journal of Marketing,* 21(10): 5-44.

Murray, E. J. (1964). *Motivation and Emotion.* New Jersey: Prentice Hall.

O'Leary, J., D. Field and G. Schreuder. (1974). Social Groups and Water Activity Clusters: An Exploration of Interchangeability and Substitution. In *Water and Community Development: Social and Economic Perspectives,* Field, D. et al. (ed.). Ann Arbor, MI: Ann Arbor Science Publishers.

Pearce, P. L. (1982). *The Social Psychology of Tourist Behavior.* Oxford: Pergamon Press.

Ryan, C. (1991). Tourism and Marketing–A Symbiotic Relationship? *Tourism Management.* 12(2): 101-111.

Schreyer, R., R. C. Knopf, and D. R. Williams. (1984). Reconceptualizing the Motive-Environment Link in Recreation Choice Behavior. In the Proceedings of the Symposium of Recreation Choice Behavior. Missoula, MT. March 22-23.

Tourism Canada and the United States Travel and Tourism Administration. (1989). *Pleasure Travel Markets to North America: Germany.* Prepared by Market Facts Limited. Toronto: Industry Science and Technology Canada.

Uysal, M. and L. Hagan (1993). Motivation of Pleasure Travel and Tourism. In the *Encyclopedia of Hospitality and Tourism.* Khan, M., M. Olsen and T. Var (eds.), pp. 798-810. New York: Van Nostrand Reinhold. In press.

Williams, R. D. (1984). A Developmental Model of Recreation Choice Behavior. In the Proceedings of the Symposium of Recreation Choice Behavior. Missoula, MT. March 22-23.

Yuan, S. and C. D. McDonald (1990). Motivational Determinants of International Pleasure Time. *Journal of Travel Research,* 29(1): 42-44.

Tour Operators' Role
in the Tourism Distribution System:
An Indonesian Case Study

William C. Gartner
Thamrin Bachri

SUMMARY. Tour operators function as intermediaries in the tourism distribution system linking producers and consumers. Their expertise in packaging tourism products allows for more offerings to a wider range of tourists. This study examined the role tour operators fill in packaging travel to developing countries using Indonesia as a case study. Many developing country governments, including Indonesia, have assumed active roles in tourism development. The results of this study indicate that the active role should include a focus on tourism's distribution channels, especially tour operators, if some of the problems common to developing countries' tourism development efforts are to be overcome.

INTRODUCTION

The travel decision process has been a subject of substantial investigation (Mathieson and Wall, 1982; Woodside and Sherrell, 1977; Woodside

William C. Gartner is Director and Associate Professor, Tourism Center, 248 C Classroom Office Building, 1994 Buford Avenue, St. Paul, MN. Thamrin Bachri is affiliated with the International Labour Organisation, JL. M.H. Thamrin 13, P.O. Box 1075, Jakarta 10010, Indonesia.

[Haworth co-indexing entry note]: "Tour Operators' Role in the Tourism Distribution System: An Indonesian Case Study." Gartner, William C., and Thamrin Bachri. Co-published simultaneously in *Journal of International Consumer Marketing* (The Haworth Press, Inc.) Vol. 6, No. 3/4, 1994, pp. 161-179; and: *Global Tourist Behavior* (ed: Muzaffer Uysal) The Haworth Press, Inc., 1994, pp. 161-179. Multiple copies of this article/chapter may be purchased from The Haworth Document Delivery Center [1-800-3-HAWORTH; 9:00 a.m. - 5:00 p.m. (EST)].

and Lysonski, 1989; Schmoll, 1977; Mouthinho, 1987). Most of the travel decision models have their roots in early consumer behavior research such as that produced by Howard and Seth (1969), Engel, Kollat and Blackwell(1968), Nicosia (1966) and Gilbert (1991). Inherent in all travel decision models is an information search process. Information search behavior can be either internal or external. An internal search is based on an individual's previous experiences or internal store of knowledge about a destination. An external search consists of actively seeking and acquiring information about a destination. The extent of information search behavior depends on many factors including prior experience, perceived risk, variations in price, composition of the vacation group and novelty of the destination (Capella and Greco, 1987; Woodside and Pitts, 1976; Snepenger et al., 1990).

McIntosh and Goeldner (1990: 257) argue that travel demand is a function of propensity and resistance. Resistance is inversely related to demand, meaning as a resistance component increases demand for travel to a particular destination decreases. Economic distance, cultural distance, and quality of host services constitute part of the resistance component of demand. For long haul international travel these three resistance factors should be operational. Therefore information search behavior, in the case of international travel, would involve identification of the means to overcome resistance.

Developing country economies are characterized by income disparity with large numbers in lower income classes, high levels of unemployment and underemployment, dependence on agricultural and extractive industries, and high levels of foreign ownership, especially in the service sector (Mathieson and Wall, 1982). To overcome these problems governments engage in active forms of tourism development (Jenkins and Henry 1982). This might include government development of resources for tourism or managerial assistance by setting tourism objectives and passing legislation to accomplish those objectives. Negotiating agreements with foreign companies or assisting them in bringing in international tourists is also a form of active involvement.

Exotic images, a theme found in much of the promotional literature produced by developing countries (Britton, 1979) has the potential to increase cultural distance. Although exotic images are also responsible for increasing propensity to travel, they are directed primarily at institutionalized mass tourists. Cohen (1974) describes institutionalized mass tourists as purchasers of complete travel packages where familiarity can be maintained by journeying within an environmental bubble. Tour operators handle all the details of foreign travel allowing the foreignness of the destination to be observed but not truly experienced. Britton (1982) argues that metropolitan enterprises, defined as large companies located in tourist generating countries, control international transport. Hoivik and Heiberg (1980) list international airlines and cruise ship companies as the primary metropolitan enterprises controlling international travel. Tour operators often negotiate discount fares for package tours with metropolitan enterprises.

The ability of tour operators to combine travel products and offer them to customers at prices generally lower than those available to individuals provides travel economy and convenience for a significant segment of tourists. As previously mentioned it also reduces cultural distance by cocooning or enclosing travelers in an environmental bubble. Product packaging and selling through operators represents a significant portion of the international travel business. Waters (1978: 28) states that in 1978 more than forty percent of U.S. residents traveling overseas purchased a package tour. Touche Ross and Company (1975) estimated that eight percent of U.S. tourists are so dependent on packaged tour products that they would not travel if they were not available. A tour operator will have more influence in the travel decision process and hence become more important both to the traveler and destination area the greater the distance from point of visitor origin to destination (WTO, 1977). They are often the first and most influential link in the tourist flow chain (IUOTO, 1976).

The dependence of developing countries on foreign tour operators derives fundamentally from the expertise of these operators as producers and wholesalers of tourism related services, their knowledge of the market, particularly the international market, and their access to the relevant complimentary services whereby a total package of tourism related services can be provided. For example, tourists depend on tour operators as sources of, presumably, expert information about product quality and consumption expectations. Harris and Katz (1986) label tour operators specialists in the areas of marketing, public relations, and management because of their skill in linking a country's touristic products and services to the traveler.

The United Nations (1982) identified three areas where tour operators provide necessary services to both travelers and developing countries. Tour operators are considered specialists in marketing and distribution of tourist related services and can achieve higher sales volume than single service providers. Second, given the high price elasticity of demand for international travel, the ability of tour operators to obtain low cost charters is crucial and finally, tour operators can arrange packages that can be mass marketed on the basis of their brand name and quality assurance. In other words, tour operators are able to reduce economic distance (low cost charter), cultural distance (providing complete packages), and increase quality of host services (brand name and quality assurance). The resistance component of demand is thereby reduced, resulting in an increase in total demand.

Another important role of tour operators as identified by McLellan and Noe (1983) and Bitner and Booms (1982) is as a gatekeeper of information. Tour operators provide information about destinations even if travelers do not choose to use their services. This source of information can be considered an induced image formation agent critical to the perceptions travelers hold about different destination areas. Murphy (1983) agrees that information dissemination by tour operators contributes to the image travelers hold about certain areas. Lapage and Cormier (1977) state that a major function of tour operators is to create attractive destination images. McLellan and Foushee (1983) argue that country images to a great extent work to influence the image held by tour operators and ultimately their clients. The role tour operators provide by distributing information organizes the information search process for the individual. External sources for information are minimized for the individual if they choose to use the services of a tour operator.

In most industries the supplier or producer has full or at least decisive control over the product including pricing, quality, and the manner in which it is distributed. Tourist service providers are an exception. According to Hawkins and Hudman (1989), the distribution sector of tourism is much stronger and travel intermediaries have far greater power to influence and direct consumer demand when compared to their counterparts in other industries. The distribution channel in tourism creates the link between the producers of tourism services and their customers. Often tour operators are the distribution link and the channel between producers and consumers of international tourism products. Since tourism products are experiential and consumed on site, tour operators are an integral link in the distribution system (Morrison, 1989). Unlike other products which flow from producer to consumer, tourists flow to the product. This inverted distribution system relies on intermediaries to perform much more than simple delivery services.

The importance of tour operators in the tourism economy of developing countries led to a study of American tour operators' perceptions of Indonesia as a preferred tourist destination. The study had the following specific objectives:

1. To determine the image of selected tourism related services in Indonesia held by American tour operators;

2. To document opinions regarding factors that affect the tour operators' decision to include Indonesia as part of their travel offering;
3. To document perceived difficulties by tour operators in selling Indonesia as a tourist destination;
4. To develop a corporate profile of tour operators currently packaging tours to Indonesia and investigate frequency of business activity within the country with perceptions of services;
5. To compare these results, from what is essentially a case study, to the larger body of knowledge regarding tour operators' role in the economic development of developing countries.

The sample population for the study was U.S. tour operators currently operating in Indonesia as identified by the Indonesian Tourism Promotion Office, Los Angeles. It is probable that this source would not identify all U.S. based tour operators conducting business in Indonesia. However, two concerns directed the sample selection effort. First, the Indonesian government has expressed its desire to assume a more active, managerial role in the country's tourism development effort. The efficacy of its U.S. based information office provides some measures to assess the success of this effort. Second, there was no single, or even a few sources, where a list of all tour operators selecting Indonesia as a travel destination could be obtained.

BACKGROUND

Indonesia is comprised of 13,667 islands making it the world's largest archipelago. Its location close to the equator makes for a tropical climate and due to its prehistoric land linkages with Australia and Asia, the flora and fauna are quite diverse and in some cases island specific. Cultural diversity is also an important attraction which has received substantial development attention (Adams, 1990). The number of tourists visiting Indonesia has been steadily increasing. Approximately 1.3 million people visited the country in 1988 which was a 22.7 percent increase from 1987 (Department of Tourism, 1989). The largest number of foreign visitors come from Singapore, Japan, Malaysia and Australia, accounting for over 100,000 visitors annually. The United States market is much smaller with approximately 61,000 U.S. visitors to Indonesia in 1988. However the Indonesian government views the U.S. as a strong market with the potential for large expansion. Indonesia has embarked on an aggressive strategy to open up more destinations within the country for tourists, relaxed visa regulations for select countries, improved lodging, food service and transportation facilities, increased promotional efforts and helped package attractions for marketing through international tour operators. The importance of tour operators to Indonesia is underscored by the estimated 34 percent of tourist business in Indonesia due to international tour operators (Department of Tourism, 1989). The stated tourism development policies of the Indonesian government resemble the active (managerial and developmental) role outlined by Jenkins and Henry (1982).

METHODS

As previously mentioned the sample population for the study consisted of all American tour operators registered with the Los Angeles Indonesian Tourist Promotion office. Sixty tour operators were identified. Those identified currently provide package tours and other travel services within the Indonesian archipelago.

The data collection instrument was a mail questionnaire. The questionnaire was divided into four sections. The four sections requested information regarding tour operators' perceptions of tourism attractions and services within Indonesia, factors affecting decisions to include Indonesia as part of their travel packages, perceived difficulties in developing packaged tours to Indonesia, and a corporate profile and history. Items selected for inclusion were based on attributes or services the Indonesian government officials felt were important to future positioning of its touristic products.

In the first section respondents were asked to rate selected services in Indonesia on a five-point Likert-type scale anchored by the bi-polar adjectives Poor (1) and Excellent (5). The second section asked for level of agreement/disagreement on nine factors that may effect a tour operator's decision to package Indonesia. Questions in this section were constructed using a five-point Likert-type scale anchored by the bi-polar adjectives Strongly Disagree (1) to Strongly Agree (5).

The third section included seven statements utilized to ascertain the level of difficulty encountered when packaging tours to Indonesia. Respondents were able to answer using a five-point Likert-type scale anchored by the bi-polar adjectives Very Difficult (1) and Very Easy (5). The last section collected information on the total number of years of experience as a tour operator, years of experience packaging tours to Indonesia and the sources of information utilized to assist in packaging tours to Indonesia.

The mail survey questionnaire was pre-tested using seven tour operators from the Southern California area. Changes were made to the questionnaire form based on their responses. On July 11, 1990, surveys were sent to all sixty tour operators identified as packaging tours to Indonesia. Telephone calls were made to all tour operators who had not returned completed surveys two weeks after the initial mailing. August 15, 1990 was the final date for receiving completed surveys.

Most of the results are reported in terms of mean scores. However, in an attempt to further investigate the perceptions American tour operators have of travel services important to tour operators, frequencies and Pearson-product moment correlations were utilized. Specifically, Pearson-product moment correlations were used to investigate the amount of time tour operators had been in business overall, the number of years of experience packaging tours to Indonesia, the number of trips packaged to Indonesia annually with their perceptions of Indonesian tourism services, and the degree of difficulty in obtaining assistance from the Indonesian government.

RESULTS

Fifty-one usable surveys were returned, six were undeliverable and three were returned only partially completed. Adjusting for nondeliverables, there was a 94.4% return rate.

Ten travel service attributes in Indonesia were evaluated by the respondent group (Table 1). The highest mean scores, indicating good to excellent service, were for the attributes "Opportunity for rest and relaxation"

TABLE 1. Perceived Image of Service Related Attractions

Type of Service	Mean	Rank
Quality of accommodation	3.20	5
Quality of restaurants	3.12	6
Cleanliness of environment	2.78	7
Local transportation	2.30	8
Reliability of computerization of information and reservation	2.14	10
On-time arrivals and departures	2.25	9
Pleasant attitude of service personnel	3.57	3
Receptiveness of local people to tourists	4.04	2
Opportunity for rest and relaxation	4.12	1
Safety and security	3.51	4

Poor[1]   Excellent[5]

(4.12) and "Receptiveness of local people to tourists" (4.04). Six of the service attributes were rated above the midpoint of three on the five-point scale and four were evaluated below the midpoint or closer to the Poor end of the scale. The lowest mean scores were recorded for the service attributes "Reliability of computer services for information and reservations" (2.14) and "On time arrivals and departures" (2.25). Those service attributes rated the highest were more of an intangible nature and can be considered of value to the tour operator's clientele, and those rated the lowest were more related to the efficient functioning of the tour operator's business.

Respondents indicated their degree of agreement on nine statements related to factors influencing their decision in selecting Indonesia as part of their travel offering (Table 2). The highest levels of agreement were recorded for the statements "Indonesia is a country rich in tourism resources" (4.65), and "Indonesian people are friendly and hospitable" (4.41). Only two statements received aggregate mean scores below the midpoint of three indicating disagreement with the statements. Those statements were "Indonesia provides adequate information regarding tourism facilities, prices and services" (2.10) and "The quality of tourism facilities and services is excellent" (2.62). It is also interesting to note that respondents did not overwhelmingly agree with the statement "Indonesia is the most attractive country in Asia" (3.42). The feeling that other

TABLE 2. Opinion About Factors that Affect U.S. Tour Operators in Selecting Indonesia as Part of Their Travel Offering

Factor	Mean	Rank
Indonesia is a country rich in tourism resources	4.65	1
Indonesia is the most attractive country in Asia	3.42	7
Indonesia is a fascinating destination for tourists	4.24	3
The quality of tourism facilities and services is excellent	2.62	8
Indonesia provides adequate information regarding tourism facilities, prices, and service	2.10	9
Travel to Indonesia is safe	3.96	4
Cost of developing tours to Indonesia is reasonable	3.67	6
Indonesian people are friendly and hospitable	4.41	2
Airfare to Indonesia is reasonable	3.80	5

Strongly Disagree[1]   Strongly Agree[5]

countries in Asia are more attractive indicates Indonesia's touristic image may not be strong enough to compensate for inadequate services.

The trend noticed above appears to be repeated. Statements that relate more to client satisfaction have higher levels of agreement than those that relate to efficient operation of the tour operator's business.

Further investigation of the perceived difficulties in packaging Indonesia as a travel destination reveals that tour operators encounter many problems when trying to acquire information and necessary services. Respondents indicated their degree of difficulty in acquiring six information or travel related services instrumental for trip packaging. Each one received an aggregate mean score less than three indicating that all were perceived as difficult or very difficult to obtain. The lowest mean score was for "Obtaining assistance from the Indonesian Tourism Promotions Office in Los Angeles" (2.04) followed closely by "Obtaining enough information on facilities, prices and services in Indonesia" (2.10). The highest mean score was recorded for "Securing space on domestic flights" (2.96) although this was still considered difficult (Table 3). These results appear to indicate that tour operators demand a certain level of quality services be provided and Indonesia does not sufficiently satisfy the demand for those services. Because of the importance of tour operators to the tourism economy in Indonesia and due to the expressed desire of the Indonesian government to increase travel from the United States, it appears that major improvements in support services to American tour operators should become a priority task for the Indonesian government. Although the expressed tourism policies of the Indonesian government indicate it is taking an active role in tourism development, one of its primary functions, assisting tour operators develop package tours, does not seem to be proceeding very well.

In order to more fully investigate tour operators' perceptions of Indonesia's provision of tourist related services, a corporate profile of the respondent group was constructed and then selected information was compared to some of the previously reported perceptions using Pearson-product moment correlations. For example, the number of years tour operators had been in business was compared with perceptions of the service attributes, factors that effect decisions in selecting Indonesia as a destination, and expressed degree of difficulty in packaging tours to Indonesia. The same analysis was performed for the number of years of experience packaging tours to Indonesia and number of tours packaged to Indonesia annually.

The corporate profile reveals that the average number of years the respondent group had been in the tour business was approximately 14, with the average operator having slightly over five years experience con-

TABLE 3. Perceived Difficulties in Developing and Packaging Indonesia as a Tourist Destination

Category of Choice	Securing Space for Domestic Flight N = 51 Mean = 2.96		Booking Hotel in Indonesia N = 49 Mean = 2.78		Selling Indonesia due to Time/Distance Factors N = 51 Mean = 2.84	
	f	%	f	%	f	%
1. Very Difficult	5	9.8	2	3.9	3	5.9
2. Difficult	11	21.6	20	39.2	18	35.3
3. No Opinion/Neutral	16	31.4	16	31.4	15	29.4
4. Easy	19	37.3	13	25.5	14	27.5
5. Very Easy	0	0.0	0	0.0	1	2.0

Category of Choice	Obtaining Enough Information N = 50 Mean = 2.10		Assistance from Tourist Promotion Office in L.A. N = 51 Mean = 2.04		Contracting and Utilizing Local Transportation N = 50 Mean = 2.42	
	f	%	f	%	f	%
1. Very Difficult	9	17.6	17	33.3	10	19.6
2. Difficult	28	54.9	16	31.4	17	33.3
3. No Opinion/Neutral	12	23.5	17	33.3	16	31.4
4. Easy	7	2.0	1	2.0	6	11.8
5. Very Easy	7	2.0	0	0.0	0	0.0

ducting tours to Indonesia and the average number of tours arranged annually over 14. The number of tours arranged annually had a range of between 1 to 100 with a median of ten (Table 4).

When considering only the number of years a tour operator had been in business with the perception of service attributes and factors affecting packaging Indonesia, four significant linear (.05 level of probability) relationships resulted. As the number of years of experience as a tour operator increased, respondents were more likely to upgrade their perception of the quality of restaurants, receptiveness of local people and the safety and security of Indonesia as a travel destination. Respondents were also less likely to perceive securing enough hotel space in the country as a problem. However, the analysis between the number of years of experience packaging tours to Indonesia with the above factors revealed different results. There was a significant negative correlation between the number of years experience conducting tours to Indonesia and the perception of the country as safe. Also, tour operators were more likely to experience difficulty in securing space on domestic flights as the number of years of experience packaging Indonesia increased. As the number of tours packaged annually increased, six negative significant correlations were noted. The more tours respondents packaged to Indonesia annually, the less likely they were to view Indonesia as a safe destination, the Indonesian people as friendly and hospitable and airfare to Indonesia as reasonable. They were also more likely to view securing space on domestic flights as difficult, securing enough hotel rooms as difficult and obtaining assistance from the Los Angeles office as difficult (Table 5).

It appears from these results that tour operators have certain expectations as their business builds, in terms of preferential service, and that these services are not adequately being met by the Indonesian government or providers of inbound services. Quite possibly the negative correlation noted as the number of tours conducted to Indonesia annually increases and the perception that Indonesian people are less friendly and hospitable is not necessarily a reflection of the indigenous people's hospitality but may be more a perception of local business contacts being unable or unwilling to negotiate price and space for inbound services. Obviously these results deserve to be more carefully investigated as it is apparent that the principal tour operators, those important to increasing U.S. travel market share, do not feel that provided services are adequate.

When sources of information utilized for packaging tours to Indonesia were investigated very few respondents indicated they used government provided services. Only 3.2 percent used the National Tourist office in Djakarta and 12.6 percent indicated they used the Indonesian Tourist

TABLE 4. Corporate Profile: Years as Tour Operator, Years Conducting Tours to Indonesia, and Average Number of Tours Conducted to Indonesia Yearly

	Number of Years as Tour Operator	Number of Years Conducting Tours to Indonesia	Number of Tours Arranged to Indonesia Yearly
Mean	13.78	5.39	14.38
Median	14.00	5.00	10.00
Range	6-25	2-15	1-100
Standard Deviation	4.78	2.52	17.01

TABLE 5. Pearson-Product Moment Correlations Coefficient Between Years Experience, Experience with Indonesia, Number of Tours per Year in Indonesia and Service Attributes, Difficulties in Arranging Tours, and Factors Affecting Travel Decisions

Factors	Number of Years Experience as a Tour Operator	Number of Years Conducting Tours to Indonesia	Number of Tours Conducted Annually to Indonesia
Quality of Restaurants	.29*		
Receptiveness of Local People	.32*		
Safety and Security	.33*		
Travel to Indonesia Is Safe		−.28*	−.39†
Indonesian People Are Friendly and Hospitable			−.43†
Airfare to Indonesia Is Reasonable			−.45†
Securing Space on Domestic Flights		−.28*	−.40†
Securing Sufficient Hotel Rooms	.30*		−.29*
Obtaining Sufficient Information from the L.A. Office			−.35*

* Significant at .05 level of probability.
† Significant at .01 level of probability.

Note: Only significant correlations are shown. Factors not significantly correlated with any of the three categories were omitted.

Promotion office in Los Angeles. The most important sources of information were airlines (36.2%), followed by hotels (24.4%) and other independent tour operators (22.8%) (Table 6). Obviously tour operators have found ways to obtain the information they need even if the sources are not their first preference. As mentioned earlier, Britton (1982) argues metropolitan enterprises control a large share of tourist traffic to developing countries. The above results do not refute that claim as it appears tour operators extensively utilize these sources. What is not so clear however is tour operators would continue to use those sources if needed services could be obtained from a host government organization. The high percentage of tour operators that have experienced difficulty in obtaining assistance from the Indonesian government (Table 3) might be indicative of why metropolitan enterprises control so much of the travel to developing countries. If Indonesia is typical of developing countries, which have initiated active government involvement programs for tourism development, tour operators' reliance on metropolitan enterprises for assistance in packaging tours should continue.

Respondents do not appear to package Indonesia as a separate destination. Over ninety-two percent of the respondents include another country in their package, with Singapore as their first choice. Thailand and Malaysia are also popular joint-offering countries (Table 7). These results indicate that American tour operators do not perceive Indonesia as having sufficient touristic attractions or quality of services to stand alone as a single destination. It may also indicate a belief on the part of American tour operators that the institutionalized American tourist demands multiple destinations on what amounts to a high cost, high time allocation, trip. Earlier findings indicating that respondents did not view Indonesia as the

TABLE 6. Sources of Information Utilized for Developing Tourism to Indonesia (N-51)

Source of Information	f	%
National Tourist Office	4	3.2
Independent Tour Operators	29	22.8
Hotels	31	24.4
Airlines	46	36.2
Tourist Promotion Office	16	12.6
Others	1	0.8
Total	127*	100.0

* equals more than 51 due to multiple response.

TABLE 7. Countries Included with Indonesia in an Asian Tour Package

Country	f	%
1. Thailand	43	84.3
2. Singapore	47	92.2
3. Brunei Darussalam	4	7.8
4. Malaysia	43	84.3
5. Phillipines	20	39.2
6. Other (Hong Kong and China)	20	39.2
Total	177*	

* equals more than 51 due to multiple response.

most attractive country in Asia reinforce the importance of multiple offerings, especially if tour operators' images of a country are an important image formation source for prospective travelers. Since Indonesia appears vulnerable to substitution, more effort with regards to provision of quality services is needed. Efforts on the part of the Indonesian government to open up more areas for tourism may help increase length of stay but they may also prove ineffectual if fundamental problems remain unresolved.

CONCLUSIONS

The results presented above provide direction for the Indonesian government and private sector providers of tourist services for the improvement of their travel delivery system. They also help understand how tour operators operate in at least one developing country and reinforce findings from earlier studies (Britton, 1982; Britton, 1979; and Jenkins and Henry, 1982). The importance of tour operators, especially for international travel, has been documented, and attempts to increase travel flows from the U.S. market to Indonesia should concentrate on this significant segment of the market. The question of why U.S. tour operators continue to sell Indonesia when it appears that there exist significant barriers in obtaining information and services within the country is probably due to Indonesia's overall appeal in the U.S. market. The strong ratings given to the attributes of "Opportunity for rest and relaxation," "Receptiveness of local people to tourists," and "Pleasant attitudes of service personnel" indicate that tour operators perceive their clients will be welcomed and accepted in Indonesia. The fact that tour operators strongly agree with the statements,

"Indonesia is a country rich in tourism resources" and "Indonesia is a fascinating destination for tourists," indicates that the attraction base is one demanded by their clients or is an image presented to their clients to increase sales. It also reinforces Britton's (1979) argument that a predominant developing world image is one of exotic people and places. In competing for customers tour operators must include destination attractiveness as one of the intangible qualities they market (Whipple and Thach, 1988). The image of Indonesia appears strong in terms of attractions and hospitality and this image is projected through the agents to their customers. However, the operators are concerned about the overall tourism experience for their clients and this can be affected by inefficient in-country services. Price elasticity also enters into the decision process and Indonesia must be aware the tour operators do not view that country as the most attractive in Asia. Therefore, difficult to obtain services with higher than expected prices may lead to destination substitution. Tourism demand could be increased by reducing economic distance for tour operators. The more difficult it is to obtain needed information, reserve domestic airline space or book blocks of hotel rooms, the more time consuming and expensive it becomes for tour operators.

Indonesia, similar to many other developing countries, has come under increasing pressure to find means of sustainable economic development which is not easy given the large population base of the country. Traditional natural resource industries (timber, agriculture, fisheries) are coping with stock depletion at the same time that demand for development increases. Tourism provides an opportunity to help balance the economic base of the country. Documentation of the tour operators' role in expanding foreign exchange earnings, especially in Indonesia, indicates that more attention needs to be given to this tourism distribution channel. Questions that need to be addressed immediately include: Are there measures which can be undertaken to improve the services for international tour operators? Are there opportunities for the Indonesian government in particular and all developing countries in general to provide information and assistance in obtaining needed services directly to tour operators, thereby reducing dependency on metropolitan enterprises? Are tour operators' expectations of discount fares and preferential bookings realistic and in keeping with sustainable development policies? Is there room for immediate expansion of the tourism industry in Indonesia or should this be planned over a period of time? What role does the government and private sector play in the provision of services to international tour operators?

This study has certain limitations that must also be recognized. The sample population consisted of tour operators registered with the Indonesia

Tourism Promotions Office, Los Angeles. It is probable that many other tour operators from the U.S. are operating in Indonesia but do not use the Los Angeles headquarters. The results which show the ineffectiveness of that office in providing adequate service, and the relatively few respondents who still use them, provide substance for the above statement. It is possible that tour operators have probably found other more reliable industry sources for information and services assistance. It is also possible that tour operators are more satisfied with these other sources and do not find it as difficult, as the study population, in arranging tours to Indonesia. Therefore this study may overemphasize the problems with Indonesian tour packaging in the United States. Conversely it is not known whether certain tour operators have stopped operating in Indonesia entirely because some of the identified difficulties. What is known is that those who were surveyed are not satisfied with the present system and would like to see some improvement. This constitutes a call for action and even with the sample population limitations there appears to be enough evidence to study the tourism distribution channel and find ways to make it operate more efficiently.

This study also investigated a different approach to estimating difficulties in securing needed travel services. The Pearson-product moment correlations reveal that tour operators heavily involved in packaging tours to Indonesia are the ones experiencing the most difficulty. As an operator increases their business in the country they are more likely to be confronted with increasing problems of securing adequate services. This principal or heavy half segment is an excellent predictor of problems others will encounter if they choose to take advantage of Indonesia's attempts to increase travel to the country. What is not known is if the same problems are encountered by other international tour operators in other countries. Is this Indonesian case study an example or an exception? Careful attention will have to be given to resolving some of the present problems of tourism's service delivery system in Indonesia if the government's expansion effort are to be fruitful. Careful attention will also have to be given to studying how other countries, with active government involvement in tourism development, are dealing with their own tourism service delivery channels, especially the part affecting international tour operators.

REFERENCES

Adams, K. (1990). "Cultural Commodization in Tana Toraja." *Cultural Survival Quarterly*, 14(1): 31-34.

Bitner, J. and Booms, H. (1982). Trends in Travel and Tourism Marketing: The Changing Structure of Distribution Channels. *Journal of Travel Research*, 20(4), 39-44.

Britton. R. (1979). "The Image of the Third World in Tourism Marketing." *Annals of Tourism Research*, 6(3): 318-329.

Britton. S. (1982). "Political Economy of Third World Tourism." *Annals of Tourism Research*, 9(3): 331-358.

Capella, L. and Greco A. (1987). "Information Sources of Elderly for Vacation Decisions." *Annals of Tourism Research*, 14(1): 148-151.

Cohen, E. (1974). "Who is a Tourist? A Conceptual Classification." *Sociological Review*, 22: 527-553.

Department of Tourism, Post and Telecommunication, Directorate General of Tourism Republic of Indonesia and WTO. (1989). *Final Report: Marine Tourism Plan for Indonesia*. Jakarta: Euroconsult-Gitarama Consortium.

Engel, J; Kollat, D. and Blackwell, R. (1968). *Consumer Behavior. New York:* Holt, Rinehart, and Winston.

Gilbert, D. (1991). "An examination of the Consumer Behavior Process Related to Tourism." In progress in *Tourism, Recreation and Hospitality Management*, Volume Three, C.P. Cooper (Editor, London), pp. 78-105: Behaven Press.

Harris, G. and Katz, K. M. (1986). *Promoting International Tourism: How to Increase the Flow of Foreign Visitors to Local Areas*. Los Angeles: The Americas Group, 60.

Hawkins, D. E. and Hudman, L. E. (1989). *Tourism in Contemporary Society: An Introductory Text*. Englewood Cliffs, NJ, 149-161.

Hoivik, T. and Heiberg, T. (1980). "Centre-Periphery Tourism and Self-Reliance." *International Social Science Journal*, 32 (1): 69-98 (from S. Britton, 1982).

Howard, J. and Seth, J. (1969). *The Theory of Buyer Behavior*. New York: John Wiley.

IUOTO, International Union of Official Travel Organizations. *The Impact of International Tourism on the Economic Development of the Developing Countries* (1976). Geneva: World Tourism Organization (from S. Britton, 1982).

Jenkins, C. and Henry, B. (1982). "Government Involvement in Tourism in Developing Countries." *Annals of Tourism Research*, 9(4): 499-521.

LaPage, W. F. and Cormier, P. L. (1977). "Images of Camping: Barriers to Participation?" *Journal of Travel Research* 15(4), 21-25.

Mathieson A. and Wall, G. (1982). *Tourism: Economic, Physical and Social Impacts*. London: Longman.

McIntosh. R. and Goeldner, C. (1990). *Tourism: Principles, Practices and Philosophies*. New York: John Wiley.

McLellan, R. W. and Foushe, K. D. (1983). "Negative Images of the United States as Expressed by Tour Operators from Other Countries." *Journal of Travel Research*, 22, 2-5.

McLellan, R. W. and Noe, F. P. (1976). "Source of Information and Types of Messages Useful to International Tour Operators." *Journal of Travel Research*, 8(3): 27-30.

Morrison, A. (1989). Hospitality and Travel Marketing. Albany, NY: Delmar Publishers, Inc.

Mouthinho, L. (1987). "Consumer Behavior in Tourism." *European Journal of Marketing* 21(10): 1-44.
Murphy, P. E. (1983). Perception of Attitudes of Decision Making Groups in Tourists Center. In *The Image of Destination Region*. Stabler, M. J, 133-160. New York: Croom Helm, Inc.
Nicosia, F. (1966). *Consumer Decision Processes: Marketing and Advertising Implications*. Englewood Cliffs, NJ: Prentice Hall.
Schmoll, G. (1977). *Tourism Promotion*. London: Tourism International Press.
Snepenger, D., Meged, K., Snelling, M., and Worral, K. (1990). "Information Search Strategies by Destination-Naive Tourists." *Journal of Travel Research*, 29(1): 13-16.
Touche Ross and Company (1975). *Tour Wholesaler Industry Study*. New York.
United Nations Center on Transnational Corporations (1982). Transnational Corporations in International Tourism. New York: United Nations Publication.
Waters, S. R. (1978) *Travel Industry World Yearbook: The Big Picture*, 28. New York: Child and Waters, Inc.
Whipple, W. and Thach, V. (1988). "Group Tour Management: Does Good Service Produce Satisfied Customers?" *Journal of Travel Research*, 27(2): 16-21.
Woodside A. and Lysonski, S. (1989). "A General Model of Traveller Destination Choice." *Journal of Travel Research* 27(4): 8-14.
Woodside, A. and Pitts, R. (1976). "Effects of Consumer Lifestyles, Demographics and Travel Activities on Foreign and Domestic Travel Behavior." *Journal of Travel Research* 14(3): 13-15.
Woodside, A. and Sherrell, D. (1977). "Traveler Evoked, Inept and Inert Sets of Vacation Destinations." *Journal of Travel Research* 16(1): 14-18.
World Tourist Organization (WTO) (1976). *Factors Influencing Travel Demand and Leading to the Redistribution of Tourist Movements*. WTO-AVDA. Del Generalissimo, 59-Madrid-16.

"De Higher de Monkey Climb, de More 'e Show 'e Tail": Tourists' Knowledge of Barbadian Culture

Graham M. S. Dann

SUMMARY. International tourists the world over have been portrayed by some commentators as superficial nitwits. Simply seeking pleasure in exotic enclave resorts, and both physically and psychologically removed from the lives of the destination people they purport to visit, such tourists seem to pay scant regard to host culture–particularly if it is of the Third World variety. This paper attempts to examine this assertion by exploring other theoretical positions and by means of an empirical investigation of metropolitan tourists visiting the typical developing Caribbean island of Barbados. The paper recommends that studies such as this one should be conducted, not only to provide a comprehensive picture of what travelers really know about the places and people they visit, but also to delineate related market segment(s) and demand.

INTRODUCTION

"De higher de monkey climb, de more 'e show 'e tail."
"Where did you get that from?"
"It's in this local newspaper here."

Graham M. S. Dann, is affiliated with the University of the West Indies, Barbados.

[Haworth co-indexing entry note]: " "De Higher de Monkey Climb, de More 'e Show 'e Tail": Tourists' Knowledge of Barbadian Culture." Dann, Graham M. S. Co-published simultaneously in *Journal of International Consumer Marketing* (The Haworth Press, Inc.) Vol. 6, No. 3/4, 1994, pp. 181-204; and: *Global Tourist Behavior* (ed: Muzaffer Uysal) The Haworth Press, Inc., 1994, pp. 181-204. Multiple copies of this article/chapter may be purchased from The Haworth Document Delivery Center [1-800-3-HAWORTH; 9:00 a.m. - 5:00 p.m. (EST)].

181

"What on earth does it mean?"

"It's probably got to do with natives climbing trees–coconuts–something like that."

"Monkeys? Tails? So what's that to us? Listen, we only came to visit this place, didn't we?"

"Relax. Have another rum punch. Then we'll go for a dip in the pool."

The foregoing imaginary dialog typifies a conversation between two "mass" tourists (Smith, 1989) who, after purchasing an all-inclusive package to a Third World enclave resort, have just been confronted for the first time with a strange element of indigenous culture. Since the predominant motive for their vacation is escape amidst familiarity (English, 1986; Rivers, 1972), they are unlikely to be interested in novel experiences of an alien culture which could threaten their unbridled pursuit of leisure. They, and maybe millions of other like-minded individuals, have been described as superficial nitwits and cultural dopes (Boorstin, 1964), barbarians (Nitford, 1959), suntanned destroyers of culture (Turner and Ash, 1975), even as fanaticists temporally equipped with power (Fussell, 1980). Their "pleasure first" principle renders them either unwilling or unable to seek out the "authentic" (Turner and Ash, 1975) from the lives of the destination people who surround them–at a safe distance. Those permitted to enter their hedonistic "environmental bubbles" (Cohen, 1972) are restricted to local purveyors of rest and recreation (maids, couriers, servants, entertainers, taxi drivers, middlemen, and other marginal types provided by the tourism industry–English, 1986; van den Berghe, 1980). There are to be no unpleasant surprises, no culture shocks (Pearce, 1982). All must follow the language of social control employed by the holiday brochure (Dann, 1988). Only in this way will the promises of the advertising blurb be fulfilled and satisfaction be achieved.

THE OTHER SIDE OF THE STORY

There are several commentators who take exception to the above scenario and question its accuracy. MacCannell (1976), for example, arguing from a neo-Durkheimian semiotic position, believes that tourists are engaged in a post-modern "sacred" quest for authenticity. In escaping the pressures of their tedious metropolitan environments, they attempt to discover their true selves by experiencing the real world of others. Unfortunately, the tourism establishment thwarts this aspiration by supplying a series of false fronts and staged cultural experiences.

While accepting that the idea of "tourist as moron" is oversimplistic and stereotypical, Cohen (1988) nevertheless disagrees with MacCannell to the extent that the former maintains that the search for authenticity is an emergent and changing reality, one that is not universally applicable to *all* tourists. Such a quest depends, for instance, on the degree of alienation in the home environment (Rivers, 1972), the phenomenological mode of touristic experience pursue (Cohen, 1979), and the manner in which different individuals define their varying life situations (Teas, 1988) (rather than how these are interpreted by intellectual analysts).

According to Cohen (1979, 1982), tourists' experiences can be arranged on a continuum ranging from the recreational, diversionary, experiential and experimental to the existential. This continuum stretches between familiarity and strangeness, from the mass tourist who delights in the creature comforts of the enclave resort to the adventuresome nomad who opts for meaningful encounters with members of the host population. Since the majority of tourists tend to fall into the first two categories (Boorstin asserts that they all do, while MacCannell tends to assume that they comprise the last three categories), this naturally raises the question as to the mass tourist's need for authenticity. Cohen (1982) argues that the mass tourist is not simply the gullible victim of the machinations of the tourism industry. Rather, he or she, while being aware of staged authenticity, nevertheless agrees to go along with the game that is being played with connivance from both parties, in a similar fashion to an individual's becoming engrossed in a detective story.

Whether one accepts the interpretation of MacCanell or that of Cohen, there is still a shared view that the basis for travel lies in the disorienting home environment of the potential tourist. Sometimes the quest for self identity is expressed as a search for the other, an elective center beyond the individual's immediate surroundings, one which is located in a different culture. Only by journeying beyond the ordinary can one restore meaning to life (Cohen, 1979; 1982).

Within a micro-functionalist framework, Crompton (1979) maintains that individuals experience cultural disequilibrium in their personality systems. In order for a new balance to be achieved, they seek tension relief at a higher level through novelty (curiosity, adventure, etc.), and often too in the desire to learn more about the lives of others. Need satisfaction can thus be understood as a motive for travel, just as can the related sociopsychological needs of escape, self-evaluation, relaxation, prestige, enhancement of kinship relations and facilitation of social interaction. Since these various needs are internally generated, they may be collectively considered as "push" factors, logically and temporally prior to the complementary attractions ("pull" factors) of any tourist destination (Dann, 1981). Seen in this light, the desire to experience another culture is proportionate to the perceived lack of coherence in the tourist's own culture, or, as Teas (1988: 40) would say:

> Travelers seek to redefine (American) culture by learning how other peoples answer the same problems of living.

So far, the consensus from "the other side of the story" seems to be that, through travel, the culture of "alter" can somehow respond to deficiencies in "ego," and that such a learning experience will vary according to individual needs, alienation, and how situations are defined. Thus the basis for understanding tourist motivation is grounded primarily in demand ("push") rather than in supply ("pull").

Far less clear is what is intended by "culture." In order to resolve this complex issue in which a plethora of descriptions abound, it is often worthwhile to follow a working definition from which other conclusions derive. Agreement or disagreement can then link back to such a point of departure. Here the initial premise selected is taken from Geertz (1977: 13-14), who believes that culture comprises "webs of significance manifested in (a people's) behavior." Thus, in order to learn and understand the symbolic meanings of what "other people are up to," we need not necessarily become members of that society, but we do have to be able to communicate with them.

Applied to tourism, there will be those who are attracted to a destination by learning more about the lives of others and those who prefer to seek pleasure within their own company. The former (alocentric) group becomes similar to the anthropologist or ethnographer (Crick, 1989); the latter (psychocentric) derives leisure from the internal environment (Plog, 1972). It is thus possible to speak of "cultural tourism" as catering to the demands of those who are fascinated with the picturesque, local color and the peasantry (Smith, 1989), or the context which surrounds the unique identity of a people–even though most tourists are not motivated by such interests (Wood, 1984). Nevertheless, cultural tourism will exert its greatest influence among those who wish to compare the lives of others with their own. In so doing, they may bring back cultural trophies and relate experiences to those who stayed behind, thereby somehow enhancing their status (Dann, 1981; Moeran, 1983).

SOME EMPIRICAL INVESTIGATIONS

There have been numerous empirical investigations which have explored the effects of tourism on indigenous culture and cultural patrimony.

These impact studies have been very well summarized and reviewed by Dogan (1989).

Generally, such works have focused on various institutionalized facets of life of the host community (e.g., crime, race relations, morality), and many have attempted a cost-benefit analysis seeking to measure the net effect of tourism on a destination society (Mathieson and Wall, 1982). A few have tried to control simultaneously for the effects of allied factors (e.g., modernization, industrialization, the mass media). Even less have examined the reverse process, i.e., the impact of tourism on the tourist.

Nevertheless, there are some noteworthy illustrations of this last category. Smith (1955), for example, looked at the effects of travel on young American students touring Europe, and eventually concluded that, while there had been some reduction in ethnocentrism and authoritarianism as a result of the experience, there was little modification of deep rooted attitudes. Pool (1958), however, discovered that, where such change did occur, more often than not it was predicated on type of personality and what the traveler (in this case the American businessman) hoped to discover.

Later, Triandis and Vassiliou (1967) extended this type of work to the realm of stereotyping. More specifically, by comparing two groups–American military personnel and Greek students–they were able to examine the effects of interaction on heterostereotypes (images of another group) and autostereotypes (self-image). Due to intercultural contact, the Americans saw themselves more positively while devaluing the Greeks, whereas the Greeks managed to evaluate Americans more positively without denigrating themselves (Pearce, 1982: 210).

Subsequently, Pearce (1977) conducted a study of British package tourists traveling to Greece and Morocco, who were apparently more interested in having a good time among themselves than even they were in meeting the local inhabitants or studying their culture. Nevertheless, and simply on account of visiting these places, albeit for only a short two to three week period, many of these young travelers modified their views on a number of attributes of Greeks and Moroccans and also on one of their own characteristics (that of relative wealth). Writing some five years afterwards, Pearce (1982: 199) concluded that the effects of intercultural contact are predicated on the tourist's affluence, motivation, transience and sociological status in the host community.

Finally, a large scale survey was conducted by Tourism Canada (1987) which examined 53 factors which long haul tourists looked for in selecting a North American vacation destination (cf. Taylor, 1988). One of these factors was "opportunities to increase one's knowledge," and this was ranked in first position by the French, third by visitors from the UK and Japan, and eighth by those from Germany. In the last three cases it was further possible to identify a "culture and nature" segment comprising historical sites, unique culture groups, museums, art galleries, different cultures, wildlife and birds. This segment, which represented roughly 1 traveler in 8, was most evident among "enthusiastic independents," which included young, single, university educated, residents of large cities, frequent travelers, and those who had been exposed to books and other printed material relating to the destination area.

THE CARIBBEAN CONNECTION

Two decades ago, Lunberg (1972: 111) observed that over 90 percent of U.S. visitors to the Caribbean journeyed there for purposes of pleasure. This statistic was contrasted with that for Europe, where 25 percent of American adults with a college education accounted for 50 percent of all those thus destined by air (Lundberg, 1972: 117). Given that the latter case is explained in terms of the propensity to travel abroad increasing with education, and that this factor in turn is related to a search for knowledge, truth, understanding and the urge to learn (Lundberg, 1972: 116), it follows that Caribbean tourism is characterized by a marked absence of such motivation. Just why there should be this discrepancy may be accounted for in terms of the absence or presence of historical sites, the quest for roots, etc. Yet Lundberg (1972: 117) offers an additional explanation in relation to educational travel and its lack of universal applicability when he points out:

> This is not to say that every traveler learns. He may be a mere spectator in his journeys. Humans learn from an environment only to the extent that they respond to it.

It is this "lack of response" among Caribbean bound tourists which has evoked a wave of criticism from a number of commentators on the Caribbean scene. Harrigan (1974), for instance, likens the exploitative relationship between the white tourist in the luxury hotel and the servile black attendants to a massa-slave situation. Perez (1973-4) speaks of neocolonialism, Naipaul (1969) of racism. Michael Manley, former prime minister of Jamaica, alludes to a sense of shame experienced by his people, with the knowledge that the tourist, far from wishing to meet them, prefers instead to become slowly drunk in his hotel room (Britton, 1980). By way of further generalization, English (1986: 53) notes:

For "sun-lust" tourism, the chief element in North-South tourism, its dominant theme is invariably one of self-indulgence, evident both in the travel brochure and at the hotel. Culture and people are downplayed, except perhaps to emphasize their primitiveness.

The few survey-style impact studies of tourism in the Caribbean (e.g., Brathwaite, 1991; Sethna, 1980), while highlighting a number of negative effects (e.g., declining morality, AIDS, drugs, prostitution, homosexuality), nevertheless show that, by and large, these are offset by such economic benefits as increased foreign exchange, employment and improvements in the infrastructure. At the same time, Brathwaite's (1991) study of Barbados (and similar findings in St. Lucia, Tobago and Curacao) reveal that host perceptions of visitors' motives are regarded principally in terms of rest and relaxation rather than any desire to interact with members of the host society.

Another recent study, conducted by an anthropologist (Wright, 1989), and adopting a case method approach among vendors and other "beach people," reinforces the local view that "most tourists to Barbados are of the 'sea, sand and sex' variety" and that generally they are indifferent to Bajan culture (Wright, 1989: 109). Visitors to Barbados thus come to "refresh themselves; to get a tan, swim, drink, eat, dance and take advantage of the local amenities. Some Barbadians lament the fact that most tourists are not interested in experiencing their culture but prefer hedonistic pastimes (Wright, 1989: 61). The foregoing sentiment is reinforced by "the self perception that Barbadian culture is somehow lesser than other forms of life" (Wright, 1989: 27). Just why this should be so is explained as follows:

> Tourists that are generated from the metropole are often perceived as coming from a more powerful, relevant place, thus creating a perception that the local culture is subsidiary to the important places and activities of the world. (Wright, 1989: 61)

Such alienated self-denigration in turn leads to the commoditization of culture–the tourism establishment glorifies the inglorious days of slavery by staging floor shows with natives in plantation attire. Local art forms (e.g., steel drum making and basketry) are trinketized, creating a devaluation of indigenous culture as something "quaint, outdated and merely another saleable commodity" (Wright, 1989: 70).

Yet, in spite of the many useful insights gained from such studies, none has fully attempted to explore the accuracy of the descriptions they provide of the tourists themselves. More to the point, there is an absence of information on tourists' knowledge of local culture, and hence, by implication, about the assertions made in relation to tourists "en masse" whenever such knowledge is lacking.

METHOD

In order to investigate the foregoing missing link, and as part of a larger study of visitor motivation and satisfaction in Barbados, it was decided to include a number of questions relating to tourists' awareness of nine cultural items. During February 1989, 535 tourists who had been on the island four days or more were sampled on a quota basis. In the absence of an alternative reliable sampling frame, quotas were drawn up proportionately matching respondent profiles (age, sex, generating country, type of accommodation) according to the same percentage frequency distribution evidenced in February of the previous year.

In order to derive typical cultural items it was first necessary to differentiate material (e.g., arts, crafts) and non-material culture (Mathieson and Wall, 1982), and to distinguish culture as inanimate (e.g., architecture, paintings), animated (e.g., festivals, presentations of historical events), or related to the daily lives of a people (e.g., language, work dress, gastronomy) (Ritchie and Zins, 1978). It was this latter non-material living sense which was adopted, since how a given people thinks, speaks and acts is more germane to the intercultural contact engendered by tourism than, say, works of literature or archeological discoveries. Ziolwenska (1989: 41) comes close to the idea when she instances such cultural items as "wooden huts, richly carved roadside chapels, women rushing for Sunday church services in striped skirts."

Concentrating on this interpretation of culture, two items were selected which characterized traditional living/interactional arrangements–the chattel house and the rum shop, respective foci of the West Indian family and community. These were followed by two items relating to indigenous food and drink: cou-cou and corn 'n oil. Recreational activities were represented by cricket and the tuk band, the latter also being a vehicle for the transmission of folk songs. Two local sayings were added to the list–"above and below" and "de higher de monkey climb, de more 'e show 'e tail," as was a typical nonverbal mannerism–the chupse.

Although the nine items could not claim to be exhaustive of nonmaterial living culture, it was felt by a number of independent experts that they were sufficiently representative in order to capture something of the way of life of the destination people. At the same time, since not all the items were unique to Barbados, some having become adopted through the process of acculturation, it might be possible to discern whether such a distinction formed part of tourists' cultural knowledge.

As a further refinement of the latter, it was readily acknowledged that mere acquaintance with an item would not in itself constitute adequate knowledge. Additionally it would be necessary to demonstrate sufficient understanding of an expression (Geertz, 1973). Since the meaning of each contained two or more essential features, responses were deemed "correct" where this condition was fulfilled. Replies containing only one such characteristic were rated as "half correct," and "incorrect" answers comprised the remainder of the cases in which interviewees had either heard of or experienced the item in question. Absence of data signified that the respondent had not previously heard of or experienced a given item.

What ensues is an item by item commentary, a ranking according to percentage meanings assessed as correct or half correct, an inter-variable analysis, a discussion and a few concluding recommendations.

ITEM BY ITEM COMMENTARY

Rum Shop

In a Barbadian/Caribbean context, Collymore (1970: 90) describes such an establishment as "a small shop where rum and some other alcoholic drinks are sold, together with such commodities as bread, cheese, sliced ham, etc., and a place where men gather to discuss the topics of the day." Potter and Dann (1987: xxxviii) further note that a rum shop frequently acts as a rural grocery store, and Marshall (1986b: 279) adds that it is "an informal community center, where tongues are loosened, politics discussed and rumors spread."

When respondents who had heard of/experienced a rum shop were subsequently asked to elaborate on its meaning, examples of correct answers included: "a small drinking tavern found in the village," "a place where people hang out and drink rum" and "a village pub where you get rum." But those which captured the essence of this male bastion of conviviality and alcoholic assembly were: "men come to drink rum, bet, play cards and argue" and "a little open shack where men go and drink and play games." Instances of half correct replies were: "a bar," "a place that makes rum," "alcohol" and "I'm a rum runner."

Chattel House

According to Potter and Dann (1987: xxxvi), a chattel house is "a rectangular wooden house, generally set on a pile of rocks. Such vernacular houses are movable, reflecting the fact that they are owned by the occupant, whilst the land is rented, often from plantations, at peppercorn rents. The standard gable-roofed chattel house may measure little more than 5.4m by 2.7m." The Concise Oxford Dictionary (Fowler and Fowler, 1959: 199) further observes that the word "chattel" refers to a movable possession, usually in the plural–as in "goods and chattels." Thus, in a Barbadian context, a chattel house is a wooden movable property, often located on a tenantry, which can be easily dismantled (Wilder, 1986: 147-8; 211).

Featuring this transient quality were such correct answers as: "little houses that sit on the land and can be moved," "black Bajan home from the British period, not attached to the land" and "a house which can be moved from its site," while half correct replies included: "small village house," "traditional wooden house" and "style of Barbadian house." Incorrect responses contained the following misinterpretations: "a dance hall," "where the slaves were," "a furniture store," "church," "liquor store," "money lender," "caravan" and even "a brothel."

Cricket

The Concise Oxford Dictionary (Fowler and Fowler, 1959: 284) describes cricket as "an open air game played with ball, bats and wickets, between two sides of eleven players each." In the local setting, Cozier (1986: 281) states that cricket was introduced almost two centuries ago by the British military and was subsequently engaged in by the white planters and merchants, who, from 1877, played it at their respective clubs of Pickwick and Wanderers. Later, the majority black population became involved, so much so that today it is virtually a national religion and way of life. For many non-Commonwealth visitors, however, the rules of the game seem quite incomprehensible.

Several respondents managed to include correctly a number of salient characteristics of the game. They referred to its English origin and the fact that several people from the Caribbean excelled at it as a national sport. Some even mentioned famous Barbadian cricketers like Garfield Sobers, while others spoke of the inter-island Red Stripe tournament. They additionally referred to its being played on a grass pitch and noted that it had bowlers, fielders and batsmen, using a ball and bat. In some respects also it was said to resemble baseball. A few further alluded to the complexity of the regulations and described the game as both lengthy and boring. While half correct answers highlighted just one of these features (the most frequent being that cricket was a game or sport), incorrect responses confused it with soccer, croquet, hockey, tennis, and even water sports. Other incorrect replies included references to bugs and cockroaches, presumably an allusion to the jumping chirping insect whose name is derived from the French "criquer" –to creak (Fowler and Fowler, 1959: 284).

Cou Cou/ Coo Coo/ Couscous

This item was included since, together with flying fish, it constitutes the Barbadian national dish (Potter & Dann, 1987: xxxvi). Cou cou is a semolina-like mixture made from stirring corn meal, okras, water, salt and butter (Springer, 1983: 171), although Indian corn, guinea corn, breadfruit, bananas, yams and potatoes can be used instead of corn meal (Collymore, 1970: 27). Wood (1973: 44) adds sugar to the recipe and substitutes coconut milk for water, while Springer (1986: 271-2) observes that any salt fish can be the accompaniment. The latter authority further notes that cou cou is inspired from the African "foo-foo," and, when turned out from the bowl on to the plate, resembles a golden mound whose central well is filled with gravy.

Most of the correct answers identified the corn meal ingredient, while a few mentioned okra and the fact that cou cou was the national dish when eaten with flying fish. Interestingly, two respondents likened cou cou to the Arabrian couscous. This reply was also adjudged to be correct since the indigenous fare of the Mahgreb, although made from wheat grain, and often accompanied by meat, saffron, harissa (a hot sauce) or yoghurt, is similarly steamed (albeit over a broth) and semolina-like in consistency and appearance (Roden, 1979: 290-294; cf. couscous (sou)–Fowler & Fowler, 1959: 277). Two more interviewees employed the name used in the Caribbean Leeward islands–"fungi"–(cf. Springer, 1983: 166), while one legitimately referred to "callaloo" (dasheen leaves, ochroes, crab, garlic, onion and hot pepper) as a West Indian accompaniment (cf. Wood, 1973: 44). Half correct replies described cou cou as simply food or a local dish, without elaborating on either its ingredients or method of preparation. While the most common erroneous response was "a bird" or "clock" (no doubt the onomatopoeic "cuckoo" (cf. Fowler & Fowler, 1959: 829)), there were also references to "coconut," "cocoa," "fish" and "root."

Tuk Band

Marshall (1986a: 235-241) describes a tuk band as a small male group of wandering minstrels which travels from village to village playing popular tunes, while inviting people to join in with their own compositions. The band usually comprises a drummer and a flautist and some members dress up as donkeys, bears or pregnant women. It origin goes back over 120 years and it is now usually only seen at Crop Over and on other public holidays and festivals. The name "tuk" is said to be derived from the "boom-a-tuk" sound of the big log drum whose seductive beat can lead to a "wuk up" (provocative dance employing a predominant hip movement).

Most of the correct answers focused on the homemade instruments (flutes and drums) and a few referred to the masquerading of the players, while the half correct responses were less specific. Incorrect replies included: "native bank," "item of clothing," "little shop," "man who sells food," "something to lie glasses on" and "a dress for Mardi Gras."

Corn 'n Oil

Collymore (1970: 27) describes corn and oil as a drink compounded of rum and falernum, the latter name being derived from Falernian or vinum Falernum–the ancient Ager Falernus of Campania (Collymore, 1970: 39), for which Springer (1983: 174) provides the ingredients (lime juice, white rum, granulated sugar, water and almond essence).

The majority of correct answers similarly provided the combination of the two main alcoholic beverages, while the half correct replies simply referred to corn 'n oil as a drink or liqueur. Incorrect responses focused on oil (cooking oil, frying oil, sun tan oil), corn (corn cob, food, vegetable, sweet, barbecue, popcorn), both (corn oil, oil from corn) or neither (whisky, a pudding, staples).

Chupse/Stupse

Collymore (1970: 22-23) describes a chupse as a sound made by a pouting of the lips and sucking in air between the teeth. He quotes Allsopp (1950) as observing that, although it is indicative of distrust or sulking (with almost closed eyelids), there are chupses of amused tolerance (an oral shrugging of the shoulders, self-admonition, offense/abuse, provocation, disdain (with raising of eyebrow) and sorrow (quick serial, with shaking of the head from side to side). They range from "the small effortless chupse of indifference to the thin hard chupse of mere disdain and the long liquid vibrating chupse which shakes the rafters and expresses every kind of defiance."

While only one respondent managed to capture two or more features ("suck your teeth in disgust"), quite a few provided either the nonverbal behavior (teeth sucking) or the signification (annoyance, disgust, "vex," displeasure, etc.). Without further elaboration, one mentioned its African origin, and another referred to its use by a popular Caribbean comedian–Paul Keens Douglas. Typical misconceptions included: "front porch," "verandah," "steps," "kiss," "chicken farm," "chips," "Chinese food," "a dance," and even "whistling at girls."

"De Higher de Monkey Climb, de More 'e Show 'e Tail"

Forde (1986: 257) supplies the following meaning for this Barbadian proverb: "the more one shows off, the more one's faults are brought into the open."

Some respondents related the saying to social status by indicating that the higher the social position, the more likely it was that a person would reveal his/her true feelings/colors, be exposed, and hence attract criticism. Whereas these and similar replies were not absolutely consonant with the original expression, they were adjudged sufficiently close in meaning to merit a correct answer. While simply "showing off," "being big headed" or "open to ridicule" were deemed to be only half correct, literal interpretations, such as "a monkey," "climbing a coconut tree," etc., were evaluated as incorrect responses.

Above and Below

As Collymore (1970: 1) so aptly observes in the local Barbadian context, "if you were told that Mr X was "above the house," you wouldn't expect to observe him hovering over the roof; you would look for him somewhere to the windward (east) side of the building." Below, on the other hand, is to the leeward (west) (Collymore, 1970: 9). These directional markers (which are far from comprehensive in their subtle meanings) stand in sharp contrast to standard English usage (cf. Fowler and Fowler, 1959: 4; 108) and are often a source of great confusion to Anglophobe visitors.

Nevertheless, some respondents were aware of the east/west-right/left distinction and were consequently awarded full marks. Others, who spoke only of directions without being more specific, were adjudged to be only half correct. Incorrect replies included: "above average, below average," "heaven and hell," "scuba diving," "water and land" and "upstairs and downstairs."

RANKING OF ITEMS

From Table 1, it can be seen that the ranking of items 1-4, 6 and 9 according to the combined correct and half correct replies followed the

TABLE 1. Ranking of Nine Cultural Items According to Percentage Responses (n = 535)
Heard or Experienced

Item	Percent correct meaning	Percent half correct meaning	Percent incorrect meaning	Percent neither heard nor experienced	Ranking correct and half correct	Ranking heard and experienced
Cricket	9.0	69.3	3.2	18.5	1	1
Rum shop	6.7	52.5	1.3	39.5	2	2
Cou Cou	8.6	26.5	6.9	58.0	3	3
Chattel House	5.0	22.6	4.9	67.5	4	4
Tuk Band	3.0	9.7	1.9	85.4	5	7
Above & Below	2.1	9.9	3.9	84.1	6	6
Chupse	0.2	9.0	3.4	87.4	7	8
Corn 'n Oil	2.4	6.6	7.3	83.7	8	5
De Higher de Monkey climb, de More 'e Show 'e Tail	3.6	5.2	1.3	89.9	9	9

ranking of heard and experienced. However, with items 5, 8 and 7 (due to greater percentages of incorrect responses), the ranking of heard and experienced respectively changed to 7, 5 and 8.

The items fell naturally into three categories:

- above average knowledge: cricket and rum shop
- below average knowledge: cou cou and chattel house
- substandard knowledge: tuk band, corn 'n oil, chupse, above and below, and last, but not least–de higher de monkey climb de more 'e show 'e tail.

Thus classified, it can be seen that above and below average scores were obtained for items which are non-destination specific (cricket and cou-cou are extra-regional, and rum shop and chattel house are Caribbean in nature). By contrast, substandard scores (with the exception of chupse) are recorded for items which are Barbadian in character. Such a patterning suggests that cultural knowledge flows from the general to the particular, and that persons are more likely to be familiar with instances of acculturation (e.g., cricket) than with indigenous cultural features (e.g., corn 'n oil). Alternatively stated, and as an hypothesis worthy of ulterior exploration: just as the distinctions between nationalities and national boundaries are becoming increasingly blurred (cf. Dann, forthcoming), so too does cultural knowledge tend to assume a parallel conceptual fuzziness.

INTER-VARIABLE ANALYSIS

A more detailed inspection of the data showed that there were only 37 individuals (just 6.9 percent of the sample) who gave two or more completely correct replies to the 9 cultural stimuli (2 with 5 correct replies, 2 with 4, 5 with 3 and 28 with 2).

When these more knowledgeable respondents were subsequently examined according to their backgrounds, no significant differences with respect to the remainder of the sample were found for gender, occupation, education, marital status, religion or traveling companion.

However, these same persons were overrepresented:

- in the 30-37 and 59+ age groups
- among those with Canadian and Caribbean backgrounds
- among repeat visitors

The second finding is certainly not surprising, given the similarities between West Indian and Barbadian culture. The Canadian connection, however, is less obvious, and without additional data, an explanation for the relationship would be simply speculative. The association between familiarity with cultural items and repeater status was anticipated to the extent that those who had visited the island before might have been more prepared than first-timers to venture forth into unexplored territory, thereby acquiring more cultural knowledge. Yet it cannot always be assumed that frequency of visit always results in enhanced knowledge of local culture, since, theoretically at least, tourists could return to a similar enclave establishment and remain oblivious to the local life surrounding them.

For this reason, it was decided to examine the category of visitor accommodation in more detail. It will be recalled that the 535 tourists had already been sampled according to where they were staying and that the actual distribution of this variable closely approximated that of the previous year. Properties had been classified in declining order by price and degree of comfort as shown in Table 2.

When Chi-square tests were subsequently carried out over all nine cultural items, it was established that for five of them knowledge was *inversely* and significantly associated with type of visitor accommodation, as in Table 3. In other words, the lower the category patronized, the greater the cultural knowledge displayed.

Now if category of accommodation is simply interpreted as a function of income, a similar association with cultural knowledge should have been reflected in the related variables of occupation and education. The fact that the latter *failed* to register significant relationships therefore suggests an alternative hypothesis, namely that those frequenting more moderately priced establishments did so out of preference, more specifically since typically they were smaller non-enclave properties located closer to the destination people. This choice in turn may have led to greater interaction between host and guest, resulting in enhanced knowledge of the majority of local cultural items.

Finally, two other sets of variables were inspected. One related to the sources of information about the island, the other to predominant type of motivation.

Returning to the 37 most knowledgeable respondents, it was observed that here there was above average reliance on four sources of information:

- articles written in newspapers and magazines, travelogues, etc.
- residents of the island
- persons who had previously visited the island and
- home-based special interest groups.

In other instances (i.e., books, electronic media features, print/audio-visual advertisements, brochures, travel agents and industry personnel, professional contacts and former residents) there were no noticeable differences

TABLE 2. The Visitor Sample According to Category of Accommodation

Category	Description	Frequency	Percent
A	Luxury hotels with restaurants	156	29.1
B	First class hotels and apartment hotels with self-catering facilities	125	23.4
C	Second class hotels and apartment hotels	123	23.0
D	Third class hotels and guest houses	131*	24.5
ALL		535	100.0

* includes 15 individuals staying in private homes

TABLE 3. Significant Inverse Relationships Between Cultural Items and Category of Accommodation

Cultural Item	Chi-Squared	d.f.	Probability
Rum Shop	19.3	3	0.001
Cou Cou	37.2	3	0.001
Tuk Band	12.9	3	0.020
Chupse	33.7	3	0.001
De Higher de Monkey climb de More 'e Show 'e Tail	9.6	3	0.050

between the most knowledgeable individuals and the remainder of the sample. The most knowledgeable thus resembled Tourism Canada's (1987) "culture and nature" segment to the extent that they relied on the printed word. They differed, however, with respect to the importance attached to "word of mouth." Here the Barbados sample placed far greater emphasis on this factor, and it was this difference (particularly as it applied to local residents as a source of information) which arguably led to their enhanced cultural knowledge.

As regards type of motivation, there was only one noteworthy variation between the 37 individuals and the others. The overall mean ranking of motives in declining importance is given in Table 4. However, in the case of the most knowledgeable tourists, the fourth and fifth motives were reversed, i.e., to learn more about another country had increased in relative importance. The difference, though slight, nevertheless emphasizes the greater significance attached to the educational motive allocentric travelers, and serves to illustrate that those who wish a learning experience will see to it that their goal is accomplished in terms of acquiring cultural knowledge.

DISCUSSION

In a paper which describes tourism in terms of "sun, sex, sights, savings and servility," Crick (1989: 331) observes that:

> The tourist-local relationship is odd in many ways. One member is at play, one is at work; one has economic assets and little cultural knowledge, the other has cultural capital but little money.

TABLE 4. Ranking of Travel Motives by Visitors to Barbados

Motive	Rank
To relax/unwind	1
Enjoyment	2
Escape from daily routine	3
To get away from bad weather at home	4
To learn something about another country	5
To experience something completely different	6
To meet a new set of people	7
To be able to tell friends about the experience	8
Health reasons	9
Self-discovery	10

Tourists are therefore "out of culture"–they do not belong to the destination community since they have stepped out of the ordinary and into the ludic and liminoid realm (Crick, 1989 : 332). According to Crick (1989: 328) it thus follows that "tourism is about our culture, rather than their culture," and that very few tourists are genuinely concerned with the life of the destination people they purport to visit.

Teas (1988: 39) reaches a similar conclusion when she notes that:

> If the goal of travel is to experience other cultures, travelers choose to buffer themselves with western comforts and conversation, so that the travel experience becomes a visual one.

Bruner (1991) makes the additional point that, although tourist advertising declares that western travelers bound for Third World destinations will return refreshed and renewed–as transformed persons–the reality of the situation is that they are relatively unchanged. Instead, the primitive and untouched cultures which they visit become drastically and adversely affected.

When the foregoing picture of self-indulgent tourists having scant regard for local culture (English, 1986) is combined with the observation that there is very little scientific evidence about the active and passive processes for learning about different peoples with a view to mutual understanding through tourism (Taylor, 1988: 58), it is clear that much of the discourse about the superficiality of the tourist is at the level of description or assertion.

The present study has attempted to remedy the situation to the extent that knowledge of destination culture was tested in relation to a number of visitor profile and other variables. In the event, it was discovered that such knowledge was generally quite low, and that it became increasingly limited the more specific it was to the visited culture. However, the very fact that some knowledge was present, and the realization that it varied in degree and depth, does not permit the 'carte blanche' description of the tourist as a mindless nitwit (Boorstin, 1964). Nor can one accept the position adopted by MacCannell (1976) that somehow all tourists are engaged in a sacred quest for identity in the other. Indeed this motive for travel appeared last in the rankings (cf. Table 4).

Instead, Cohen's (1979, 1982, 1988) view appears to gather more support from this investigation. Certainly the majority of these tourists fell into his recreational and diversionary modes. Yet there were some, albeit a minority, who gained from intercultural contact with the host society. It was found, for instance, that age, cultural background, repeater status, sources of information, motivation and category of accommodation had some part to play in opening a certain type of visitor to cultural awareness of the way of life of the destination people. In particular, the last of these variables–choice of accommodation–was seen as being more than simply an indicator of discretionary income, education or occupation. Rather, the physical proximity of the establishment to the host community and the greater approximation of its facilities to those of the residential population were seen as being more conductive to tourist-local interaction than the enclave five-star property. As a predisposition to so-called "alternative tourism" (Dann, 1992), this in turn could lead to a matching of the educational motive for travel with enhanced knowledge about indigenous culture.

CONCLUSION AND RECOMMENDATIONS

Given that only a minority of tourists visiting Barbados approached the experiential, experimental and existential end of Cohen's (1979) continuum, while the majority was clearly in the modes of mass tourism, what are the implications for the local travel industry? Should business just proceed as usual in an 'ad hoc' fashion, hoping to attract more and more visitors regardless of quality and effects, without any ulterior investigation into policy, promotion and research?

The findings of the Tourism Canada (1987) study suggest that far greater attention than hitherto paid needs to be concentrated in the area of market segmentation and psychographics (Lawson, 1991; Mayo and Jarvis, 1981; Plog, 1972; 1987). Admittedly its profile of "enthusiastic independents" disposed to "culture and nature" tourism differed in many respects from the Barbados bound minority of the culturally knowledgeable, yet the size of the two segments was quite similar. However, the truth of the matter is that relatively little has been done in Barbados to identify key market segments, in spite of the appearance of all-inclusive hotels and the emergence of such specific cultural packages as heritage tourism and sports tourism. Instead of placing the accent on an analysis of demand, the emphasis has instead been focused on supply, in the rather illusory hope that demand will take care of itself. Hence, in the absence of an adequate data base, the local Board of Tourism has attempted to market entire countries–the United States, Canada and Great Britain for instance–without apparently realizing that nationality itself is often an inadequate predictor variable, and that attitudes and behavior of specific market segments rarely coincide with national boundaries (cf. Dann, forthcoming).

As to enhancing cultural awareness among visitors, several strategies can be employed to ensure that greater numbers of international travelers know more about the destinations they visit. When studies such as this have been cumulatively conducted to reveal significant cultural gaps, adequate steps can be taken to fill them. In-flight educational videos, for instance, can be shown, which do more than simply portray local people in stereotypical roles and as fantasy stage props to the sun, sand and hotel, revealing them instead in the typicality of their everyday lives. Short pre-trip courses can also be run at community colleges, universities, consulates and embassies, featuring illustrated talks and opportunities for questioning citizens or former residents of the destination area. Travel agents and industry personnel on familiarization visits can see to it that they come back equipped with more than just a list of hotels and restaurants or a mere smattering of local culture, and instead become true culture brokers, instilling enthusiasm in their clients from what they have authentically experienced. The possibilities are seemingly endless, and, with a little imagination, could easily extend to compilers of documentaries and brochures, to tour operators and couriers, in fact to all who come into direct or indirect contact with international travels.

Yet throughout this growing process, the focus must surely be on a genuine and non-superficial knowledge which is imparted to the potential tourist (the pleasure seeking as well as the culture oriented). After all, clients are becoming ever discerning, and, sooner or later, they are going to appreciate that: "de higher de monkey climb, de more 'e show 'e tail."

REFERENCES

Allsopp, R. 1950. The Language We Speak. Kyck-over-al, October.

Boorstin, D. 1964. The Image: A Guide to Pseudo Events in American. New York: Harper & Row.

Brathwaite, F. 1991. Socio-Cultural Impacts of Tourism in Barbados. Port of Spain; UN-ECLAC.

Britton, R. 1980. Let Us Handle Everything. The Travel Industry and the Manipulation of the Travel Experience. USA Today: 45-47.

Bruner, E. 1991. Transformation of Self in Tourism. Annals of Tourism Research, 18: 238-250.

Cohen, E. 1972. Toward a Sociology of International Tourism. Social Research 39: 64-82.

_____ 1979. A Phenomenology of Tourist Experiences. Sociology, 13: 179-201.

_____ 1982. The Pacific Islands from Utopian Myth to Consumer Product. The Disenchantment of Paradise. Cahiers du Tourisme, serie B, no. 27.

_____ 1988. Authenticity and Commoditization in Tourism. Annals of Tourism Research, 15: 371-356.

Collymore, F. 1970. Notes for a Glossary of Words and Phrases of Barbadian Dialect. 4th edn. Barbados: The National Trust.

Cozier, T. 1986. Cricket– the National Religion. Pp. 281-284 in Wilder.

Crick, M. 1989. Representations of International Tourism in the Social Sciences: Sun, Sex, Sights, Savings and Servility. Annual Review of Anthropology, 18: 307-344.

Crompton, J. 1979. Motivations for a Pleasure Vacation. Annals of Tourism Research, 6: 408-424.

Dann, G. 1981 Tourist Motivation: An Appraisal. Annals of Tourism Research 8: 187-219.

_____ 1988. The People of Tourist Brochures. Paper presented to the First Global Conference–Tourism, A Vital Force for Peace. Vancouver, October.

_____ 1992. Predisposition towards Alternative Forms of Tourism among Tourists Visiting Barbados: Some Preliminary Observations. In V. Smith and W. Eadington (eds.), Tourism Alternatives. Potentials and Problems in the Development of Tourism. Baltimore: University of Pennsylvania Press.

_____ (Forthcoming.) Limitations in the Use of 'Nationality' and 'Country of Residence' Variables. c. 6 in D. Pearce and R. Butler (eds.), Tourism Research: Critiques and Challenges. London: Routledge.

Dogan, H. 1989. Forms of Adjustment: Socio-Cultural Impacts of Tourism Research, 16: 216-236.

English, E. 1986. The Great Escape: An Examination of North-South Tourism. Ottawa: North-South Institute.

Forde, A. 1986. Words of Wisdom: 40 Bajan Proverbs. Pp. 256-257 in Wilder.

Fowler, H. & F. Fowler (eds.). 1959. The Concise Oxford Dictionary of Current English. Oxford: Clarendon Press.

Fussell, P. 1980. Abroad. British Literary Traveling between the Mars. New York: Oxford University Press.

Geertz, C. 1973. The Interpretation of Cultures. New York: Basic Books.

Harrigan, N. 1974. The Legacy of Caribbean History and Tourism. Annals of Tourism Research 2: 13-25.

Lawson, R. 1991. What is Psychographic Segmentation? Pp. 445-455 in R. Bratton, F. Go and J. Ritchie (eds.), New Horizons in Tourism and Hospitality Education, Training and Research. Calgary: World Tourism Education and Research Centre, University of Calgary.

Lundberg, D. 1972. The Tourist Business. Chicago: Institutions/Volume Feeding Magazine.

MacCannell, D. 1976. The Tourist. A New Theory of the Leisure Class. New York: Schocken.

Marshall, T. 1986a. Bajans Come Back to Calypso. Pp. 235-241 in Wilder.

_____ 1986b. A Very Sweet Thing: The Story of Rum. Pp. 278-279 in Wilder.

Mathieson, A. and G. Wall. 1982. Tourism: Economic, Physical and Social Impacts. London: Longman.

Mayo, E. and L. Jarvis. 1981. The Psychology of Leisure Travel. Boston: CBI.

Mitford, N. 1959. The Tourist. Encounter 13: 3-7.

Moeran, B. 1983. The Language of Japanese Tourism. Annals of Tourism Research, 10: 93-103.

Naipaul, V. 1969. The Middle Passage. New York: Penguin Press.

Pearce, P. 1977. The Social and Environmental Perceptions of Overseas Tourists. Unpublished D. Phil thesis, University of Oxford.

_____ 1982. Tourists and Their Hosts: Some Social and Psychological Effects of Inter-Cultural Contact. Pp. 199-221 in S. Bochner (ed.), Cultures in Contact. Oxford: Pergamon.

Perez, L. 1973-4. Aspects of Underdevelopment. Tourism in the West Indies. Science and Society, 37: 473-480.

Plog, S. 1972. Why Destination Areas Rise and Fall in Popularity. Paper presented to Southern California Chapter of Travel Research Association, October.

_____ 1987. Understanding Psychographics in Tourism Research. Pp. 203-213 in J. Ritchie and C. Goeldner (eds.), Travel, Tourism and Hospitality Research. New York: Wiley.

Pool, I. 1958. What American Travelers Learn. Antioch Review, 18 (4): 431-446.

Potter, R. and G. Dann. 1987. World Bibliographic Series, no 76–Barbados. Oxford: Clio Press.

Ritchie, J. and M. Zins. 1978. Culture as a Determinant of the Attractiveness of a Tourism Region. Annals of Tourism Research, 5: 252-267.

Rivers P. 1972. The Restless Generation: A Crisis in Mobility. London: Davis-Poynter.

Roden, C. 1979. A Book of Middle Eastern Food. Harmondsworth: Penguin.

Sethna, R. 1980. Social Impact of Tourism in Selected Caribbean Countries. Tourism Planning and Development Issues. Washington DC: George Washington University.

Smith H. 1955. Do Intercultural Experiences Affect Attitudes? Journal of Abnormal and Social Psychology, 51 (3): 469-477.

Smith, V. 1989. Introduction. Pp. 1-17 in V. Smith (ed.), Hosts and Guests: The Anthropology of Tourism. 2nd edn. Philadelphia: University of Pennsylvania Press.

Springer, R. 1983. Caribbean Cookbook. London: Pan Books. 1986. The Land of Flying Fish and Cou Cou. Pp. 271-272 in Wilder.

Taylor, G. 1988. Understanding Through Tourism. Pp. 58-60 in L. D'Amore and J. Jafari (eds.), Tourism–A Vital Force for Peace. Montreal: L. D'Amore Associates.

Teas, J. 1988. I'm Studying Monkeys. What Do You Do? Youth and Travel in Nepal. Pp. 35-41 in N. Graburn (ed.), Kroeber Anthropological Society Papers, nos 67-68. Berkeley: Department of Anthropology, University of California.

Tourism Canada. 1987. Pleasure Travel Markets to North America. Ottawa: Tourism Canada.

Triandis, H. and V. Vassiliou. 1967. Frequency of Contact and Stereotyping. Journal of Personality and Social Psychology, 7: 316-328.

Turner, L. and J. Ash. 1975. The Golden Hordes: International Tourism and the Pleasure Periphery. London: Constable.

Van den Berghe, P. 1980. Tourism as Ethnic Relations: A Case Study of Cuzco, Peru. Ethnic and Racial Studies, 3(4): 377-391.

Wilder, R. (ed.). 1986. Insight Guides–Barbados. Singapore: APA Productions.

Wood, B. 1973. Caribbean Fruits and Vegetables. London: Longman.

Wood, R. 1984. Ethnic Tourism, the State and Cultural Change in Southeast Asia. Annals of Tourism Research 11: 353-374.

Wright, J. 1989. The Toured: The Cultural Impact of Tourism in Barbados. Unpublished MA thesis, University of Southern California.

Ziokolwska, E. 1989. Folk Culture and Ethnographic Tourism. Problems of Tourism, XII (3): 41-49.

Long-Term Impact of a Mega-Event on International Tourism to the Host Country: A Conceptual Model and the Case of the 1988 Seoul Olympics

Yong-Soon Kang
Richard Perdue

SUMMARY. The purposes of this study are to present a conceptual framework for identifying and understanding the long-term impacts of a mega-event on international travel to the host country and to apply a component of that conceptual framework in an analysis of international visitation to Korea as a result of the 1988 Summer Olympic Games. Study results indicate (1) mega-events do have a long-term impact on the international tourism to the host country; (2) that impact is greatest in the year following the event and diminishes over time; and (3) in the case of Korea, the value of the benefit realized in a three-year period is estimated to be $1.3 billion.

Yong-Soon Kang is a member of the Doctoral Program in Marketing, and Richard Perdue is Professor of Tourism Management, both at the College of Business and Administration, University of Colorado at Boulder, CO 80309-0419.

The authors wish to acknowledge the cooperation of Korea National Tourism Corporation in obtaining data for this study; special thanks go to Mr. Jegal Sang-Ho and Mr. Kwon Yong-Jip. The authors would also like to thank the Editor of this volume, Muzaffer Uysal, and two anonymous reviewers for their valuable assistance with this article.

[Haworth co-indexing entry note]: "Long-Term Impact of a Mega-Event on International Tourism to the Host Country: A Conceptual Model and the Case of the 1988 Seoul Olympics." Kang, Yong-Soon, and Richard Perdue. Co-published simultaneously in *Journal of International Consumer Marketing* (The Haworth Press, Inc.) Vol. 6, No. 3/4, 1994, pp. 205-225; and: *Global Tourist Behavior* (ed: Muzaffer Uysal) The Haworth Press, Inc., 1994, pp. 205-225. Multiple copies of this article/chapter may be purchased from The Haworth Document Delivery Center [1-800-3-HAWORTH; 9:00 a.m. - 5:00 p.m. (EST)].

INTRODUCTION

Although the definition of a "mega-event" is still unclear (Jafari, 1988), researchers began to use the term over the last decade as a "mega" version of a "hallmark event" which has been defined as a "Major one-time or recurring event of limited duration, developed primarily to enhance the awareness, appeal, and profitability of a tourism destination in the short and/or long term" (Ritchie, 1984, 2). In addition, mega-events also include international events that are not necessarily "developed primarily" for tourism purposes but can "serve" to promote a destination. Thus, a parsimonious definition of a mega-event is "an event with (1) a large number of participants or visitors and (2) worldwide publicity" (Socher & Tschurtschenthaler, 1987, 103).

Hosting a mega-event requires a large financial commitment from the host country or committee. For example, the budget for Seoul Olympic Organizing Committee was U.S. $900 million while total Olympics-related spending by Korea has been estimated at $3.1 billion (McBeth, 1988). Further, these budget figures may not include all of the related infrastructure investments. Spain, the host of the 1992 Summer Olympics, the Seville World's Fair, and a 500-year celebration of Columbus's voyage to the New World has invested $23 billion in railway and other infrastructure improvements (Morais, 1988).

What are the justifications for these expenditures? One frequently cited benefit of hosting such events is the potential improvement in awareness and image of the hosting city or country as an international tourism destination (e.g., Ahn, 1987; Hall, 1987; Pyo, Cook & Howell, 1988; Ritchie, 1984; Ritchie & Smith, 1991; Sparrow, 1989). However, little is known about the effects of mega-events on international tourism, particularly over the long-term. For example, beyond the immediate participation effects, does a mega-event affect long-term tourism to the host country? And, if yes, how is that effect manifested? Answers to these two questions can be used both to improve the cost benefit analysis of potential mega-events and to enhance the tourism effects of a mega-event.

The purposes of this study were (1) to develop a conceptual framework to identify and understand the long-term impacts of a mega-event on international travel to the host country, and (2) to apply a component of that conceptual framework in an analysis of international visitation to Korea as a result of the 1988 Summer Olympic Games.

MEGA-EVENTS AND INTERNATIONAL TRAVEL FLOWS

Impact of the Olympic Games on Tourism

Although mega-events are frequently and often extravagantly covered by mass media, only a limited number of studies on the impact of mega-events have been published in academic journals (Goeldner & Long, 1987). Of the two Olympic Games held in 1988, only the impacts of the Winter Games in Calgary have been relatively well documented due mainly to the continued efforts of one researcher. Ritchie, in a series of research works has chronicled and analyzed the impact of the Olympics on host region awareness and resident attitudes and reactions over a five-year study period (e.g., Ritchie & Aitkin 1984; Ritchie & Lyons, 1990; Ritchie & Smith, 1991).

In contrast, assessments of the tourism impacts of the Seoul Summer Olympics are limited, especially in the Western literature. Ahn (1987) provides an extensive list of possible impacts, but relatively little data. Additionally, a Korean journal, *Study on Tourism*, carried three articles on the impact of the Seoul Olympics during the 1987-1991 period. One of these articles was on Olympic visitor perceptions of Korea (Ahn, Var & Kim, 1989). The second article, on Korean resident perceptions and evaluations of the Olympics, found that many residents strongly believed that the Korean government and tourism industry overspent both in promoting the Olympics and in tourism infrastructure developments (Kim, 1989). In the third article, Hyun (1990) attempted to measure the magnitude of the Olympic's impact on inbound tourism to Korea. By using a simple regression of annual time-series data, Hyun estimated the probable number of visitors to Korea in 1988 if the Olympic Games were not held. He then calculated the impact of the Olympics by subtracting the trend figure (1.70 million) from the actual arrival figure (2.34 million). In reality, the number of visitors to Korea had been increasing for eight consecutive years reaching 1.87 million in 1987 (Ministry of Transportation and Korea National Tourism Corporation [MOT & KNTC], 1987). Hyun's study is valuable in that it is the only known attempt to statistically estimate the impact of the Seoul Olympics on international tourism. However, Witt (1989, 169) suggests such univariate time-series forecasting methods lack theoretical foundation.

Long-Term Impact on Tourism. In this paper, "short-term" refers to a period that includes immediately before, during, and after the event (e.g., a two-month period surrounding the two-week-long Olympics) during which international tourism statistics are directly influenced by event participation; "long-term" is defined as the periods before and after the "short-term," beginning with announcement of the mega-event and end-ing at some point in the future yet to be determined.

In 1974, Ritchie and Beliveau (1974, 19) stated that "until a systematic analysis of the long-run impact of such events is reported, all investments in hallmark events must be conservatively treated as short-term ex-penses." Since then, the long-term aspects of a mega-event's impact on tourism have frequently been mentioned, but research has continued to focus on short-term impacts.

Witt and Martin (1987) reviewed five econometric studies of tourism de-mand which included a mega-event variable. Those studies identified and esti-mated three types of mega-event impacts on international tourism: (1) de-crease in outward tourism from the mega-event host country, (2) increase in inward tourism to the host country, and (3) either increase in inward tourism (by joint tours) or decrease in inward tourism (by substitution) to the destinations adjacent to the host country. However, none of those articles estimated the long-term effects of a mega-event on international tourism.

Two recent works provide some clues about the long-term tourism effects of a mega-event. Sparrow (1989, 256-257) suggested two alterna-tive scenarios regarding the duration of the impact, a short-term scenario characterized by "a quick return to normalcy" and a long-term scenario which creates "a new plateau for tourism growth." Ritchie and Smith (1991) report results from a longitudinal survey on international aware-ness of Calgary; the results indicate that awareness of Calgary increased rapidly prior to the Games then has decreased gradually over the period of time following the Games.

A Conceptual Framework

The conceptual framework presented in Figure 1 attempts to capture the essential linkages by which a mega-event may produce long-term impacts on international travel to the host country. The initial/direct effects of hosting a mega-event include (1) increased mass media coverage in the world community, (2) improvements and expansion of tourism infrastruc-ture and tourism services, (3) possible increase in tourism promotional activities by the host tourism industry to capitalize on a favorable market-ing environment, and (4) an influx of participants and tourists during the event period.

Mass Media, Awareness, and Image. By definition, a mega-event is characterized by its magnitude of participation and worldwide publicity. Publicity of an Olympic Games begins far in advance and reaches its apex during the Games period; for example, sites for the 1988 Olympic Games

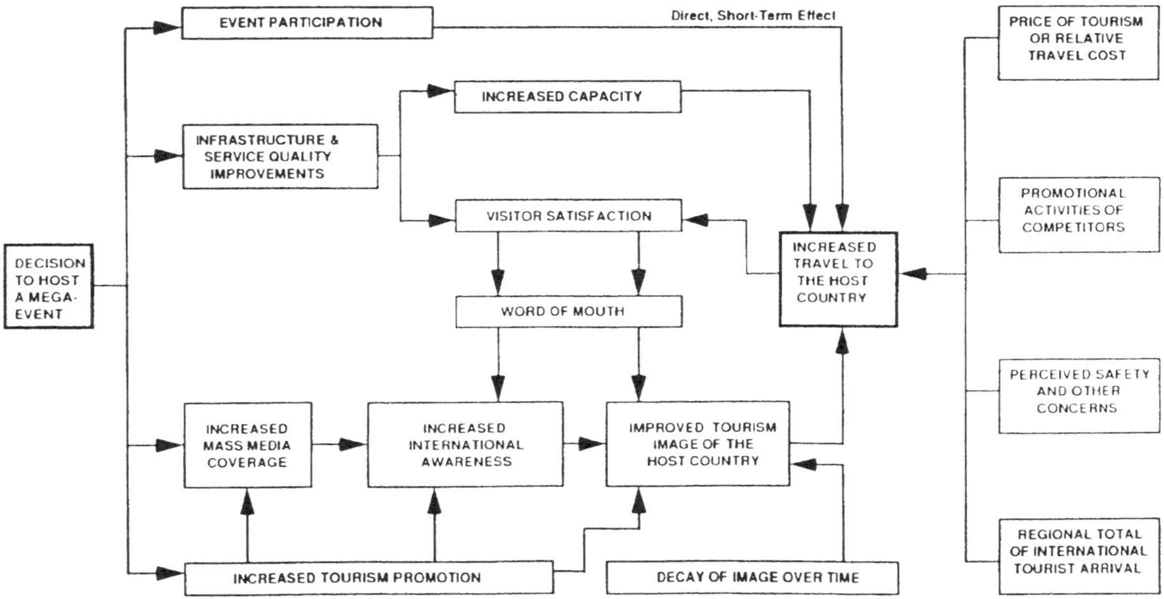

FIGURE 1. Impact of a Mega-Event on International Tourism: A Conceptual Framework

were decided on September 30, 1981 with international publicity. Further-more, "The pre-event printed media build up sometimes even appears greater than the event itself. . . . television brings the event almost better to the non-ticket holders many miles away" (Hiller, 1989, 120). The exten-sive media coverage translates into a higher level of awareness of the host city or the country; furthermore, if the media coverage of the host country is favorable–which is true in most cases–the worldwide publicity should result in a renewed, stronger, and better image of the host city and country.

Event Participation. Hiller (1989) reports that 36,000 non-Canadians visited Calgary during the two-week Winter Games period and millions of people came to Vancouver over the five-month World Expo period. Given the "mega" attractive power of the event, the number of foreign partici-pants during the event period varies depending mainly on the duration of event and the capacity–accommodations and transportation–of the host region. The immediate effect of a mega-event on international tourism to the host country, therefore, may or may not be significant.

Infrastructure and Service Improvements. A mega-event necessitates "mega" facilities. Typically, commercial accommodation and public transportation facilities–prerequisites to the future tourism growth–are re-furbished and expanded during the event preparation, providing both nec-essary facilities for the event and an opportunity to improve the quality of future tourism services.

Visitor Satisfaction and Word-of-Mouth. Sparrow (1989) suggests that resident support of mega-events enhances the quality of experience for mega-event participants. Further, the improved tourism services and facili-ties resulting from mega-event development will enhance the visitor satis-faction in the ensuing periods. The word-of-mouth communications stem-ming from this enhanced visitor satisfaction are essential to the long-term international tourism impact of the mega-event.

Image Decay and Promotional Activities. As shown by Ritchie and Smith (1991), the positive image and awareness of the host community, resulting from the mega-event promotion, publicity, and word-of-mouth communications, will decay over time. However, the host country's tour-ism industry, especially the government tourist board, may counter this image decay by intensifying its promotional activities.

Prices and the Final Outcome. Directly or indirectly the various factors outlined above are consequences of hosting a mega-event; all of them, except for the decay of image, potentially contribute to a long-term in-crease in the international tourism to the host country. However, these effects do not occur in a vacuum. External factors, particularly those related to the actions of competitors and overall cycles in international tourism, also affect visitation to mega-event host countries. First, economic theory postulates that demand for a destination is a function of price, specifically vis-à-vis the price of visiting alternative destinations (Yarbrough & Yarbrough, 1991). Second, the promotional efforts of competitors may also influence international tourism patterns (Baile, 1989). Third, safety concerns may also have a impact on international tourism; for instance, the dramatic 23 percent decrease in U.S. citizen travel to Europe in 1986 was largely due to the "threat of terrorist activities" (U.S. Travel Data Center [USTDC], 1987, 48-49).[1]

Finally, since international tourism in general and travel to Asia in particular has been increasing steadily (e.g., Waters, various years), the impact of a mega-event should be measured on a relative basis, i.e., market share. Thus, the key issue is determining how well the host country's tourism performs vis-à-vis its competition after controlling to whatever extent possible the effects of price and other factors.

THE CASE OF THE 1988 SEOUL OLYMPIC GAMES

Event Participation: Short-Term Impact

Ahn et al. (1989) report that 240,000 foreign visitors attended the Seoul Olympic Games. However, this figure does not reflect the short-term effects of the Games on inbound tourism to Korea. The Olympic Games period (September 17-October 2) fell within the peak season of Korean tourism. Olympic visitors may have "crowded out" or replaced a large number of potential tourists who would have otherwise visited Korea during the event period. Furthermore, an important negative aspect of mega-events is the potential short-term increase in travel prices, particularly for accommodations (Hall, 1989; Pyo, Cook & Howell, 1988), which may have discouraged some non-event tourists from visiting Korea.

The short-term incremental visitation to Korea due to the Olympics was estimated in two ways. An estimate was obtained by first calculating the average proportion of annual visitation occurring during September and October of the previous five years (i.e., 1983-1987), then an "expected" number of visitors during the two months of 1988 was estimated by multiplying that average proportion by the total visitation of the year. Incremental visitation was then estimated by subtracting the actual number of visitors during those months of 1988 from the "expected" number. An alternative estimate was obtained by subtracting the average number of visitors during September and October of the adjacent years (i.e., 1987 and

1989) from the actual arrival figure during those months of 1988. Using these procedures the net incremental impact of the Olympics on tourism during the two months of 1988 was between 39,000 (first procedure) and 55,000 visitors (second procedure) or approximately 47,000 visitors.

Promotion and Publicity of Korean Tourism

Korea National Tourism Corporation (KNTC), the government tourist office of the Republic of Korea, steadily increased its overseas marketing budget during the 1980s even after adjusting for inflation; however, there is not a noticeable discrete increase in promotional spending before or during the Olympics[2] (Figure 2). Although this increased promotional spending may have increased visitation to Korea, its effect on Korea's market share cannot be identified without comparable data from competing destinations and some measure of effectiveness of spending across the tourist boards.

Figure 2 also shows the annual number of mass media articles pertaining to Korean tourism which appeared in the U.S.A. and Europe as compiled by KNTC's overseas offices and their hired clipping services. The number increased gradually until 1986, doubled in 1987, and continued to grow after the Olympics, particularly during 1990.

Awareness of Seoul, Korea as an Olympic Site

No direct measure of the longitudinal changes in the image of Korea has been conducted. However, Ritchie and Smith (1991) report four-year (1986-1989) longitudinal data on awareness levels in Europe and the U.S. of 10 Olympic host cities including Seoul. Since their study included both past and future host cities, it is possible to reorganize their findings as if the survey were conducted for a single site over a 19-year period[3] (Figure 3).

The only departure from an otherwise consistent pattern in Summer Olympics host city awareness is the case of Moscow. The 1980 Summer Olympic boycott by the U.S. and its allies dramatically reduced international public interest in the Moscow Games, with observed impact on destination awareness. Still, these results show both the increase in international awareness prior to the Olympic Games and the following awareness decay.

Other Factors

In preparing for the Olympics, Korea dramatically expanded its tourism infrastructure. For instance, the annual growth rate in the total number of

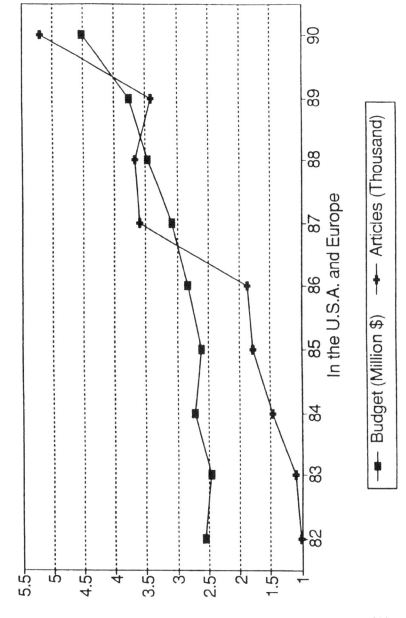

FIGURE 2. Korea's Promotional Budget and Publicity

In the U.S.A. and Europe

— ■ — Budget (Million $)   — ◆ — Articles (Thousand)

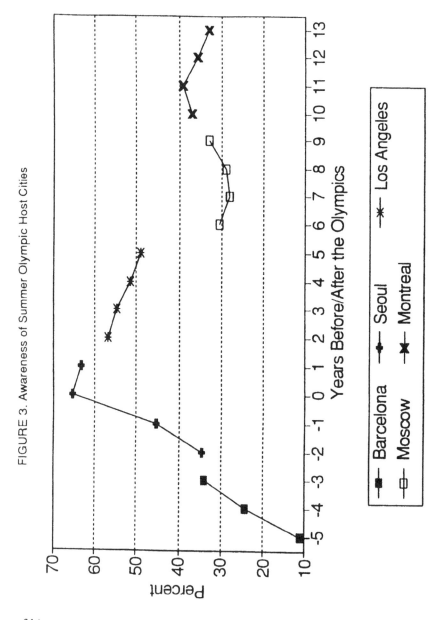

FIGURE 3. Awareness of Summer Olympic Host Cities

214

rooms at registered "tourist hotels" for 1987 and 1988 was 10.8 percent and 20.8 percent, respectively, while the averaged growth rate for the preceding seven years (1980-1986) was 4.6 percent (MOT & KNTC, 1990).

Visitor satisfaction during the Olympic period was high. Based on a survey of the Olympic visitors conducted immediately before visitor departures, Ahn et al. concluded, "Most foreign tourists perceive Korea as a positive and favorable travel destination" (1989, 118). Except for some potentially negative publicity about safety issues (e.g., Wadden & Pardau, 1988) which may have affected short-term tourism during the Olympic year, the available data on the Seoul Olympics generally supports the model presented in Figure 1.

STATISTICAL ANALYSIS

In addition to the preceding analyses, the long-term impact of the Seoul Olympics on international visitation to Korea was statistically estimated with regional market share as the dependent variable and travel price and the mega-event as independent variables.

Data and Models

To measure and compare the relative performance (i.e., regional market share) of tourist destinations, it is necessary to define a set of competing destinations. For this analysis, Japan, Taiwan, Hong Kong, and Thailand were defined as the primary competitors of Korea[4] resulting in a five-country comparison. Four destinations including Korea are in Northeast Asia whereas Thailand is a Southeast Asian country. Thailand was included for two reasons. First it staged a very successful "Visit Thailand Year 1987" (Economist Intelligence Unit, 1988), allowing an opportunity to examine the effect of another mega-event. Among Southeast Asian destinations Thailand draws the largest number of international tourists. Southeast Asia is the closest competitor of Northeast Asia on an interregional basis. Thus, the inclusion of Thailand allows an opportunity to assess the levels of interregional competition. Japan, Taiwan, and Hong Kong have not staged any event that approaches a "mega" size during the period included in this study.

Market Share. Annual international visitor arrival totals for the period 1980 through 1990 were obtained for each country using the annual statistical reports from World Tourism Organization (WTO) and Pacific Asia

Travel Association (PATA). Regional market share for each country was obtained by dividing the number of visitors to the destination by the total numbers of visitors to the five destinations. In 1988, for example, the number of visitors to Korea was 2.34 million while the total of the five countries (including Korea) was 17.52 million; Korea's market share was 13.36 percent.

Price of Tourism. The price measures of tourism to the five destinations were established using the dollar amounts set by the "Maximum Travel Per Diem Allowances for Foreign Areas" (U.S. Department of State) that have been developed to audit international travel by U.S. Government civilian employees. Use of these price data eliminated the tedious and fallible process of combining the exchange rates and domestic travel price information for all countries. The adequacy of adopting the travel allowance as the price measure may be inferred from the following excerpt:

> The travel per diem allowance is intended to substantially cover the cost of lodging and meals at adequate, suitable and moderately-priced facilities including costs for mandatory service charges, tips, taxes and related incidentals such as laundry and dry cleaning. (U.S. State Department, June 1990)

Since the rate is revised monthly, the mid-year rate for the capital city of each country was used.[5] The relative price of travel to each country was a percentage coefficient calculated by dividing its own price by the average price of the other four countries. In 1988, for instance, price of Korean tourism (Per Diem Allowance) was U.S. $144.00 while the average price of the four alternative countries (excluding Korea) was $178.00; therefore, Korea's relative price was $80.90 in that year.

Alternative Approach: Four-Country Model. In addition to the above procedure involving five countries (five-country model), an alternative model that includes only the four Northeast Asian countries was developed to assess the effect of inclusion or exclusion of Thailand. The procedures used for this four-country model were analogous to the five-country model; for instance, total visitation to the four countries, instead of five, was used in calculating the market share.

Mega-Event Factor: Olympic Impact Curve

A hypothetical "Olympic impact curve" which represents the expected longitudinal impact of the mega-event was derived from Ritchie and Smith's (1991) Summer Olympic host city awareness data presented in Figure 3. Since awareness is a necessary condition for any impact, the longitudinal impact size would be proportional to the awareness level (Figure 4).

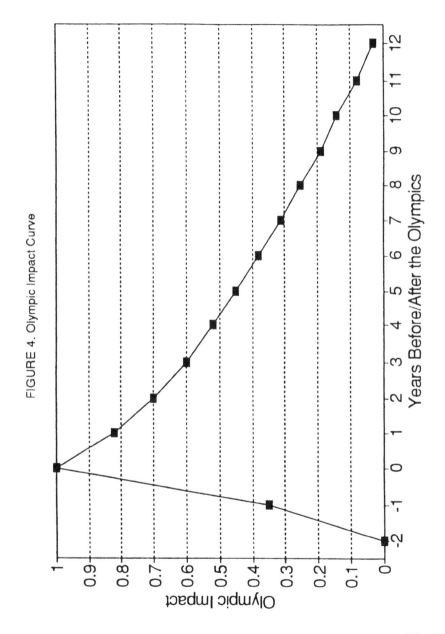

FIGURE 4. Olympic Impact Curve

The shape of the awareness curve was estimated using OLS regression; specifically, the declining part was estimated as a negative logarithmic function of time with a dummy variable for the boycotted Moscow Olympic.[6] Two modifications were made in converting the awareness curve into the impact curve: (1) the awareness curve was shifted out by a year, and (2) the curve below the awareness level of two years before or thirteen years after the Games was ignored. The first modification embodies the expectation of a one-year time lag between awareness and actual impact (i.e., international travel). The second modification reflects limitations imposed by the available data.

In accordance with the foregoing assumptions and procedures, the mega-event variable was given the following values: zeroes (0s) for the years before the event, 0.35 for the event year, 1.00 for the next year, 0.82 for the second year, 0.70 for the third year, and so forth.

Statistical Procedures

To take advantage of higher degrees of freedom, data from multiple countries were "pooled" together to test the overall adequacy of the selected independent variables (relative price and event) in explaining the behavior of the dependent variable (regional market share). Two pooled regressions–a simple regression model with relative price as the independent variable and a multiple regression model with the relative price and the event variable as independent variables–were run on the five-country pooled data (n = 55) and the four-country pooled data (n = 44) respectively. The estimation was conducted by using the "pooled cross-section time-series" procedure available in the *Shazam Econometrics Computer Program* (White et al., 1990). Kmenta's (1986, 618-622) "cross-sectionally heteroskedastic and time-wise autoregressive model" was used with a modification that allowed the researchers to keep the first observation of each cross-section. In pooling the data, the event variable for non-event countries was defined as zero.

Additionally, two models specific to Korea were estimated using the OLS method. The expectation was that these "focused" models would better fit Korea's data than the "pooled" models although at a lower degree of freedom (n = 11).

RESULTS AND DISCUSSION

Multiple-Country Pooled Models

Table 1 summarizes the results of the regression analyses. While relative price was an important determinant of regional market share in all of

TABLE 1. Results of Statistical Analyses

Models	d.f.	Price		Event		R^2	F
		parameter estimate	t-stat	parameter estimate	t-stat		
Five-Country Pooled Models							
(1) Simple Price Model	53	−0.036	−6.69***	n/a	n/a	0.457	44.71
(2) Price-Event Model	52	−0.042	−7.37***	4.42	8.30***	0.655	49.45
Four-Country Pooled Models							
(3) Simple Price Model	42	−0.044	−4.73***	n/a	n/a	0.348	22.38
(4) Price-Event Model	41	−0.045	−5.20***	2.02	2.12**	0.438	15.98
Models for Korea							
(5) Five-Country Model	8	−0.038	−1.90*	2.12	4.29***	0.846	21.91
(6) Four-Country Model	8	−0.078	−5.21***	3.47	7.89***	0.960	94.99

Note:
• The R^2s for models (1) through (4) are "Buse's R-squared" (Kenneth et al., 1990, 85) which lie between zero and one and represent "the proportion of weighted variation in y explained by regression" (Judge et al., 1985, 32).

• Significance level of t-statistics (one-tailed test): * at alpha = .05 (95%); ** at alpha = .025 (97.5%); and *** at alpha = .005 (99.5%).

the analyses, the addition of the mega-event variable significantly improved the performance of the models, improving the R^2 coefficients from .457 to .655 in the five-country model and from .348 to .438 in the four-country model. All of the t-statistics for the regression coefficients were significant at alpha below .05 level.

Models for Korea

As noted earlier, separate models focusing on Korea were estimated. Model 5 in Table 1 is based on the market share and relative price data of Korea from the five-country pool and model 6 is based on four-country data. The Durbin-Watson test statistics for these two models were 1.778 and 2.228, respectively, indicating the absence of first-order autocorrelation. Again, in these models, relative price and the mega-event demonstrate strong relationships with Korea's market share. Individual t-statistics and model F-statistics are highly significant. The higher R^2 value of .96 from the four-country-based model 6 implies that Japan, Hong Kong and Taiwan are closer competitors/substitutes for Korea than Thailand.

Estimate of Total Impact

Both of the pooled models identify a statistically significant mega-event impact on long-term tourism. Because of its high explanatory power, model 6 was chosen to estimate the number of incremental tourists to Korea (and tourist receipts) due to the Olympics, resulting in the following equation:

$$\text{Market Share} = 23.712 - 0.0777 \text{ (Relative Price)} + 3.4662 \text{ (Event Factor)}$$

The direct impact of the 1988 Seoul Olympics is estimated at U.S $1.3 billion in additional tourist receipts or one million additional visitors between 1988 and 1990 (Table 2).

Two simplifying assumptions were made to extend the estimate of total impact into future years: total inbound tourism to Northeast Asia will grow constantly, and per capita tourist spending in Korea will grow at the same rate at which future revenue is discounted.[7] Incremental tourist receipts for the eleven additional years (from 1991 till 2001) is U.S. $2.6 billion, resulting in an estimated total tourism benefit from the Olympics of approximately $3.8 billion.

TABLE 2. Estimate of Olympic Impact on Korean Tourism

Year	(a) Increased Market Share due to the Olympic Games	(b) Regional (four country) Total of Tourist Arrival	(c) Incremental Number of International Tourist Arrival	(d) Average Tourist Receipts per Visitor	(e) Increase in Tourist Receipts due to the Games
	(percent)	(thousands)	(thousands)	(U.S. $)	(U.S. $000)
1988	1.213	12,220	148	1,395	206,460
1989	3.466	12,928	448	1,304	584,192
1990	2.842	14,062	400	1,203	481,200
Total			996		1,271,852

Note:
(a) is based on model 6 in Table 1; (b) is the total visitation of Korea, Japan, Hong Kong and Taiwan; (c) is obtained by multiplying (a) with (b); (d) is data from KNTC; and (e) is the product of (b) and (c).

CONCLUSIONS

The study presents a conceptual framework for identifying and understanding the long-term effect of a mega-event on international tourism to the host country. A portion of this framework was used to measure the magnitude of 1988 Summer Olympic Games on long-term tourism to Korea.

There are several limitations which must be considered in generalizing the findings of this study. First, the length of the time-series is limited; availability of data inhibited inclusion of the years before 1980. Further, although four years have elapsed since the Seoul Olympics, it is still premature to totally evaluate the long-term effect which may extend to a decade or more.

Second, even though this study involves five destinations, the study should be considered a case study focusing on a single region of East Asia. The five study destinations share important geographical characteristics which would not be found easily in other regions such as Europe or the Americas. Four of the destinations are either actual or political (e.g., Korea) islands, and Thailand has relatively little border traffic. Further research examining other types of settings is needed.

Third, prior to the Seoul Olympics, Korea was a less known, "emerging" country in international tourism. Thus, the Olympic impact may be greater for Korea than for an established destination such as Los Angeles, the site of 1984 Summer Olympics. Again further research in other settings is needed.

In this study, the case of the 1988 Seoul Olympics was analyzed according to a conceptual framework which posits that a long-term impact is generated primarily through improvement of facilities and services, media coverage, and word-of-mouth communication under the general price context of demand theory. Overall, the results conform to the general framework. Evidence drawn from existing research and the analyses presented in this study appear to support the following conclusions: (1) Mega-events do have a long-term impact on international tourism to the host country; (2) That impact is greatest in the year following the mega-event and diminishes over time, perhaps as long as ten years; and (3) In the case of Korea, the value of such impact over the three years (1988-1990) was estimated to be U.S. $1.3 billion.

Additionally, two generalizations concerning international tourism behavior are derived from the foregoing analyses. First, consumer reaction to a mega-event is lagged and protracted. Although the amount of media coverage and consumer awareness of host destinations increase sharply during the preceding years, it is only during and after the event year that visitation increases significantly. The one-year lag identified in this study implies that consumers need a preparation period following media publicity for future vacation scheduling.

Second, the strong price-market share relationships identified in this study indicate that international tourism is price sensitive in the aggregate. A mega-event and its related media publicity alters the price-share relationship, in effect shifting the demand curve for the host country.

NOTES

1. The quick recovery of European travel in the next year (USTDC, 1989) suggests that such negative impact may be very short-term.

2. The annual budget figures were obtained from KNTC and include major categories of the marketing budget for the U.S. and European markets; the annual budget amounts in current dollars were adjusted for the U.S. Consumer Price Index.

3. The unweighted average awareness in the U.S. and Europe was used.

4. China and Macau were not included because of their small share of international tourism and data availability.

5. Whenever possible June rates were used. However, for 1984, 1986, and 1987 May rates were used and for 1983 August rates were used.

6. Both linear and logarithmic functions fitted the data equally well ($R^2 = .95$); however, the logarithmic function was preferred because a linear function would imply a negative level of awareness.

7. The ten-year (1981-1990) arrival trend was extrapolated using simple regression and the per capita spending of 1990 was used as the base.

REFERENCES

Ahn, Jong-yun. (1987). The Role and Impact of Mega-Events and Attractions on Tourism Development in Asia. In AIEST (Ed.), *The Role and Impact of Mega-Events and Attractions on Regional and National Tourism Development*, Vol. 28 (pp. 133-186). St-Gall, Switzerland: AIEST.

_____, Var, Turgut & Kim, Yong-kwan. (1989). An Investigation of Olympic Tourists' Perception of Korea. *Study on Tourism*, 13 (pp. 109-121). Seoul, Korea: The Korea Academic Society of Tourism.

Baile, J. Gerald. (1989). International Travel Patterns. In S. Witt & L. Moutinho (Eds.), *Tourism Marketing and Management Handbook* (pp. 231-234). New York: Prentice Hall.

Economist Intelligence Unit [EIU]. (1988). Thailand. In EIU (Ed.), *International Tourism Reports*, 3 (pp. 69-85). London, U.K.: EIU.

Goeldner, Charles R. & Long, Patrick T. (1987). The Role and Impact of Mega-

Events and Attractions on Tourism Development in North America. In AIEST (Ed.), *The Role and Impact of Mega-Events and Attractions on Regional and National Tourism Development*, Vol. 28 (pp. 119-131). St-Gall, Switzerland: AIEST.

Hall, Colin Michael. (1987). The Effects of Hallmark Events on Cities. *Journal of Travel Research*, 26 (Fall), 44-45.

_____. (1989). Hallmark Tourist Events: Analysis, Definition, Methodology and Review. In Geoffrey J. Syme et al. (Eds.), *The Planning and Evaluation of Hallmark Events* (pp. 3-19). Brookfield, VA: Avebury.

Hiller, Harry H. (1989). Impact and Image: the Convergence of Urban Factors in Preparing for the 1988 Calgary Winter Olympics. In Geoffrey J. Syme et al. (Eds.), *The Planning and Evaluation of Hallmark Events* (pp. 119-131). Brookfield, VA: Avebury.

Hyun, Jin-kwon. (1990). The Impact of 1988 Seoul International Olympics on Inbound Tourism in Korea. *Study on Tourism*, 14 (pp. 235-245). Seoul, Korea: The Korea Academic Society of Tourism.

Jafari, Jafar. (1988). Tourism Mega-Events. *Annals of Tourism Research*, 15 (2), 272-273.

Judge, G., Hill, R., Griffiths, W., Lutkepohl, H. & Lee, T. (1985). *The Theory and Practice of Econometrics* (2nd ed.). New York: John Wiley.

Kim, Joung-man. (1989). Resident Perception of the Impact of the Seoul Olympics on Korean Tourism. *Study on Tourism*, 13 (pp. 27-40). Seoul, Korea: The Korea Academic Society of Tourism. (Published in Korean.)

Kmenta, Jan. (1986). *Elements of Econometrics*. New York: Macmillan.

McBeth, John. (1988, April 7). Sporting Seoul Awaits the Five-Ring Circus. *Far Eastern Economic Review*, pp. 42-46.

Ministry of Transportation and Korea National Tourism Corporation. (Various years). *Annual Statistical Report on Tourism*, Seoul, Korea: KNTC.

Morais, Richard C. (1988, September 19). Sun, Sea and a Will to Change. *Forbes*, pp. 76-79.

Pyo, Sungsoo, Cook, Raymond & Howell, Richard L. (1988). Summer Olympic Tourist Market—Learning from the Past. *Tourism Management* (June), 137-144.

Ritchie, J. R. Brent. (1984). Assessing the Impact of Hallmark Events: Conceptual and Research Issues. *Journal of Travel Research*, 23 (Summer), 2-11.

_____ & Aitken, Catherine E. (1984). Assessing the Impacts of the 1988 Olympic Winter Games: The Research Program and Initial Results. *Journal of Travel Research*, 23 (Winter), 17-25.

_____ & Beliveau, Donald. (1974). Hallmark Events: An Evaluation of a Strategic Response to Seasonality in the Travel Market. *Journal of Travel Research*, 13 (Fall), 14-20.

_____ & Lyons, Marcia M. (1990). Olympulse VI: A Post-Event Assessment of Resident Reaction to the XV Olympic Winter Games. *Journal of Travel Research*, 30 (Winter), 14-23.

_____ & Smith, Brian H. (1991). The Impact of a Mega-Event on Host

Region Awareness: A Longitudinal Study. *Journal of Travel Research*, 30 (Summer), 3-10.

Socher, Karl and Tschurtschenthaler, Paul. (1987). The Role and Impact of Mega-Events: Economic Perspectives–The Case of the Winter Olympic Games 1964 and 1976 at Innsbruck. In AIEST (Ed.), *The Role and Impact of Mega-Events and Attractions on Regional and National Tourism Development*, Vol. 28 (pp. 103-117). St-Gall, Switzerland: AIEST.

Sparrow, Mark. (1989). A Tourism Planning Model for Hallmark Events. In Geoffrey J. Syme et al. (Eds.), *The Planning and Evaluation of Hallmark Events* (pp. 250-262). Brookfield, VA: Avebury.

U.S. Department of State, Allowances Staff, Per Diem and Temporary Lodging Section. (various years). *Maximum Travel Per Diem Allowances for Foreign Areas: Section 925*. Washington DC: Department of State.

U.S. Travel Data Center [USTDC]. (Various years.) *The Economic Review of Travel in America*. Washington DC: USTDC.

Wadden, Paul & Pardou, Stuart. (1988, July 6.) Seoul's Olympian Security Threat. *The Wall Street Journal*, p. 25.

Waters, Somerset R. (Various Years). *Travel Industry World Yearbook: The Big Picture*. New York: Child & Waters.

White, Kenneth J., Wong, S. Donna, Whisltler, Diana & Haun, Shirley A. (1990). *Shazam Econometrics Computer Program: User's Reference Manual Version 6.2*. New York: McGraw-Hill.

Witt, Stephen F. (1989). Forecasting International Tourism Demand: Univariate Time Series Methods. In S. F. Witt & L. Moutinho (Eds.), *Tourism Marketing and Management Handbook* (pp. 169-174). New York: Prentice Hall.

Witt, Stephen F. & Martin, Christine A. (1987). Measuring the Impacts of Mega-Events on Tourism Flows. In AIEST (Ed.), *The Role and Impact of Mega-Events and Attractions on Regional and National Tourism Development*, Vol. 28 (pp. 213-219). St-Gall, Switzerland: AIEST.

Yarbrough, Beth & Yarbrough, Robert. (1991). *The World Economy: Trade and Finance*, (2nd ed.). Chicago: Dryden Press.

Health Tourism:
A New Positioning Strategy
for Tourist Destinations

Jonathan N. Goodrich

SUMMARY. This article defines the novel concept of health tourism, provides a brief historical overview, reports on an exploratory study of health tourism relative to the Caribbean, and *extends* the concept by adding other dimensions of health tourism (e.g., ecotourism, travel health care service) to that originally proposed by Goodrich and Goodrich (1987). This is followed by a discussion of market segmentation and medical facilities, and suggestions for future research. Health tourism can be a new and effective positioning strategy for tourist destinations.

INTRODUCTION

In the early 1980s, the concept of health-care tourism was developed. This concept was eventually published (Goodrich and Goodrich, 1987), and spawned more research in the USA and the UK. This article reports on parts of an ongoing study of health tourism, with *emphasis* here on the Caribbean. The main purpose of the article is three-fold: (1) to provide a brief overview of the novel concept of health tourism developed by Good-

Jonathan N. Goodrich is Professor of Marketing, College of Business Administration, Florida International University, Miami, FL 33199.

[Haworth co-indexing entry note]: "Health Tourism: A New Positioning Strategy for Tourist Destinations." Goodrich, Jonathan N. Co-published simultaneously in *Journal of International Consumer Marketing* (The Haworth Press, Inc.) Vol. 6, No. 3/4, 1994, pp. 227-238; and: *Global Tourist Behavior* (ed: Muzaffer Uysal) The Haworth Press, Inc., 1994, pp. 227-238. Multiple copies of this article/chapter may be purchased from The Haworth Document Delivery Center [1-800-3-HAWORTH; 9:00 a.m. - 5:00 p.m. (EST)].

rich and Goodrich (1987); (2) to report on an exploratory study of health tourism in the Caribbean; and (3) to add other possible dimensions to the concept since its origination.

WHAT IS HEALTH TOURISM?

Health tourism is defined as the attempt on the part of a tourist facility (e.g., hotel) or destination (e.g., Baden, Switzerland or Bath, England) to attract tourists by *deliberately* promoting its health-care services and facilities, in addition to its regular tourist amenities. These health-care services may include medical examinations by qualified doctors and nurses at the resort or hotel, special diets, acupuncture, transvital injections, vitamin-complex intakes, special medical treatments for various diseases such as arthritis, and herbal remedies (see Table 1).

Based on this explanation, there are many countries with health tourism facilities, such as Switzerland, Germany, Austria, Hungary, the USA, the UK, and some Caribbean Islands (e.g., Jamaica and the Bahamas). Some cities or resorts in these countries have grown up around thermal springs and concomitant health facilities. Hollywood celebrities, statesmen, and ordinary tourists visit such resorts for rest and relaxation as well as for treatment of various ailments. The concept of health tourism has also spread to many cruise lines (e.g., Carnival, and Royal Caribbean) which now offer some of the services listed in Table 1. These services will spread as we enjoy higher incomes, devote more time to leisure/recreational activities, and seek longer, healthier lives.

BRIEF HISTORICAL PERSPECTIVE

It is said that many people in ancient times traveled to nearby rivers and mineral springs for the alleged curative properties and for relaxation. For example, we hear of such people dipping and bathing in the Nile River (the world's longest river), in the Ganges River in India, in the Yangtze River in China, and in the River Jordan in Jordan, to be cleansed physically and spiritually. Or, the ancient Romans and English visited Bath in England to bathe in the warm springs and mineral waters and drink some of the water for its supposed health benefits (Hembry, 1990). Bath became a health resort for English society in the 1700's. The Wife of Bath is a famous character in Geoffrey Chaucer's *Canterbury Tales*.

In more modern times, some people believe that bathing in the Dead

TABLE 1. Some Typical Elements of Health-Care Treatments at Some Hotels or Resorts

---

Medical examinations in the hotel (cholesterol levels, diabetes, blood pressure, etc.)

Vegetarian or special diets

Transvital injections, and vitamin-complex treatment

Daily exercise programmes

Yoga

Acupuncture

Thermal swimming pools (indoor and outdoor)

Underwater massage (balneotherapy)

Body massages

Cellulite treatments (cellutron)

Saunas

Hydrotherapy treatments

Fango packs (mud)

Special stop-smoking programmes

Various baths, e.g., eucalyptus bath, and Turkish bath

Herbal wraps, and herbal teas

Use of sun-bed under supervision

Sessions on muscle development and relaxation techniques

Beauty treatments, such as facials, cream packs, face peeling, etc.

Sea is healthful because of its high mineral content (e.g., common salt, bromine, calcium chlorine, and potassium chloride). Health benefits are said to include cures for skin problems, and arthritis. The Dead Sea is the saltiest body of water in the world, about nine times as salty as the ocean. It lies at the mouth of the River Jordan and forms part of the border between Israel and Jordan. It covers about 400 square miles, and is called the Dead Sea because few plants and no fish except brine shrimp live in its salty waters. The extremely high salt content of the water provides buoyancy, enabling people to float with ease. Several health resorts in the area provide facilities for bathers (*World Book Encyclopedia,* 1984, pp. 49-50).

In Europe, many cities have grown up around mineral springs and health spas. Examples of such cities are Baden, Lausanne, St. Moritz, and Interlaken in Switzerland; Baden-Baden and Wiesbaden in (West) Germany; Vienna, Austria; and Budapest, Hungary (Goodrich and Goodrich, 1987). People have used mineral water since ancient times to cure such ailments as rheumatism, skin infections, and poor digestion. The waters from some foreign springs are imported to the USA, usually in glass bottles. Among these waters are the Apolinaris from Germany, Hunyadi-Janos from Hungary, and Vichy from France.

Before the Revolutionary War in the United States, residents of the American colonies traveled to the many mineral springs, seaside resorts and spas much like their European counterparts. Popular sites included Yellow Springs near Philadelphia, Stafford Springs in Connecticut, and Berkeley Springs in Virginia. Like the European spas, the American spas attracted the rich and famous, including early presidents such as George Washington and John Adams. Modern spas and resorts still attract the rich and famous, but more convenient travel and accommodations have made the spas, seaside resorts, and mineral springs more accessible to the expanding population of travelers (Babcock, 1983). The health claims of these spas and resorts–some perhaps exaggerated–are also more in line with the trim and fit consciousness of our society.

The popularity of many of the mineral springs in the USA has declined since the turn of the century, and many have gone out of business. The best known mineral springs today are at Saratoga Springs, New York; Hot Springs, Arkansas; and French Lick, Indiana. Hot Springs has been made a national park.

In the Caribbean Islands, the local people, as well as tourists, regularly enjoy sea-bathing as a healthy activity, especially on weekends. Many islands, such as Cuba, Jamaica, St. Lucia, and the Bahamas, also have mineral springs and health resort facilities, such as the Silver Reef Health Spa in the Grand Bahama Island, and Doctor's Cave Beach in Jamaica.

Cruise lines and hotels all over the world (e.g., in the Caribbean and Europe) have special fitness and wellness seminars and programs in addition to their regular spas, pools, and exercise gyms. Retail sales of home gyms have increased in the last five years as people seek the convenience of exercise at home, and more people than a decade ago visit commercial gyms regularly for workouts with weights, and aerobics. Exercise videos, such as Jane Fonda's, have become popular. Health newsletters, and television and radio programs about the interrelationship among recreation, health, regular exercise, and nutrition, are common.

Today, more and more people are becoming aware of the value of regular exercise, low-fat diets, and rest and relaxation (recreation) as part of a healthier, happier life. And traditional medicine seems to be accepting more readily the contribution of 'holistic' medicine to a healthy life (Alster 1989, Barrett 1976, Bricklin 1983, Coon 1979, Finkler 1985, Sobel 1979).

AN EXPLORATORY STUDY OF HEALTH TOURISM IN THE CARIBBEAN

The main focus of this exploratory study is on the Caribbean. During 1990 and 1991, telephone and personal interviews were conducted with 28 tourist officials at 28 Caribbean tourism offices in Miami and New York. The interviews discussed the concept of health tourism, inquired about specific facilities in each island which fit the concept, the kinds of tourists who patronize such facilities, and whether or not the health services/facilities dimension was mentioned in promotions (brochures, radio, television, etc.).

Information from the personal and telephone interviews was supplemented with similar interviews with 25 travel agents in Miami who did a great deal of Caribbean tourism business, and content analysis of 250 regular tourism brochures and literature from Caribbean countries. These Caribbean countries included Jamaica, the Bahamas, the Virgin Islands, Barbados, Trinidad and Tobago, St. Lucia, Grenada, Antigua, St. Kitts, St. Vincent, the Cayman Islands, Guadeloupe, Martinique, and St. Martin. The purpose of the content analysis was to help identify resorts that advertise their touristic health facilities or services, and the types of such services offered.

RESULTS OF THE STUDY

There were four main results of the study.

1. Content analysis of tourism brochures and literature indicated that only seven Caribbean resorts were found to advertise *specifically* their health facilities to tourists (through brochures and booklets). These resorts are the Sans Souci Hotel, Club & Spa, and Doctor's Cave Beach in Jamaica; the Silver Reef Health Spa in the Grand Bahama Island, the Bahamas;

the Diamond Mineral Baths, and Le Sport Hotel in St. Lucia; the fitness programs at the Grand View Hotel in St. Vincent; and Fort Recovery Resort in Tortola, and the British Virgin Islands.

A few comments on some of these resorts are in order here. Doctor's Cave in Jamaica has long advocated the therapeutic value of its mineral spring water and saltwater bathing. The Silver Reef Health Spa in the Grand Bahama Island, offers and *advertises* European body wraps, massages, sauna, weight room, facials, beauty salon, special diets for weight loss, and workshops on health and nutrition. The tourist can also enjoy other healthy activities there, such as water skiing, golfing, bicycling, tennis, bodybuilding, and yoga. The natural steaming spa at Diamond Mineral Baths in St. Lucia is said to be a cure for nervous disorders and hangovers. Fort Recovery in Tortola offers special diets to tourists, weight loss programs, massages, and seminars on yoga, meditation, and relaxation techniques.

2. A second finding of the study was that the primary tourist users of these resorts tended to be younger adults between the ages of 25 and 45 years old, white, and predominantly from the U.S.A. This is not surprising, since the main market for Caribbean tourism is the U.S.A., and adults between the ages of 25 and 45 generally have the income to afford leisure trips away from their country. Local Caribbean tourists also visit these resorts.

3. The Caribbean tourist offices had never before heard of the term health-(care) tourism, since it was relatively new, and did not try at any time to promote their respective islands along that dimension. One tourist officer said, "We are not in the health-care business." Strictly speaking, he is correct, but in a larger, more general sense he is not. The health of the tourist is important to the host country.

4. The Miami travel agents also had never heard of the term. However, when it was explained to them, four of the twenty-five mentioned one or more of the resorts alluded to earlier, e.g., Doctor's Cave Beach in Jamaica, and the Silver Reef Health Spa in the Grand Bahama Island.

OTHER DIMENSIONS OF HEALTH TOURISM

One of the purposes of this article is to extend the original concept of health tourism developed by Goodrich and Goodrich (1987), and defined earlier. Other possible dimensions of health tourism emanated from discussions with other colleagues and graduate students, and from my own private thoughts about the concept. These additional dimensions are mentioned below. They include medical treatment of the sick from other countries, travel health care services, ecotourism, and the AIDS crisis.

The Sick from Latin America and the Caribbean

Many sick people suffering from heart, liver, kidney and eye ailments, and other diseases, often come from Latin America and the Caribbean to the USA for medical treatment. Many of them then take vacations in the USA after their operations or treatments, often staying with friends and relatives in the USA. No firm data exist at a central repository in the USA about such tourists. Travel agencies, tourist and convention bureaus, and tourist offices do not normally compile such data, which, of course, is difficult to obtain. Hospitals keep information about their foreign patients proprietary. However, it is believed, for example, that somewhere between 12,000 and 15,000 patients from Latin America and the Caribbean visit Miami and Houston each year for various medical treatments, spend a short vacation (e.g., 7-21 days) afterwards, then return home. Some become residents or citizens of the USA later on.

Travel Health Care Service

There is a growing, yet not so visible activity in some parts of the world, such as New York, Miami, Houston, and Barbados, where consultants provide registered nurses, doctors, professional nursing escorts and ancillary health care services to travelers to these and other places. Typically, the medical professional accompanies the tourist–most times older tourists, although not necessarily so–from his/her homeland to and from the tourist destination for medical treatment, and sometimes just for a vacation, or both. This service is an extension of the one dealt with in the previous section. It may also include recommendations to stay at a hotel(s) that offers particular services, referral to other doctors and health professionals, and making airline bookings and other travel arrangements.

An example of a company that provides the travel health care service referred to here is Tomorrow's Level of Care, Inc. (TLC), a New York-based network of health professionals providing assistance to travelers who are in need of long or short-term care, or "mature" travelers who are experiencing a change in lifestyle (Webley 1991).

Ecotourism

The term ecotourism evolved within the past 10 years. It is a derivative of the words ecology and tourism, and depicts the global concern for

environmental protection, cleanliness, safety, and health for tourists and
the local people, by tourists and local people at the tourist destinations
(Fridgen 1991, pp. 168-177), as well as the urge to seek out the natural
wonders of the world. The practice of ecotourism is reflected all over the
world (e.g., the U.S.A., Caribbean, South America, and Africa) in such
things as preservation of "nature" parks, forests, lakes and rivers, and
wild life; laws and ordinances against air, water and noise pollution; and
the growing number of nature tours for tourists to see the unspoiled hinter-
lands of countries such as Jamaica, Brazil, Guyana, Ireland, Australia,
Canada, Kenya and Zambia. Touristic brochures, booklets, and television
advertisements about these countries reveal this trend toward ecotourism.

Ecotourism is sometimes called "green tourism." It is a relatively new
type of market positioning for tourist destinations, or an additional positioning to capture new tourist markets (in addition to heritage tourism,
ethnic tourism, sports tourism, resort tourism, and so on). (See Gayle and
Goodrich 1992.)

The AIDS Crisis

It is estimated that about 1,000,000 people in the USA have the AIDS
virus (or about 1 in 250,000 persons). Similar numbers exist for South
America, and Asia, and many more are infected in Africa and other parts
of the world. The spread of AIDS has focused more attention on the health
of a country's population and its tourist visitors. These concerns are reflected in print and electronic advertisements promoting safe sex, use of
condoms, the dangers of intravenous drug use and the dangers of sex
tourism. There is even talk of testing tourists for the AIDS virus before
they are allowed (or disallowed) to visit a country. If the AIDS virus
continues to spread rapidly and no cure is found for AIDS within the next
5 years we may see the implementation of such testing programs for
tourists (and visiting business people).

Cruise Ships

Cruise holidays are popular in many parts of the world, such as the
Mediterranean and the Caribbean. Some popular cruise lines are Carnival,
Cunard, and Royal Caribbean. Most countries have laws and regulations
relative to dumping of garbage and other waste matter at sea, off their
coastlines. Obviously, these laws are protective measures against polluting
and destroying beaches, fish life, and water supplies–all fragile, and a part
of the touristic ecosystem.

DISCUSSION

There are other facets of the *original* concept of health tourism (Table 1) which were not empirically studied here because of the lack of data, and which include market segmentation, and medical facilities at destinations. These other aspects are discussed briefly below.

Market Segmentation

Market segmentation is a well-known concept and strategy (Smith 1956; Frank et al. 1972; Engle et al. 1972). Bases for market segmentation include geographic, demographic, psychographic, price, usage and benefits. In the *original* health tourism concept, there are at least two possible approaches to segmentation of the consumer market:

* health
* income

On the basis of health, advertising appeals could be directed at people with various afflictions, such as high cholesterol levels and obesity. These people would form the core 'health segment.' Advertising appeals could also be directed at people who wish to maintain their youthful vigor and appearance. Advertising slogans could focus on such things as preventive health, remedial health, holistic medicine, education, and an active lifestyle.

On the basis of income, some hotels or resorts may cater to the high-income segment who can afford the high prices for the health services at the resort. Other resorts may cater to middle-class clients, furnishing similar services and facilities as the 'high class' resorts, but with much less extravagance.

These two bases for segmenting the health tourism market are not mutually exclusive–they overlap. The author believes that appealing to people on the basis of their health, i.e., preventive health care, or present affliction, would be the better focus of the two segmentation methods. Such an appeal cuts across income, age, geography, benefits, and other segmentation approaches. Furthermore, with the growing health consciousness among peoples of the world, the health-care appeal seems appropriate.

Medical Facilities

Traditionally, tourist destinations appeal to tourists by promoting the variety of attractions, excellent convention centers, delightful cuisine, modern and beautiful accommodations, climate, opportunities for rest and relaxation, etc. Tourist destinations may attract more visitors by mentioning their excellent medical facilities in addition to their other touristic attributes and attractions. Such mention could be made in public relations pieces and other literature mailed from the tourism department of one city to another, from chambers of commerce, offices of public officials, and in speeches of government officials to conventions. The medical staff at the health facilities should be first class so as to maintain high quality services. Ideally, they should be fluent in at least two languages (e.g., English and Spanish) since they will deal with people from different countries.

FUTURE RESEARCH

Health tourism has the potential for many future research studies. Some of these are:

- comparison of health tourism in Europe and the USA;
- large-scale study of market segmentation relative to health tourism;
- forecasting studies of the demand for this type of tourism at a destination;
- a study of users versus non-users of health tourism facilities; and
- the economic value and scope of health tourism.

A few thoughts on these research areas are presented here. First, this research seems to suggest that health tourism as originally defined in this article began in Western Europe, although one can never really be sure. Second, it appears that the meaning of the word 'spa' has changed over time and means different things to different people. Many people in Europe, for instance, think of a spa as the equivalent of a mineral spring sometimes harnessed commercially, and with attendant facilities for bathers. In the USA, the term is also used to describe a type of 'hot tub' or jacuzzi.

Third, research discussion with some European scholars, as well as European and American tourists, seems to indicate that many Europeans view going to the spa as a regular part of their social activity, and a part of their everyday culture since early times. This has only been the case in the USA in the last 20 years or so. Fourth, the concept of health tourism is so novel, and becoming multidimensional, that studies on the topic have been fairly narrowly focused to be manageable.

Fifth, the author is presently conducting a study on health tourism in

Cuba, which has some large mineral springs. Cuba is also promoting a new kind of health tourism, i.e., advertising itself to other Caribbean Islands–primarily through word-of-mouth–as a place for good, but inexpensive, medical treatment. In other words, "why go to the USA for medical treatment when you can have the same treatment in Cuba for much less money?" (Discussion with Cuban-born economist, Maria Dolores Espino, Florida International University.) Will this effort succeed? Only time will tell.

Finally, a study of the economic impact of health tourism would be fascinating and informative, but difficult to do because of (a) the normal problems in collecting economic impact data; (b) the fluid definitional boundaries of the health tourism concept; and (c) the novelty of the concept and hence the absence of good data organized along the lines of health tourism.

CONCLUSIONS

This paper discussed the novel concept of health tourism and *added* other dimensions. The concept can be described as the attempt on the part of a tourist facility or destination to attract tourists by *deliberately* promoting its health services/facilities (as well as its other usual touristic amenities, e.g., hotel accommodations, water sports, golfing, and scenic tours). The health services could include medical check-ups, minor surgery, special diets, vitamin-complex treatments, herbal remedies, thermal swimming pools, and so on (Table 1).

Tourism's health-care component is not new. It has existed for many centuries in many countries of the world, e.g., Switzerland, Germany, Austria, Jamaica, Hungary, the USA and the UK. What is fairly new, however, is the concept of health tourism as a deliberate and growing marketing strategy. It can be a positioning strategy for some hotels or resorts in a world that is becoming more health conscious. Health tourism can, however, become subject to quackery, so self-regulation and careful government scrutiny are imperative.

Like many pilot studies on novel concepts, this study has a few weaknesses. First, one of the objectives of the study–to profile users of health tourism services–was not fully achieved. This was due largely to the novelty of the concept and general lack of information in the tourism literature, at travel agencies and other tourism organizations. But this was not sufficient reason to abort the study–it encouraged the author to explore the idea further. The second weakness of the study is that, given the small sample, the external validity of the findings is limited. More studies are needed. Finally, health tourism is found in countries that do not appear in this study. Review of tourism information from such countries would be useful and interesting. I hope, however, that this article will stimulate further studies on the fascinating subject of health tourism, and reveal other dimensions and issues.

REFERENCES

Alleyne, George (1990). "The Health/Tourism Interaction," *The Courier* (Africa-Caribbean-Pacific-European Community). (July-August), 67-68.

Alster, Kristine B. (1989). *The Holistic Health Movement.* Alabama: University of Alabama Press.

Babcock, Judy (1983). *The Spa Book: A Tour of Health Resorts and Beauty Spas.* New York: Crown Publishers.

Barrett, Leonard E. (1976). *The Sun and the Drum: African Roots in Jamaican Folk Tradition.* London: Heinemann Educational Books.

Bricklin, Mark (1983). *The Practical Encyclopedia of Natural Healing.* Emmaus, Pennsylvania: Rodale Press.

Clymer, R. Swinburne (1963). *Nature's Healing Agents.* Philadelphia, PA: Dorrance & Co.

Conway, David (1973). *The Magic of Herbs.* New York: E. P. Dutton.

Coon, Nelson (1979). *Using Plants for Healing.* Emmaus, PA: Rodale Press.

Engle, J. F., Fiorillo H. F., and Cayley, M.A. (1972). *Market Segmentation: Concepts and Applications.* New York: Holt, Rinehart and Winston.

Finkler, Kaja (1985). *Spiritualist Healers in Mexico.* New York: Praeger.

Frank, Ronald E.; Massy, William F.; and Wind, Yoram (1972). *Market Segmentation.* Englewood Cliffs, NJ: Prentice Hall.

Fridgen, Joseph D. (1991). *Dimensions of Tourism.* East Lansing, Michigan: Educational Institute of The American Hotel & Motel Association.

Gayle, D. J. and Goodrich, J. N. (1992, forthcoming). *Tourism Marketing and Management in The Caribbean.* London, England: Routledge Publishers.

Goodrich, J. N. and Goodrich, G. E. (1987). "Health-Care Tourism: An Exploratory Study." *Tourism Management* (September), 217-222.

_____ "Health-Care Tourism," reprinted in S. Medlik (ed.), *Managing Tourism* (pp. 108-114). Oxford, England: Butterworth-Heinemann Ltd.

Hembry, Phyllis M. (1990). *The English Spa, 1560-1815: A Social History.* London, England: Athlone Press.

Smith, W. R. (1956). "Product Differentiation and Market Segmentation an Alternative Marketing Strategies." *Journal of Marketing* (July), 3-8.

Sobel, David S. ed. (1979). *Ways of Health: Holistic Approaches to Ancient and Contemporary Medicine.* New York: Harcourt Brace Jovanovich.

Webley, Peter (1991). "Travel Health Care Service Now Available in Barbados." *Caribbean Today,* (May), 6.

World Book, Inc. (1984). *The World Book Encyclopedia.* Chicago, D, volume 5, pp. 49-50.

Projecting Western Consumer Attitudes Toward Travel to Six Eastern European Countries

Ken W. McCleary
David L. Whitney

SUMMARY. A study of six Eastern European countries (Bulgaria, Czechoslovakia, "East" Germany, Hungary, Poland and Rumania) was conducted using the Delphi technique. A panel of experts from the United States and Canada made projections regarding travel to Eastern Europe and explored consumer motivations and perceived risks (psychological, financial, safety, social and functional) relative to travel to each of the six countries. An overall assessment of the importance of tourism in the future development of the countries was made. The effects of six possible constraints which impact consumer travel were also assessed.

INTRODUCTION

The world is changing rapidly. Perhaps there is no better illustration of rapid change than has been seen on the European continent in the last few

Ken W. McCleary is Professor, Department of Hospitality and Tourism Management, Virginia Tech, Blacksburg, VA 24061. David L. Whitney is Professor, Department of Marketing and Hospitality Services Administration, Central Michigan University, Mt. Pleasant, MI 48859.

The authors wish to thank Judith Zacek of the Institute of Certified Travel Agents for identifying Certified Travel Counselors specializing in Europe.

[Haworth co-indexing entry note]: "Projecting Western Consumer Attitudes Toward Travel to Six Eastern European Countries." McCleary, Ken W., and David L. Whitney. Co-published simultaneously in *Journal of International Consumer Marketing* (The Haworth Press, Inc.) Vol. 6, No. 3/4, 1994, pp. 239-256; and: *Global Tourist Behavior* (ed: Muzaffer Uysal) The Haworth Press, Inc., 1994, pp. 239-256. Multiple copies of this article/chapter may be purchased from The Haworth Document Delivery Center [1-800-3-HAWORTH; 9:00 a.m. - 5:00 p.m. (EST)].

239

years. Economic alliances, diminished hostilities, the loosening of economic barriers and the new freedom of most of the former Soviet Bloc countries represent changes which are likely to dramatically affect markets and trade relations.

The study reported here projects the behavior of Western consumers of foreign travel relative to six Eastern European countries. The six countries include: Bulgaria, Czechoslovakia, Hungary, Poland, Rumania and "East" Germany. Although "East" Germany has some obvious dissimilarities to the other five countries, the former German Democratic Republic allows for some interesting comparisons with more independent countries. The goal of the study, which used the Delphi methodology, was to predict the future of tourist development, travel behavior and barriers to tourism relative to the six Eastern European countries.

BACKGROUND

Tourism is often touted as an economic savior. Perhaps a more realistic view of tourism than that of savior, is that it has potential for rapid development in an increasingly shrinking world. Tourism is often considered a good economic alternative because it is an industry that can be more easily developed than some goods producing industries that require high technology and a highly skilled labor force. Tourism can provide a good source of foreign exchange and is seen as a relatively clean industry.

Of course, there are other issues to consider in pursuing tourism development. The scale to which tourism should be integrated into local communities or kept as an enclave, separating it to a great extent from the local culture needs to be considered (Jenkins 1982). A case can be made that there are some similarities between the emerging democracies of Eastern Europe and other developing countries. Britton (1982) points out that there is a danger of increased dependency on developed countries as tourist enterprises come under the control of large-scale foreign enterprises. While tourism is already becoming important to the Hungarian economy (Hungary 1989), it would be wise for countries such as Rumania and Bulgaria to consider the impact of tourism on community life. Macnaught (1982) suggests that there are at least six potential negative impacts on local communities. As noted in the introduction, the goal of this article is to predict what will happen with regard to tourism development in Eastern Europe. It is not our purpose to advocate whether development should take place nor to attempt to say how it should take place.

Regardless of the social implications, tourism is becoming a priority industry in Eastern Europe (Waters 1990). While development is not always easy, with large capital outlays necessary for both infrastructure and superstructure construction, some countries are already meeting with success in developing tourism. For example, Hungary has shown that even with modest tourist resources, it can attract a substantial number of tourists from both the East and the West (Medlik 1990).

Western Europe has long been a popular destination for North American travelers and there is speculation that the newly opened countries of Eastern Europe will become popular travel destinations for Western travelers as well. Again using Hungary as an example, Witt (1991, p. 182) noted that the country is in the top 40 international tourism earners at thirty-eighth position, attracting 14.2 million tourist arrivals from abroad. In the past, the majority of visitors to the former Soviet satellite counties have come from neighbors or other Eastern Bloc countries. For example, one source estimated that in 1988, 85 percent of visitor arrivals in Czechoslovakia came from a combination of the German Democratic Republic, Poland and Hungary (Medlik 1990, p. 96). Another source notes that 1988 visitor arrivals from the West accounted for only 6.8 percent of all foreign tourists and that 75 percent of the tourists from other East European countries were simply excursionists, that is, travelers staying less than 24 hours (Czechoslovakia 1989, p. 28).

Meeting the Needs of Tourists from the United States

The acceptance of a travel destination by Western consumers depends to a great degree on the attractions available and the degree to which a country is able to handle tourist needs. While there are those tourists that may fit with Plog's (1974, 1990) allocentric characteristics, attracting large numbers of tourists, and therefore foreign exchange, requires attracting mass tourism. The majority of Western tourists expect a comfortable level of accommodations and the availability of restaurants and other facilities to meet their needs. The problem of lack of capacity to accommodate tourists is illustrated by the estimate that Czechoslovakia's foreign tourism demand is double its handling capability (Czechoslovakia 1989).

From a marketing perspective, it would seem to be important for Eastern European countries that want to develop tourism to gain a basic understanding of how they are perceived by Western consumers. Expectations and destination image are frequently used by travelers in selecting a place to visit (Reilly 1990). A country's image may or may not be accurate and it can be changed with proper planning.

METHODOLOGY

Data for this study came from a panel of travel and tourism experts in the United States. Members of the panel consisted of two types of experts: travel professionals and tourism educators. Both groups received the same questions, but their responses were tabulated separately. This allowed the researchers to see if a similar consensus was arrived at by each group and served as a validity check for the Delphi questionnaire.

Panel Participants

The panel of travel industry professionals was drawn from a list of 54 potential participants provided by the Institute of Certified Travel Agents in November of 1990. The Institute screened its membership to ensure that those suggested for the panel had experience in booking travel to Europe.

A total panel membership of at least 20 participants was sought. Previous studies have found this number to be the minimum acceptable (Yong, Keng and Leng 1989). Because a balance between industry and academic experts was sought, at least 10 of each was considered desirable.

Due to the nature of the Delphi process, some attrition from the original panel is expected during each round of questioning. Yong, Keng and Leng (1989) experienced a 30% drop in one classification of their panel just between the first and second rounds. Therefore, the number of panel members selected at the beginning was higher than the minimum target of 20 experts because of expected attrition, as suggested by Green, Hunter and Moore (1990).

Industry professionals were contacted by phone and the study described to them. Out of the list of 54 Certified Travel Agents, actual contact was made with 36 agents and 29 agreed to participate in the study. Some of the agents could not be contacted after repeated attempts, several felt they did not have time to participate and four felt they were not qualified.

Tourism experts for the academic panel were drawn from the membership of the Society of Travel and Tourism Educators. In addition to being a member of STTE, potential participants were selected only if they were teaching or had taught a course or courses in tourism at the college level. From a list of 49 possible participants, 31 were actually contacted and 29 agreed to participate in the study. Only one of the 31 contacted declined to participate because of a perceived lack of expertise.

The Delphi Technique

The Delphi model or technique is a speculative approach to forecasting events and is particularly useful for medium and long-term forecasting.

While Delphi results in qualitative rather than quantitative projections, it is useful in situations where conditions have not allowed for the generation of appropriate historical data upon which to base quantitative forecasts. This may be the case where social, economic and political conditions have changed dramatically as they have in Eastern Europe. In an examination of several tourism studies, Calantone, Di Benedetto and Bojanic (1987) observed that: "Forecasts may yield results which are only marginally better than 'guessing' by an experienced professional" (p. 37).

Delphi then, is a subjective, qualitative process. One of the appropriate uses for qualitative methods is for predicting the future from today's knowledge base (Makridakis and Wheelwright 1977). To do this, it relies on the opinions of experts in the field. The reliability of the process lies in the level of expertise of the participants (Uysal and Crompton 1985) and the degree to which a consensus of opinion is reached.

The Delphi Process

The use of the Delphi process and its technical development has been documented by Linstone and Turoff (1975). Many Delphi studies seek to assign probabilities to the occurrence of future events. For example, experts might be asked to indicate how likely there is to be a lasting peace in the Middle East. They would then assign figures such as a 60 percent probability, 90 percent probability, etc., and the results of the study are usually expressed in terms of the degree of probability of an event happening (Uysal and Crompton 1985). Because these degrees of probability are not accurate from a statistical standpoint anyway, the study reported here did not assign probabilities, but rather sought direction of agreement with statements related to tourism development. For example, the panel was asked to indicate their degree of agreement, on a nine-point scale, with the following statement: In general, Western tourists will visit Bulgaria for a family vacation. The same statement was then given for the other five countries so that comparisons could be made. The means of the responses were then examined to determine the extent and direction of agreement or disagreement with each statement.

An important feature of the Delphi technique as applied in this study is that the items for the final questionnaire were based on a pre-survey of panel members. The researchers assembled a proposed list of study topics derived from the tourism literature. Panel members were mailed the list and asked to rate on a nine-point scale, the importance of each item to the development of tourism in Eastern Europe in the 1990s. Space was provided for participants to add topics which were not on the printed list.

As mentioned earlier, one problem with Delphi is that the results depend on the expertise of the panel. While the panel for this study was screened twice, each panel member was also asked to assess their own expertise. This was done both from an overall standpoint and for each individual question on the Delphi survey as well. Although the Delphi process requires that each individual remains anonymous throughout the process, a general description of the characteristics of the panel was provided to allow each member to rate their own expertise. During the first round of questioning each panel member was asked to assess their degree of confidence in their response to each question.

The final questionnaire used in the study was compiled based on the responses to the Preliminary Pre-Delphi Survey. Due to the fact that all questions had to be answered relative to all six countries in the study, only those questions rated as most important to tourism development were used. The final Delphi questionnaire consisted of 33 questions which represent ten categories. All 33 questions had to be answered for each country which meant a total of 198 responses were required. All of the 56 initial panel members responded to the Preliminary Pre-Delphi Survey. High attrition at the preliminary stage has been a criticism of previous Delphi studies (Wheeller, Hart and Whysall 1990).

Delphi ultimately seeks to attain "stability of the means" of the responses to questions. In order to achieve stability no respondent can fall more than a half point above or below the mean of the responses on the nine-point scale.

In January of 1991, panelists were mailed the first round of the Delphi questionnaire. Twenty-two travel professionals and 24 educators completed the survey in Round One. Each panelist was also asked to indicate their degree of confidence in each of their responses in Round One.

The mean responses from Round One were computed and Round Two was mailed out. The Round Two questionnaire included not only the original questions, but also revealed the group mean response for each question. Each respondent was sent a copy of their original responses in Round One and asked to compare their response to the group mean. They were then asked to fill out the questionnaire again and given the opportunity to change their responses if they desired, after seeing the combined response of the total panel to which they belonged.

As was expected considering the large number of questions and the nature of the panel, especially the portion of the panel made up of travel professionals, the drop out rate between Round One and Round Two was considerable. Thirteen travel professionals and 19 educators completed Round Two. Stability of the mean was reached for 157 of the questions for the travel professionals and 174 of the questions for the educators. This left 41 questions for Round Three for the travel professionals and 24 questions for the educators.

Ten travel professionals and 17 educators completed Round Three. Stability was met for all questions by the educators portion of the panel and all but nine questions for the travel professionals.

RESULTS

Discussion of the results of the study will begin with the panels' projections of the importance of tourism an economic force in Eastern Europe in the 1990s. The next section will discuss what travel motives are projected to be the most important in the 1990s. The panels' predictions of what constraints to tourism development are likely to be met are then explored. Finally, a discussion of how panelists think Western travelers perceive five types of risk in Eastern European travel will be presented.

Overview

Because Delphi is a subjective process, using objective quantitative techniques to interpret the data is suspect. The goal of Delphi is to identify emerging trends, not to precisely measure variables. Therefore, the format for discussion will rely primarily on the reporting of the consensus means for each portion of the panel. Furthermore, both the travel professionals' projections and the educators' opinions will be treated together where agreement occurred and only discussed separately where differences occurred.

In general, Rumania and Bulgaria were seen as the least likely to develop a viable tourism product during the 1990s. Hungary, Poland and Czechoslovakia were viewed as having above average potential for attracting Western tourists. Opinions were mixed regarding "East" Germany.

Tourism as an Economic Contributor

Panelists were asked their degree of agreement that tourism will become a primary economic force in each of the countries studied. Table 1 presents the mean responses for each portion of the panel. The responses of the professionals and educators were fairly consistent with each other, with both groups seeing Hungary as having the most potential for tourism as an economic force and listing Bulgaria and Rumania as having the least potential.

Most of the panels' rankings are consistent with economic data published by other organizations. For example, Witt (1991) cites World Tourism Organization data that puts Hungary first among the six countries in terms of international tourism receipts. The data in Witt's article also show Rumania last among the six, Bulgaria towards the bottom, Czechoslovakia towards the top and "East" Germany as somewhat of a question because data were not available on the German Democratic Republic.

Perhaps the most interesting Delphi projections are for Poland. While data show Poland with only $202 million in international tourism receipts in 1989, which is less than Bulgaria, (Witt 1991, p. 183) the Delphi panel ranked it towards the top in predicted economic impact of tourism. Another point of comparison is an ASTA survey (ASTA 1990) of Eastern European travel which showed Hungary as the top destination with 41 percent of bookings. The survey listed Czechoslovakia next with 40 percent, East Germany with 35 percent, Poland with 28 percent, Rumania with 11 percent and Bulgaria with seven percent.

When examining the data, it is important to note the level of confidence indicated by respondents. For example, on Table 1 the low perceived potential for economic impact is accompanied by a lower level of confidence in respondents' opinions than for the top rated countries. In other words, even though experts see less economic impact in Rumania and Bulgaria, they are not as certain of their assessments as they are the assessments of the higher ranked countries. For most issues, industry professionals exhibited a higher level of confidence in their responses than did educators.

TABLE 1. Perceived Economic Impact of Tourism
(Tourism will be a primary contributor to the economy of the
following countries: agree = 9, disagree = 1)

Country	Professionals Rank**	Mean	Confidence*	Educators Rank**	Mean	Confidence*
Bulgaria	5/6	4.2	6.7	5	4.5	5.5
Czechoslovakia	4	6.4	7.0	2	5.9	6.8
"East" Germany	3	7.1	7.3	4	5.4	6.6
Hungary	1	7.8	7.2	1	6.7	6.6
Poland	2	7.3	6.8	3	5.8	6.1
Rumania	5/6	4.2	6.8	6	3.4	5.7

Note: *Confidence responses were on a nine-point scale with 1 = Low and 9 = High.
          **Rank order of means.

Consumer Travel Motives

Often identified motivations for travel were drawn from the tourism literature (Crompton 1979; McIntosh and Goeldner 1986; Yaun and McDonald 1990). Seven motives were selected for inclusion in the study: Enhancing Personal Prestige (ego); Educational or Cultural Enrichment; Business; Family Vacation; Recreation/Sports; Incentive Travel; and Visit Family/Explore Heritage.

Appendix 1 contains the complete set of scores for both the travel professionals and educators projections for the importance of each travel motive. Table 2 presents a summary of the motives considered the most and least important for each country. The discussion here refers primarily to Table 2. If the reader wants to conduct further analysis, such as a comparison of the actual rankings and mean scores for both subsets of the Delphi panel, this can be derived from Appendix 1.

The most important consumer travel motives are projected to be either to visit families/explore heritage or for educational/cultural enrichment. The exception is that travel professionals rated business travel as the most important motive for travel to "East" Germany. Educators placed business travel in a tie with educational/cultural enrichment as the most important motive for travel to Hungary. The reason for high placement of family/heritage motives is not difficult to explain. The strong European heritage of the United States and Canada would seem to provide a natural draw. Of course Eastern Europe has a long history and record of cultural achievement, providing ample draws for cultural/educational motives. The high ranking of business travel to "East" Germany by travel professionals is probably due to reunification which is bringing about business opportunities as the country is rebuilt and integrated into the strong "West" German economy.

There was quite a bit of distance between the highest and lowest mean rankings of travel motivations. The potential for incentive travel to Bulgaria is seen as almost nonexistent by travel professionals, receiving a mean score of only 2.0. Incentive travel was also ranked lowest for Rumania by both sets of respondents. Generally, none of the countries were seen as good sites for family vacations, with only Poland barely crossing the mid-point on the scale as ranked by educators. Indeed, family vacations were ranked as the least important travel motive for four countries by educators and three countries by travel professionals. Recreation/sports was ranked lowest for Poland and tied as the lowest motive for Hungary in the travel professional rankings. There was a great deal of consistency between the overall rankings by both Delphi subgroups.

TABLE 2. Most and Least Important Motives for Travel (by Country)

Country	Most Important Motive	
	Professionals	Educators
Bulgaria	Visit Families/Explore Heritage Educational or Cultural Enrichment (tie)	Visit Families/Explore Heritage
Czechoslovakia	Educational or Cultural Enrichment	Educational or Cultural Enrichment Business (tie)
"East" Germany	Business	Educational or Cultural Enrichment
Hungary	Visit Families, Explore Heritage	Educational or Cultural Enrichment Business (tie)
Poland	Visit Families, Explore Heritage	Visit Families, Explore Heritage
Rumania	Visit Families, Explore Heritage	Educational or Cultural Enrichment

Country	Least Important Motive	
	Professionals	Educators
Bulgaria	Incentive Travel	Family Vacation
Czechoslovakia	Family Vacation	Family Vacation
"East" Germany	Family Vacation	Family Vacation
Hungary	Family Vacation Recreation/Sports (tie)	Family Vacation
Poland	Recreation/Sports	Recreation/Sports
Rumania	Incentive Travel	Incentive Travel

Factors Inhibiting Tourist Travel

Panel members were asked to assess six items that may constrain tourist travel to Eastern Europe: International Terrorism; Political Instability Within the Host Country; Lack of Expertise in Operating Tourist Facilities; Political Instability of the Soviet Union; Lack of Marketing Ability; and Lack of a Distribution System Such as Travel Agencies.

Table 3 summarizes the results of the analysis of this part of the data. The entire Delphi panel expressed a strong level of confidence in their assessments on the inhibiting factors. The scale midpoint of 5.0 was used to determine if each factor was considered a problem for the individual country.

Responses of travel professionals indicate more problems in developing tourism than did the educators. This is perhaps due to the fact that travel professionals have a closer working relationship with Eastern Europe and have actually encountered consumer resistance related to the issues in Table 3. Consistent with other results of the study, Bulgaria and Rumania posed the most concern. There is a perceived lack of marketing ability, lack of a distribution system and lack of expertise in operating tourist facilities. Some of these shortcomings were also a concern for Czechoslovakia and Poland, but not to as large an extent.

Risk Factors

Panel members were asked to assess how much risk travelers would perceive for each country in five categories of risk: Psychological; Financial; Safety; Social; and Functional. The five categories were selected based on Jacoby and Kaplan's (1972) framework. Psychological risk is defined as the possibility that the product (tourist experience) may not fulfill self-concept. Financial risk is the possibility that the product may not be worth its monetary cost. Safety risk refers to the possibility of physical harm. The possibility that a country may not be a socially acceptable place to travel constitutes social risk. Functional risk is that the product may not perform as expected, for example, that hotels may not provide for a clean, comfortable stay.

As can be seen on Table 4, there was complete agreement on the panel that social risk would be perceived as very low for travelers and the lowest type of risk overall. The subsets of the panel disagreed on what would be perceived as the greatest risk. Travel professionals listed functional risk as being greatest for every country, although stability of the mean was not met for Hungary and "East" Germany. This is consistent with the assessment of the factors affecting development discussed in the previous section. Travel agents strongly agreed that lack of expertise in operating tourist facilities was an inhibiting factor for development in Bulgaria and Rumania and was considered a problem in the other countries, with the exception of Hungary, as well.

Educators considered financial risks to be the highest perceived risk.

TABLE 3. Factors Inhibiting Tourist Travel
(Will the country listed be constrained by the inhibiting factor listed?)*

Country	Professionals	Mean	Educators	Mean
International Terrorism				
Bulgaria	Agree	5.8	Agree	5.4
Czechoslovakia	Agree	5.4	Agree	5.2
"East" Germany	Agree	5.6	Disagree	4.7
Hungary	Agree	5.4	Agree	5.2
Poland	Agree	5.7	Neither Agree nor Disagree	5.0
Rumania	Agree	5.3	Agree	5.4
Political Instability Within the Host Country				
Bulgaria	Agree	6.9	Agree	6.7
Czechoslovakia	Agree	5.3	Agree	5.4
"East" Germany	Disagree	3.5	Disagree	3.9
Hungary	Disagree	3.8	Disagree	4.6
Poland	Disagree	4.6	Agree	5.1
Rumania	Agree	6.0	Strongly Agree	7.0
Lack of Expertise in Operating Tourist Facilities				
Bulgaria	Strongly Agree	8.0	Agree	5.8
Czechoslovakia	Agree	6.6	Disagree	4.8
"East" Germany	Agree	6.2	Disagree	4.5
Hungary	Neither Agree nor Disagree	5.0	Disagree	4.5
Poland	Agree	6.3	Agree	5.4
Rumania	Strongly Agree	8.1	Agree	5.8
Political Instability of Soviet Union				
Bulgaria	Agree	5.7	Disagree	4.5
Czechoslovakia	Agree	5.1	Disagree	4.3
"East" Germany	Disagree	3.7	Disagree	3.2
Hungary	Disagree	3.4	Disagree	3.8
Poland	Disagree	4.4	Disagree	4.3
Rumania	Agree	5.6	Disagree	4.2

Country	Professionals		Educators	
		Mean		**Mean**
Lack of Marketing Ability				
Bulgaria	Strongly Agree	8.3	Agree	6.1
Czechoslovakia	Agree	6.1	Agree	5.4
"East" Germany	Disagree	4.4	Disagree	4.4
Hungary			Neither agree	
	Disagree	4.6	nor Disagree	5.0
Poland	Agree	5.7	Agree	5.6
Rumania	Strongly Agree	8.2	Agree	6.4
Lack of a Distribution System Such as Travel Agents				
Bulgaria	Strongly Agree	7.1	Agree	5.5
Czechoslovakia	Neither Agree		Neither Agree	
	nor Disagree	5.0	nor Disagree	5.0
"East" Germany	Disagree	4.8	Disagree	3.4
Hungary	Disagree	4.4	Disagree	3.8
Poland	Disagree	4.8	Disagree	4.4
Rumania	Agree	6.6	Agree	5.9

Note: *A mean response of 7 and above was considered strong agreement that a problem existed, > 5 but < 7 was considered agreement, > = 3 but < 5 disagreement and < 3 was considered strong disagreement. 5 = neither agree nor disagree.

Physical risk was seen by the total panel as highest in Bulgaria and Rumania. This is again consistent with the assessment of inhibiting factors, as Bulgaria and Rumania were given the highest level of agreement that political instability could inhibit tourist travel (see Table 3).

LIMITATIONS OF THE STUDY

The Delphi technique has a number of limitations as discussed earlier in this article. It should be remembered that the Delphi process is subjective and that the panel is making projections based on their own personal level of understanding.

Another limitation of the study is that panel members were drawn only from the United States and Canada. It is likely that respondents were

TABLE 4. Perceived Risk for Travel

Psychological (Ego) Risk

Country	Professionals Mean	Confidence*	Educators Mean	Confidence*
Bulgaria	5.3	6.1	4.3	4.8
Czechoslovakia	5.4	6.0	4.2	4.9
"East" Germany	6.3	6.2	4.0	5.1
Hungary	5.7	6.1	4.0	5.3
Poland	6.1	6.2	4.3	5.3
Rumania	5.5	6.2	4.1	5.1

Financial Risk

Country	Professionals	Confidence*	Educators	Confidence*
Bulgaria	5.8	6.8	6.3	6.4
Czechoslovakia	5.9	6.9	5.9	6.4
"East" Germany	6.2	6.9	5.6	6.1
Hungary	6.2	7.0	5.8	6.4
Poland	6.0	6.9	6.3	6.5
Rumania	5.6	6.8	6.8	6.4

Safety Risk

Country	Professionals	Confidence*	Educators	Confidence*
Bulgaria	5.9	7.1	6.1	7.0
Czechoslovakia	5.3	6.9	5.5	6.8
"East" Germany	4.6	7.0	4.7	6.7
Hungary	4.6	7.0	5.4	6.9
Poland	5.1	7.0	5.3	7.0
Rumania	6.2	7.1	6.3	7.0

Social Risk

Country	Professionals	Confidence*	Educators	Confidence*
Bulgaria	2.6	6.8	1.6	7.1
Czechoslovakia	2.3	6.8	1.6	7.1
"East" Germany	2.3	6.8	1.3	6.8
Hungary	2.4	6.8	1.4	7.1
Poland	2.4	6.8	1.5	7.1
Rumania	2.8	6.8	1.9	7.1

Functional Risk

Country	Professionals	Confidence*	Educators	Confidence*
Bulgaria	6.8	7.2	5.6	7.2
Czechoslovakia	6.8	7.2	5.8	7.2
"East" Germany	6.6**	7.2	5.0	7.0
Hungary	6.7**	7.1	5.3	7.3
Poland	6.7	7.1	5.5	7.4
Rumania	6.5	7.3	5.6	7.1

Note: *Nine-point scale where 1 = disagree and 9 = agree.
        **Did not reach stability of the mean.

considering primarily North American tourists when answering questions. Therefore, care must be used in generalizing the results of the study to all tourists from the West. An improvement in future studies would be to include Western Europeans as panel members. This, of course, also increases the difficulty of keeping panel members active as well as the cost of the study.

CONCLUSION

It is difficult to assess what will be consumer reactions to products as complex and new as the emerging Eastern European travel destinations. The Delphi technology projects consumer attitudes based on the opinions of experts. The particular panel of experts in this study sees some major differences in how consumers view the six countries included for analysis. Based on the results presented here, it would behoove marketers in Rumania and Bulgaria to institute a plan to change image as well as to develop tourism products and distribution systems if they wish to pursue tourism as an economic tool.

The projections for tourism in Hungary in particular, and to a lesser extent, Poland, "East" Germany and Czechoslovakia, appear to be bright. Tourism marketers should take note of the motives which were found to be most attractive in each of their respective countries and capitalize on them in their consumer marketing programs. At the same time they need to examine the positive and negative elements of risk as they relate to their country and plan marketing strategies to decrease perceived risk where necessary.

REFERENCES

ASTA Surveys 500 Agents about Travel to Eastern Europe. (1990). *ASTA Notes,* (October 9) 4.

Britton, S. G. (1982). The Political Economy of Tourism in the Third World. *Annals of Tourism Research,* 9, 331-358.

Calantone, R. C., Di Benedetto, A. and Bojanic, D. (1987). A Comprehensive Review of the Tourism Forecasting Literature. *Journal of Travel Research,* (Fall), 26 (2), 28-39.

Crompton, J. L. (1979). Motivations for Pleasure Vacation. *Annals of Tourism Research,* 6, 408-24.

Czechoslovakia. (1989). *EIU International Tourism Reports,* 2, 26-41.

Green, H., Hunter C. and Moore, B. (1990). Assessing the Environmental Impact of Tourism Development Using the Delphi Technique. *Tourism Management,* (June) 111-120.

Hungary. (1989). *EIU International Tourism Reports,* 3, 38-58.

Jacoby, J. and Kaplan, L. B. (1972). The Components of Perceived Risk. *Proceedings of the Third Annual Conference of the Association for Consumer Research,* 382-393.

Jenkins, C. L. (1982). The Effects of Scale in Tourism Projects in Developing Countries. *Annals of Tourism Research,* 9, 229-249.

Linstone, H. and Turoff, M. (eds.). (1975). *The Delphi Method: Techniques and Applications.* Reading, MA: Addison Wesley Co.

Makridakis, S. and Wheelwright, S. C. (1977). Forecasting: Issues & Challenges for Marketing Management. *Journal of Marketing,* (October) 28-38.

Macnaught, T. J. (1982). Mass Tourism and the Dilemmas of Modernization in Pacific Island Communities. *Annals of Tourism Research,* 9, 359-381.

McIntosh, R. W. and Goeldner, C. R. (1986). *Tourism: Principles, Practices, Philosophies,* Fifth Edition. NY: John Wiley & Sons, Inc.

Medlik, S. (1990). Focus on Eastern Europe. *Tourism Management,* (June) 95-98.

Plog, S. C. (1974). Why Destination Areas Rise and Fall in Popularity. *The Cornell Hotel and Restaurant Administration Quarterly,* (February), 14 (4), 55-58.

Plog, S. C. (1990). A Carpenter's Tools: An Answer to Stephen L. J. Smith's Review of Psychocentrism/Allocentrism. *Journal of Travel Research,* (Spring), 28 (4), 43-45.

Reilly, M. D. (1990). Free Elicitation of Descriptive Adjectives for Tourism Image Assessment. *Journal of Travel Research,* (Spring), 28 (4), 21-26.

Uysal, M. and Crompton, J. L. (1985). An Overview of Approaches Used to Forecast Tourism Demand. *Journal of Travel Research,* (Spring), 23 (4), 7-15.

Waters, S. R. (1990). Eastern Europe, *Travel Industry World Yearbook: The Big Picture,* 4, 107-112.

Wheeller, B., Hart T. and Whysall, P. (1990). An Application of the Delphi Technique. *Tourism Management,* (June), 121-122.

Witt, S. F. (1991). The Development of International Tourism in Eastern Europe, *New Horizons Conference Proceedings,* Calgary: The University of Calgary, (181-189).

Yong, Y. W., Kau, A. K. and Leng, T. (1989). A Delphi Forecast for the Singapore Tourism Industry: Future Scenario and Marketing Implications *European Journal of Marketing,* 23 (1), 15-26.

Yuan, S. and McDonald, C. (1990). Motivational Determinants of International Pleasure Time. *Journal of Travel Research,* (Summer), 24 (1), 42-44.

APPENDIX 1

IMPORTANCE OF CONSUMER TRAVEL MOTIVATIONS

(In general, Western tourists will visit Eastern European countries for the
following reasons: agree = 9, disagree = 1)

Motive: Enhancing Personal Prestige (Ego)

Country	Professionals Rank**	Mean	Confidence*	Educators Rank**	Mean	Confidence*
Bulgaria	5/6	3.1	6.8	6	3.8	6.0
Czechoslovakia	3	4.9	6.9	4	4.9	6.4
"East" Germany	2	5.0	7.0	1	5.8	6.2
Hungary	1	5.3***	7.0	2	5.6	6.5
Poland	4	4.2	6.9	3	5.5	6.4
Rumania	5/6	3.1	6.8	5	3.9	6.0

Motive: Educational or Cultural Enrichment

Country	Professionals Rank**	Mean	Confidence*	Educators Rank**	Mean	Confidence*
Bulgaria	5	5.1	7.2	6	5.4	6.5
Czechoslovakia	1	7.3	7.4	2/3/4	7.1	7.0
"East" Germany	2/3	7.5	7.4	2/3/4	7.1	6.7
Hungary	2/3	7.5	7.4	1	7.4	7.0
Poland	4	6.8	7.5	2/3/4	7.1	7.0
Rumania	6	4.3	7.2	5	5.2	6.6

Motive: Business

Country	Professionals Rank**	Mean	Confidence*	Educators Rank**	Mean	Confidence*
Bulgaria	6	3.9	6.6	5/6	5.4	6.1
Czechoslovakia	4	6.1	6.9	2	7.1	6.5
"East" Germany	1	7.6	7.3	4	6.4	6.2
Hungary	2	7.1	7.2	1	7.4	6.5
Poland	3	6.4	7.0	3	6.9	6.7
Rumania	5	5.0	6.6	5/6	5.4	6.5

Motive: Family Vacation

Country	Professionals Rank**	Mean	Confidence*	Educators Rank**	Mean	Confidence*
Bulgaria	6	2.3	6.9	5	3.6	5.9
Czechoslovakia	4	2.7	6.9	3/4	4.3	6.0
"East" Germany	3	3.4	7.0	3/4	4.3	6.0
Hungary	1/2	4.1	7.0	2	4.6	5.9
Poland	1/2	4.1	7.0	1	5.2	6.0
Rumania	5	2.4	7.0	6	3.5	5.8

APPENDIX 1 (continued)

Motive: Recreation/Sports

Country	Professionals Rank**	Mean	Confidence*	Educators Rank**	Mean	Confidence*
Bulgaria	5	2.8	6.2	5	4.3	5.6
Czechoslovakia	3	3.8	6.2	2	5.2	5.7
"East" Germany	2	3.9	6.1	1	5.3	5.6
Hungary	1	4.1	6.1	3	5.0	5.5
Poland	4	3.6	6.2	4	4.4	5.6
Rumania	6	2.5	6.2	6	3.7	5.5

Motive: Incentive Travel

Country	Professionals Rank**	Mean	Confidence*	Educators Rank**	Mean	Confidence*
Bulgaria	6	2.0	6.3	5	3.6	5.9
Czechoslovakia	3/4	3.7***	6.4	3/4	4.5	5.8
"East" Germany	3/4	3.7	6.6	3/4	4.5	5.7
Hungary	1	4.4	6.6	1	4.9	6.0
Poland	2	3.9***	6.6	2	4.6	5.7
Rumania	5	1.9	6.4	6	3.4	5.8

Motive: Visit Families, Explore Heritage

Country	Professionals Rank**	Mean	Confidence*	Educators Rank**	Mean	Confidence*
Bulgaria	6	5.1	7.0	6	5.5	6.3
Czechoslovakia	4	6.9	7.1	3	6.9	6.3
"East" Germany	3	7.4	7.4	4	6.7	6.7
Hungary	2	7.9	7.4	2	7.3	6.5
Poland	1	8.0	7.3	1	7.8	6.8
Rumania	5	5.3	7.0	5	6.1	6.1

Note: *Confidence responses were on a nine point scale with 1 = Low and 9 = High.
         **Rank order of means.
         ***Stability of the mean was not reached on this item for this group.

Index

Page numbers in *italics* indicate figures; page numbers followed by t indicate tables.

Abbey, J. R., 83
'Above' in Barbados, 193
Accommodation
    in the Caribbean, 45-46
    cultural knowledge in Barbados
        and, 196-198,197t,198t,200
    in Eastern Europe, 241
    relationship with tour operators,
        52
    visitors to Zambia, 29
Acquired immune deficiency
        syndrome (AIDS), 234
ADSPLIT, 103-104
Advertising. *See* Marketing
Africa
    national parks, 24-25
    Zambian tourist industry, 21-36.
        See also Zambia
Age
    package vs. non-package
        travellers, 87,88
    visitors to Zambia, 33,35
Ahmed, S. A., 125
Ahn, Jong-yun, 207
AIDS (acquired immune deficiency
        syndrome), 234
AIO (Attitudes, Interests, and
        Opinions), 81
Albaum, G., 124
Alden, D. L., 128
Allen, J., 81
Allen, L. R., 140
Allocentric tourists

experiences with other cultures,
    184
sense of place, 10-11
in small island nations, 43-44
studies of, 126
Almagor, U., 36
Alone-travellers, motivation,
    149-153,154-157
Americans. *See* United States
    travellers
Anthropology, 127
Ashworth, G. J., 5,13
Asia, 102. *See also* Seoul Olympics
    and tourism
ASTA, 246
Attitudes, Interests, and Opinions
    (AIO), 81
Authoritarianism, 185

Bachri, Thamrin, 161
Back-translation, 130
The Bahamas, 231-232
Barbados
    host view of tourists, 187
    tourist awareness of culture,
        188-201
        accommodation, 197t,198t
        enhancing, 200-201
        inter-variable analysis,
            195-198
        motivation, 198-200,199t
        questionnaire, 188-189
        results of study, 188-189,194t

Basu, A., 103
Batra, R., 103
Beliveau, Donald, 208
Bello, D. C., 125
'Below' in Barbados, 193
Benefits. *See* Visitor benefits
Benefit segmentation
    advantages, 81
    limitations, 22
    by motivation, 81
Bennett, M. J., 127-128
Birks, D., 103
Bitner, J., 164
Bitner, M. J., 156
Bojanic, D., 243
Booms, B. H., 156
Booms, H., 164
Boorstin, D., 183
Braithwaite, R., 48
Branagan, D., 25
Brathwaite, F., 187
Brislin, R. W., 127, 130
British travellers
    intercultural contact, 185
    package vs. non-package, 84-98
        benefit sought, 93,94t
        data analysis, 85-86
        information sources, 90,91t
        marketing implications, 93,
            97-98
        product preferences, 93,
            95t-96t
        questionnaires, 84-85
        sociodemographics, 87,88t
        travel characteristics,
            87,89t-90t
        travel destination, 86,86t
        travel philosophy, 90-91,92t
    to the United States, 83-84
Britton, R., 163,174,176
Britton, S. G., 240
Bruner, E., 199
Bryant, B. E., 81
Buchanan, T. J., 139
Bulgaria

economic impact of tourism, 246
factors inhibiting tourism, 249,
    250-251
motives of visitors, 247,248,
    255-256
risk factors, 249-251,252
Burch, W. R., 139
Burnett, G. W., 124
Business as travel motive, 255

Calantone, R. C., 243
Calgary Olympics, 208,210
Canadians
    visiting Barbados, 195-196
    visiting the Caribbean, 46-47,54
Canadian tourist industry
    benefit segmentation, 81
    Calgary Olympics, 208,210
Caribbean tourist industry, 44-58
    cruise passengers, 55
    direct marketing, 56
    effect, 187
    expansion strategies, 50-52
    goals, 47,50
    health tourism, 231-232
    host view, 187
    mineral springs and health
        resorts, 230
    motives of visitors, 186-188
    origin of tourists, 46t-47t,52-54
    pooling resources, 57
    research, 56
    setting, 44-46,48t-49t
    special interest and niche
        markets, 57
Cateora, P. R., 128-129
Channel intermediaries. *See* Tour
        operators; Travel agents
Chattel house, 189-190
Cheek, N. H., 139
Chupse, 192-193
Cohen, E., 162,183,200
Collymore, F., 189,192,193
Conceptual equivalence, 131
Cormier, P. L., 164

Corn 'n oil, 192
Cosenza, R. M., 81
Costs. *See* Financial issues
Cou cou, 191
Country image, 164
    Eastern Europe, 241
    effect of mega-events, 208-210
Couples, travel motivation, 149-153,
    154-157
Cozier, T., 190
Crandall, R., 138,139
Crick, M., 198
Cricket, 190-191
Crompton, J. L., 81,83,125,139,141,
    183,243
Cross-cultural tourism market
        research, 123-132
    definition of cross-cultural
        tourism, 124
    factors impeding, 126-129
    lack of, 123-124
    language in, 124-126
    methodological guidelines,
        129-132
Crouch, G., 104
Crowther, G., 25
Cruise ships
    in the Caribbean, 55
    environmental regulations, 234
Cuisine in Zambia, 29,33-35
Cultural experiences
    effect on visitors, 185
    as motive, 184
        of Eastern European travellers,
            255,256
        of German travellers, 148
        visitors to North America,
            185-186
        visitors to Zambia, 33-35
Cultural tourism, 184
Culture
    defined, 184
    effect of tourism on, 184-185
    in host-tourist relationship,
        198-200

visitor awareness in Barbados,
        188-201
    accommodation and, 197t,198t
    inter-variable analysis,
        195-198
    methods for enhancing,
        200-201
    motivation and, 198-200,199t
    questionnaire, 188-189
    results of study, 189-195,194t
    visitor awareness in Caribbean,
        186-188
Czechoslovakian tourist industry
    accommodations, 241
    economic impact, 246
    factors inhibiting, 249,250-251
    motives of visitors, 247,248,
        255-256
    origin of visitors, 241
    risk factors, 252

Dann, G., 137,153,181,189
Davis, D., 81
Davis, H. L., 131,132
Davison, M., 29
Dead Sea, 228-230
"De higher de monkey climb, de
        more 'e show 'e tail, " 193
Delphi technique
    concept, 242-243
    Eastern European tourism,
        243-245
    limitations, 251-253
Demographics. *See*
        Sociodemographics
Destination image. *See* Country image
Developing countries. *See also*
        specific countries
    foreign tourism industry,
        163-165,240
    government in tourism
        development, 162
    metropolitan enterprises, 174
Diamond Mineral Baths, Saint
        Lucia, 232

Di Benedetto, A., 243
Dimanche, F., 123,131
"Dimensions of the Social Group
       Role in Pleasure Vacation"
       (Crompton), 141
Direct marketing of small island
       nations, 56
Doctor's Cave, Jamaica, 230-231
Domestic travellers
   on escorted tours, 64-75
       expectations, 68,69t,70t,71t
       meeting expectations, 72-75
       questionnaire, 65-68,67t
       sample, 64-65
   marketing approach and
       expectations, 63-64
   sociodemographic vs.
       psychographic factors, 83
Donnelly, M. A., 140
Douglas, S. P., 131
Duke, Charles R., 61

East Asia/Pacific region, 102
Eastern Europe, 239-253
   tourism as priority industry,
       240-241
   U.S. visitors
       Delphi technique for
           forecasting, 242-245,
           251-253
       economic impact,
           245-246,246t
       factors inhibiting, 248-249,
           250t-251t
       meeting needs of, 241
       motives, 247,248t, 255t-256t
       risk factors, 249-251,252t
   Western European visitors, 241
Eastern European travellers, 241
East German tourist industry
   economic impact, 246
   factors inhibiting, 250-251
   motives of visitors, 247,
       248,255-256
   risk factors, 249,252

Economic Intelligence Unit, 136
Economy and tourism, 102,240. *See*
       also Financial issues
   Africa and wildlife tourism, 25
   the Caribbean, 47,50,187
   Eastern Europe, 245-246,246t
   foreign exchange leakages, 51-52
   linkage with other sectors, 50
   tour operators in developing
       countries, 163-164
Ecosystems, small island nations and
       tourism, 42,44
Ecotourism, 233-234
Education
   methods for increasing cultural
       awareness, 201
   as travel motive, 255
Educators, view of Eastern European
       tourism, 242
   Delphi process, 243-245
   economic impact, 245-246,246t
   factors inhibiting, 248-249,
       250t-251t
   motives, 247,248t,255t-256t
   risk factors, 249-251,252t
English, E., 186-187
English language in cross-cultural
       research, 124-125
Equipment ownership, 81-82
Equivalence
   conceptual, 131
   experiential, 130-131
   measurement, 131-132
Erickson, R., 124
Escape factor, 145,149
Escorted tours, expectations, 64-75.
       See also Package tours
   foreign vs. domestic, 68,69t,
       70t,71t
   German travellers, 149-157
   meeting, 72-75
   in planning, 63-64
   questionnaire, 65-68,67t
   sample, 64-65,66t
Ethnocentrism

in cross-cultural research,
127-128
effect of travel on, 185
Europe. *See also* Eastern Europe;
specific countries
international tourism, 102
mineral springs and health spas,
230
European National Tourist Offices
(NTO), 101-119
expert system development
factors influencing budget
allocation, 115-117,116t
if-then rules, 117-119,118t
knowledge acquisition
methodology, 107-108
marketing and promotional
strategies, 113t,113-114
marketing objectives, 110-111,
111t
market segmentation and
targeting, 111-113,112t
measuring promotion
effectiveness, 114t,114-115
preliminary model,
105,105-107
steps in promotion budgeting,
108-110
functions, 102
promotion budgeting, 102-104
Europeans visiting the Caribbean,
52-53
Exotic images in promotion, 162
Expectancy-disconfirmation model,
62
Expectations. *See* Visitor
expectations
Experiential equivalence, 130-131
Expert systems
applications and limitations,
104-105
data quality, 116-117
in promotion budgeting, 105-119
factors influencing, 115-117,
116t

if-then rules, 117-119,118t
knowledge acquisition
methodology, 107-108
marketing objectives, 110-111,
111t
marketing strategies, 113t,
113-114
market segmentation and
targeting, 111-113,112t
measuring promotion
effectiveness, 114t,114-115
preliminary model, *105*,
105-107
steps in, 108-110

Factorial structure in cross-cultural
equivalence, 131
Families
German travel groups, 143,146,
149-152,154-157
motives for travel, 146,149-152,
154-157
motives for visiting Eastern
Europe, 255
type of leisure activity, 139
Family visits
marketing, 98
package vs. non-package
travellers, 87,90,97-98
Field, D. R.,137,139
Financial issues. *See also* Economy
and tourism
costs and benefits in pricing, 12
in cross-cultural research, 128
escorted tours, 72
expert systems in promotion
budgeting, 105-119
factors influencing, 115-117,
116t
if-then rules, 117-119,118t
knowledge acquisition
methodology, 107-108
marketing objectives, 110-111,
111t
marketing strategies, 113-114t

market segmentation and
targeting, 111-113,112t
measuring promotion
effectiveness, 114t,114-115
preliminary model, *105*,
105-107
steps in, 108-110
German travellers, 148
pricing
ADSPLIT model, 104
mega-event impact, 210-211
of place-products, 11-12
travel in Northeast Asian
countries, 216
promotion budgeting
ADSPLIT model, 103-104
measuring results, 103
pressures, 102-103
Seoul Olympics, 206,207
Financial risk, 249,252
Forde, A., 193
Foreign exchange, 51-52
Foreign travel, 83
Foreign travellers on escorted tours,
63-75
expectations, 63-64,68,69t,70t,71t
meeting expectations, 72-75
questionnaire, 65-68,67t
sample, 64-65,66t
Fort Recovery Resort, Tortola, 232
Foushe, K. D., 164
Fox, M., 126
Friends
German travel groups, 146,
149-153,154-157
type of leisure activity, 139
visiting as travel motive
marketing, 98
package vs. non-package
travellers, 87,90,97-98
Functional risk, 249, 252

Gartner, William C., 161
Geertz, C., 184

Geographic isolation and tourism,
41,43-44
German travellers, influence of
travel group, 141-157
data sources and analysis,
141-143
marketing implications, 153-157
motives, 143-153,144t,145t,146t,
147t,150t,151t
party characteristics, 143,143t
Germany. *See* East German tourist
industry
Gilmore Research Group, 81
Goeldner, C., 124,162
Goodrich, Jonathan N., 81,227
Government in tourism. *See also*
European National Tourist
Offices (NTO)
developing countries, 162
Indonesia, 169,176
as producers of place-products,
9-10
Great Britain, 46-47,82. *See* British
travellers
Greek students, 185
Green tourism, 233-234
Groningen, the Netherlands, 13-17

Hall, J. A., 48
Hallmark event, 206
Harrigan, N., 186
Harris, G., 163
Hawaiian Islands, 82
Hawkins, D. E., 164
Health tourism, 227-238
in the Caribbean, 231-232,
237-238
in Cuba, 237
economic impact, 237
elements, 228,229t
Europeans vs. Americans, 236
historical perspective, 228-231
market segmentation, 235
medical facilities, 235-236
other dimensions, 232-234

Heiberg, T., 163
Hensarling, D. M., 127
Heyward, J. L., 139
Hill, J. B., 140
Hiller, Harry H., 210
Hoivik, T., 163
Hong Kong, 215-216
Host-tourist relationship
  culture, 198-200
  Groningen, the Netherlands, 15
  mega-events, 210
  negative impacts, 240
  pricing systems in, 12
  Seoul Olympics, 207
  wildlife tourism in Africa, 25
Hsieh, Sheauhsing, 79
Hudman, L. E., 164
Hui, C. H., 131,132
Hungarian tourist industry
  economic impact, 246
  factors inhibiting, 250-251
  origin of visitors, 241
  risk factors, 249,252
Husbands, Winston, 21
Hyun, Jin-kwon, 207

Image. *See* Country image
Income
  health tourism marketing, 235
  package vs. non-package
    travellers, 87,88
Indonesia
  government in tourism, 169,176
  tourist industry, 165-166
  tour operators, 164-177
    corporate profile, 169-171,172t
    difficulties in securing
      services, 169-171,170t,
      173t,177
    in economy, 176
    objectives, 164-165
    other destinations in packages,
      174-175,175t
    perceptions, 167t,167-169,
      168t,175-176

questionnaire, 166-167
sources of information, 171,
  174,174t,176-177
Indonesian Tourism Promotions
  Office, 169,171,174,
  176-177
'Industrial approach' to tourism, 5-6
Information search behavior
  factors in, 162
  overcoming resistance, 162
Information sources
  mega-events, 210
  package vs. non-package
    travellers, 85,90,91t
  tour operators, 164
  visitors to Barbados, 196-198
Infrastructure
  mega-events, 206,210
  Seoul Olympics, 212,215
Institutionalized mass tourists, 162
Island nations, tourism industry
  Caribbean setting, 44-46,48t-49t
    cruise passengers, 55
    direct marketing, 56
    expansion strategies, 50-52
    national origin of tourists,
      46t-47t,52-54
    pooling resources, 57
    research, 56
    special interest and niche
      markets, 57
  distinctive characteristics, 39-40
  geographic isolation, 43-44
  political autonomy, 42-43
  size, 40-42
Iso-Ahola, S. E., 137,156,159
Item equivalence, 131

Jacobs, L. W., 81
Jacoby, J., 249
Jamaica, 230-231
Jamrozy, U., 124,135
Jansen-Verbeke, M. C., 7
Japan
  benefit segmentation, 81

cross-cultural market research, 126
tourist industry, 215-216
Jarvis, L. P., 137
Jenkins, C. L., 240
June, L., 22

Kang, Yong-Soon, 205
Kaplan, L. B., 249
Katz, K. M., 163
Keaveney, S., 128-129
Kim, Joung-man, 207
Kmenta, Jan, 218
Korea. *See* Seoul Olympics and
tourism
Korea National Tourism
Corporation, 212
Kotler, P., 17,110
Krippendorf, J., 154-155
Kruskal, J., 29

Language in cross-cultural research
barriers, 124-125,128-129
equivalence, 130-132
translation methods, 130
Lapage, W. F., 164
Latin Americans, 233
Leisure
intrinsic motivations, 139
psychological vs. sociological
view, 138
role expectations and social
norms, 140-141
sociological factors, 139-141
Life cycle and leisure participation,
140
Lundberg, D. E., 138,186

MacCannell, D., 182,183,200
McCleary, Ken W., 239
McDonald, C. D., 140
McIntosh, R., 162
McIntyre, S. H., 132
McLellan, R. W., 164

Mahoney, E. M., 82
Mak, J., 82
Manley, Michael, 186
Manning, R. E., 136
Marital status, 87,88
Market concentration, 50-51
Market diversification, 50-51,109
Marketing
budgeting decisions
ADSPLIT model, 103-104
measuring results, 104
pressures, 102-104
the Caribbean, 45
Eastern European tourist industry,
251
establishing objectives, 110
European National Tourist
Offices
objectives, 110-111
strategies, 113-114
expert systems in budgeting,
105-119
factors influencing, 115-117,
116t
if-then rules, 117-119,118t
knowledge acquisition
methodology, 107-108
marketing objectives, 110-111,
111t
marketing strategies, 113t,
113-114
market segmentation, 111-113,
112t
measuring promotion
effectiveness, 114t,114-115
preliminary model, 105-107
steps, 108-110
foreign vs. domestic travel, 63
German travellers, 136
Groningen, the Netherlands,
13-17
health tourism, 235
independent travellers, 113-114
medical facilities in promotion,
235-236

mega-events, 208-211
package vs. non-package
    travellers, 93.96-98
place-products
    difficulties, 12-13
    goals and techniques, 17-18
    pricing systems, 11-12
    pooling resources, 57
    vs. promotion, 13
    Seoul Olympics, 212.*213*
    small island nations, 50-52.56-57
    sociodemographic vs.
        psychographic factors,
        82-83
    travel group and motivation,
        153-157
Market research
    cross-cultural tourism, 123-132
        factors impeding, 126-129
        lack of, 123-124
        language, 124-126
        methodological guidelines,
        129-132
    European National Tourist
        Offices, 109
    small island nations, 56
    visitor benefits in, 22.24
Market segmentation
    benefit segmentation, 81
    demographics and
        socioeconomics in, 80-81
    European National Tourist
        Offices, 111-112.112t
    health tourism, 235
    independent vs. package
        travellers, 82-83
    product-related, 81-82
    strategy, 80
    travel groups, 157
    visitors to Barbados, 200-201
Market share, 220
Market weighting and classification,
        110,117-118
Marshall, A., 25
Marshall, T., 189,191

Martin, Christine A., 208
Mass tourists, 162,182-183
"Maximum Travel Per Diem
    Allowances for Foreign
    Areas" (U.S. Department
    of State), 216
Mayer, C. S., 128
Mayo, E. J., Jr., 137
Measurement equivalence, 131-132
Media
    coverage of Seoul Olympics, 212
    effect of mega-events, 208-210
Medical facilities in promotion,
        235-236
Medlik, S., 241
Mega-events
    conceptual model of long-term
        impacts, 207-211.*209*
    defined, 206
    financial issues, 206
    Seoul Olympics, 211-223
        awareness of Olympic site,
        212.*214*
        infrastructure, 212.215
        promotion and publicity,
        212.*213*
        short-term impacts, 211-212
        statistical models of long-term
        impacts, 207.215-223.*217*
        visitor satisfaction, 215
Metropolitan enterprises
    defined, 163
    in developing countries, 174
Mfuwe Lodge, South Luangwa
        National Park, 22,25-26
Michigan, product-related
        segmentation, 82
Morrison, Alastair M., 79,81
Morrison, M. A., 82
Moschis, G. P., 125
Moscow Olympics, 212,218
Motives for travel. *See also* Visitor
        expectations
    in benefit segmentation, 81
    in consumer behavior, 138

correlation with cultural
knowledge in Barbados,
198,199t
cultural experiences, 184,185-186
in decision-making, 136
escape amidst familiarity, 182
familiarity/strangeness
continuum, 183
intrinsic, 139
life cycle in, 140
search for authenticity, 182-183
sociopsychological factors,
138-141,183-184
theories and concepts, 137
travel group
comparisons of groups,
148-153,150t,151t
marketing implications,
153-157
pull forces, 144-145,145t,
147t,147-148
push forces, 143-144,144t,
145-147
U.S. travellers to Eastern Europe,
247,248t,255t-256t
visitors to the Caribbean, 186-188
Moutinho, Luiz, 101, 138
Moyer, W. D., 128
Multidimensional scaling (MDS), 26
Munson, J. M., 132
Murphy, P. E., 164
Myers, N., 24,25

National parks in Africa, 24-25
National Tourist Offices. *See* European
National Tourist Offices
Nederlands Bureau voor Toerism,
15-16
The Netherlands, Groningen, 13-17
Niche marketing, 52, 57
Nightlife, survey of tourists in
Zambia, 29
Noe, F. P., 164
Nolting, M., 24

Norms in leisure, 140-141
NTO. *See* European National Tourist
Offices (NTO)

O'Halloran, R. M., 127
O'Leary, Joseph T., 79, 137
Olympic impact curve, 216-218,*217*
Olympics. *See* Seoul Olympics and
tourism
O'Malley, G. L., 97
Operationalization, defined, 131
Organized tours. *See* Escorted tours,
expectations; Package tours

Package tours. *See also* Escorted
tours, expectations
benefits, 80
decision-making, 82-83
defined, 80
marketing, 113-114
traveller characteristics, 84-98
benefits sought, 93,94t
data analysis, 85-86
destination, 86,86t
information sources, 90,91t
marketing implications, 93,
97-98
philosophy, 90-91,92t
product preference, 93,95t-96t
questionnaires, 84-85
sociodemographics, 87,88t
travel characteristics, 87,
89t-90t
U.S. travellers purchasing, 163
Packaging in tourism, 7
Party size. *See* Travel group
Pearce, P. L., 137,155
Pearce, P., 185
Pearson-product moment
correlations, 173,177
Perdue, Richard, 205
Persia, Margaret A., 61
Personal communities, 139
Philosophy of travel, 85,90-91,92t

Pitts, R. E., 83
Place-products, 5-18
  consumers, 10-11
  definition and delimitation, 6-9
  Groningen, the Netherlands, as
    case study, 13-17
  marketing, 11-13,17-18
  producers, 9-10
  vs. products, 12
Plog, S. C., 10,124,126
Polish tourist industry
  economic impact, 246
  factors inhibiting, 249,250-251
  motives of visitors, 247,248,
    255-256
Political situation
  Eastern European tourism, 250
  effect on tourism, 41,42-43
Pool, I., 185
Potential Ratings in Zipcode
    Markets (PRIZM), 81
Potter, R., 189
Prestige factor
  German travellers, 147,152
  visitors to Eastern Europe, 255
Pricing. *See* Financial issues
PRIZM (Potential Ratings in
    Zipcode Markets), 81
Producers of place-products, 9-10,
    12
Product-related segmentation, 81-82
Products. *See* Place-products
Promotion. *See* Marketing
Psychocentric tourists
  cultural experiences, 184
  sense of place, 10-11
  studies of, 126
Psychographic classification
  advantages, 83
  methods, 81
  visitors to Barbados, 200-201
Psychological factors. *See also*
    Motives for travel
  social needs, 137-141
  theories and concepts, 136-137

Psychological risk, 249,252
Publicity, 208-210,212
Pullan, R., 25
Push/pull factors, 113
  concept, 183-184
  German travellers,153-154
  influence of travel group, 145-153,
    146t,147t,150t,151t

Regression analyses, 207,218-222
Reid, Laurel J., 39
Reid, Stanley D., 39
Relatives. *See* Families; Family
    visits
Repeat visitors
  to Barbados, 195-196
  to the Caribbean, 51
  package vs. non-package
    travellers, 97
Residents. *See* Host-tourist
    relationship
Richardson, S. L., 125
Risk factors, 249,251,252t
Rita, Paulo, 101
Ritchie, J. R. B., 124,206,207,208,
    210,212,216
Role expectations in leisure,
    140-141
Rumanian tourist industry
  economic impact, 246
  factors inhibiting, 249,250-251
  motives of visitors, 247,248,
    255-256
  risk factors, 249-251,252
Rum shop, 189

Safety concerns
  effect on tourism, 211
  Seoul Olympics, 215
  visitors to Eastern Europe,
    249,252
Saint Lucia, 232
Satisfaction. *See* Visitor satisfaction
Scalar equivalence, 131-132

Scale discrepancies, 7-8
Scenery
  German travellers, 147-148
  visitors to Zambia, 28-29
Schul, P., 83
Sechrest, L., 130,131
Segmentation. *See* Market
    segmentation
Self-reference criterion, 128
Seoul Olympics and tourism,
    205-223
  awareness as Olympic site,
    212,*214*
  vs. competing destinations,
    215-216
  financial issues, 206
  infrastructure, 212,215
  Olympic impact curve, 216-218,
    217
  price-market share relationship,
    216,223
  promotion and publicity, 212,*213*
  regression of annual time-series
    data, 207
  short-term impact on tourism,
    211-212
  statistical models, 218-222,
    219t,221t
  time period and value, 220,221t,
    222-223
  visitor satisfaction, 215
Shanmugam, A., 126
Sheldon, P. J., 82,126
Shopping, 33-35
Silk, A. J., 131
Silver Reef Health Spa, 231-232
Size of host economy and tourism,
    40-42
Small island nations and tourism.
    See Island nations
Smith, Brian H., 208,210,212,216
Smith, H., 185
Smith, S., 22
Smith, S. L. J., 126
Socher, Karl, 206

Social market exchange, 11
Social norms, 140-141
Social risk, 249,252
Sociodemographics
  in market segmentation, 80-81,
    82-83
  package vs. non-package
    travellers, 85,87,88t
Sociopsychological factors, 137-141
  consumer classification, 81,83
  influence on tourist behavior,
    137-141
  marketing implications, 157
  motive for travel, 155-156
  push/pull factors, 183-184
  visitors to Barbados, 200-201
Sood, J. H., 125
Sources of information. *See*
    Information sources
Southan, J., 103
South Luangwa National Park
  features, 24-25
  visitors, 25-26,28
Soviet Union, 250
Spain, 206
Sparrow, Mark, 208
Spatial scale
  Groningen, the Netherlands,
    15-16
  tourism as place-product, 7-8
Special interest markets, 52,57
Sports activities, 147,149,152,255
Springer, R., 191
Stabler, M. J., 10
Stereotypes, 185
Stewart, E. C., 127-128
Strandskov, J., 124
Study on Tourism (Korean journal),
    207
Stupse, 192-193
Stynes, D. J., 82
Suttles, S., 24
Suttles-Graham, B., 24

Taiwan, 215-216
Tanaka, Y., 126
Teas, J., 184,199
Terrorism, 250
Thailand, 215-216
Tomorrow's Level of Care, Inc., 233
Tortola, 232
Touche Ross and Company, 163
TOUREX, 105-119
  factors influencing, 115-117,116t
  if-then rules, 117-119,118t
  knowledge acquisition
      methodology, 107-108
  marketing objectives, 110-111,
      111t
  marketing strategies, 113t,
      113-114
  market segmentation and
      targeting, 111-113,112t
  measuring promotion
      effectiveness, 114t,114-115
  preliminary model, *105*,105-107
  steps in, 108-110
Tourism Canada, 82,136,142,
      158,185
'Tourist-Recreation Product,' 7
Tour operators
  accommodation suppliers and, 52
  in developing countries, 163-164
  as distribution channel, 164
  in Eastern Europe, 250,251
  enhancing cultural awareness of
      travellers, 201
  functions, 163
  Indonesia in package tours
      (study), 164-177
    corporate profiles, 169-171,
        172t
    difficulties in securing
        services, 169-171,170t,
        173t,177
    in economy, 176
    objectives, 164-165
    other destinations, 174-175,
        175t

  perceptions of, 167t,167-169,
      168t,175-176
  questionnaire, 166-167
  sample, 165
  sources of information, 171,
      174,174t,176-177
  as information source, 164
  institutionalized mass tourists,
      162-163
  meeting expectations on escorted
      tours, 72-73
  net foreign exchange, 51-52
  package vs. non-package
      travellers, 87,90
  as producers of place-products, 9
TRACE project, 105
Trade promotion, 113-114
Translations in cross-cultural
      research. *See also*
      Language
  equivalence, 130-132
  methods, 130
Transportation, 163
Travel agents
  in Eastern Europe, 251
  enhancing cultural awareness of
      travellers, 201
  knowledge of health tourism, 232
  net foreign exchange, 51-52
  package vs. non-package
      travellers, 87,90
  view of Eastern European
      tourism, 242
    Delphi process, 243-245
    economic impact, 245-246,
        246t
    factors inhibiting, 248-249,
        250t-251t
    motives, 247,248t,255t-256t
    risk factors, 249-251,252t
Travel demand, 162
Travel group
  influence on behavior, 137-138
  influence on behavior of German
      travellers (study), 141-157

data sources and analysis,
141-143
marketing implications,
153-157
motivation, 143-153,144t,145t,
146t,147t,150t,151t
party characteristics, 143,143t
motivation and type of group,
139-140
package vs. non-package
travellers
size, 87,89
Travel Health Care Service, 233
Travel philosophy, 85,90-91,92t
*Travel Tourism and Hospitality
Research* (Ritchie and
Goeldner), 124
Triandis, H., 126,185
Triandis, H. C., 131.132
Tschurtschenthaler, Paul, 206
Tuk band, 191-192

United Kingdom. *See also* British
travellers
product-related segmentation, 82
visitors to the Caribbean, 46-47
United Nations, 163-164
United States
benefit segmentation, 81
international visitors, 127
language in cross-cultural studies,
125
mineral springs and health spas,
230
visitors receiving medical
treatment, 233
United States tour operators and
Indonesia, 164-177
corporate profile, 169-171,
172t
difficulties in securing services,
169-171,170t,173t,177
objectives, 164-165
other destinations in package,
174-175,175t

perceptions, 167t,167-169,
168t,175-176
questionnaire, 166-167
sources of information, 171,174,
174t,176-177
United States travellers
in the Caribbean, 46-47,54,232
in Eastern Europe, 241-256
Delphi technique for
forecasting, 242-245,
251-253
economic impact, 245-246,
246t
factors inhibiting, 248-249,
250t-251t
meeting needs of, 241
motives, 247,248t,255t-256t
risk factors, 249-251,252t
expectations on escorted tours,
64-75
meeting, 72-75
questionnaire, 65-68,67t
results, 68,69t,70t,71t
sample, 64-65,66t
intercultural contact, 185
psychographic market
segmentation, 81
purchasers of package tours, 163
U.S. Department of State, 216
U.S. Travel and Tourism
Administration (USTTA),
82,136,142,158
Uysal, M., 1,124,135,140,243

V. V. V. Groningen, 15
VALS (Values and Lifestyles), 81
Values and Lifestyles (VALS), 81
van Raaij, W. F., 124
Vassiliou, G., 126
Vassiliou, V., 126,185
Visitor benefits
benefit segmentation, 22,81
package vs. non-package
travellers, 85,93,94t
study of, 22-24

Visitor expectations
  in determining satisfaction, 62-63
  foreign vs. domestic tours, 64-75
    meeting expectations, 72-75
    questionnaire, 65-68,67t
    results, 68,69t,70t,71t
    sample, 64-65,66t
  in tour planning, 63-64
Visitors. *See also* Host-tourist
    relationship
  allocentric vs. psychocentric, 10-11
  in Groningen, the Netherlands, 14
  of place-products
    characteristics, 10-11
    different groups, 8-9
    pricing systems, 11-12
Visitor satisfaction
  concept, 22,24
  expectancy-disconfirmation
    model, 62-63
  increasing, 62
  mega-events, 210
  Seoul Olympics, 215
  in Zambia, 25-36
    data analysis, 31-36,33t,34t,35t
    importance of benefits, 28-31,
      30t,32t
    methods, 25-27
    sample characteristics, 27-28,
      28t
    visitor profile variables, 31t
Voogd, H., 5,13

Waters, S. R., 163
Wechasara, G., 128
Whitney, David L., 239
Wildlife tourism, 28-29
Williams, R. D., 140
Wish, M., 29
Witt, S. F., 207,208,241,245
Woodside, A. G., 81,83
World Tourism Organization,
    245-246
Wright, J., 187

Zaichkowsky, J. L., 125
Zambia, 21-36
  diversifying attractions, 36
  map, *23*
  national parks, 24-25
  visitor benefits, 25-36
    importance of various benefits,
      28-31,30t,32t
    methods, 25-27
    sample characteristics, 27-28,
      28t
    visitor profile variables, 31t
    visitor satisfaction, 31-36,33t,
      34t,35t
Ziff-Levine, W., 63
Ziolwenska, E., 188

*For Product Safety Concerns and Information please contact
our EU representative GPSR@taylorandfrancis.com Taylor & Francis
Verlag GmbH, Kaufingerstraße 24, 80331 München, Germany*

T - #0071 - 230425 - C0 - 212/152/15 - PB - 9780789000965 - Gloss Lamination